Readings in World Religions

Selections from Primary Sources

Arranged with Comments by:

Gisela Webb
Seton Hall University

KENDALL/HUNT PUBLISHING COMPANY
4050 Westmark Drive   Dubuque, Iowa 52002

Contents

VI. Judaism and Christianity 169

VII. Islam 247

Introduction

Gisela Webb

T his collection of readings is not meant to replace any of the competent textbooks on world religions designed for college or university use, but rather, to provide a supplementary text for those who wish to use primary source readings. Clearly, sacred stories and other teaching tools generated within religious communities communicate the texture of religion in a way that secondary sources cannot. *Readings in World Religions* is especially designed for the one-semester introductory course in world religions in which the challenge for teachers and students is to extract some of the richness and variety of the world's religions through a streamlined examination of "documents" of six or seven traditions.

Objectives and Suggestions for Using the Text

E very instructor in a world religions course finds him/herself having to choose which religions to present, what themes or structures will be used for focus or comparison, and what methodology will be utilized. Those decisions are usually based on the training of the teacher, and this selection of readings certainly reflects my training and my recollection of readings that were valuable to me as an undergraduate. More importantly, these readings constitute a group of texts that *can* be utilized to accomplish the following objectives.

Sharing a Sense of What it Means to be Engaged in the Field of Religious Studies as well as the Understanding that the Field has its Own History and Vocabulary.

The first reading, by Mircea Eliade, while extremely dense for the undergraduate, provides a wonderful way of exposing students to the idea of comparative structures across world religions (e.g., myth, ritual) as well as to a working vocabulary used in the field of religious studies (e.g., ontology, cosmology, sacred, ritual, myth). Using Mircea Eliade necessitates a discussion on approaches (or methodologies) used to study religion and on the fact that the underlying assumptions, language, and categories (e.g., sacred vs. profane, traditional vs. historical "*man*") used in the study of religions change with time. Since much of Eliade's discussion focuses on oral cultures, we follow it with a selection from *Black Elk Speaks* which students can study as an example of Native American religious expression and analyze both in terms of structural categories that Eliade saw as characteristic of "traditional" religion, and in terms of the particular intentions, imagery, and "feel" of the text.

Communicating the Common Human Questions that Religions Ask and the Diverse Manners in Which Religions Answer Them.

Our assumption is that all religions—in their stories, rituals, art, and theological/ philosophical reflections—provide answers to certain basic questions of human existence: What is the nature and purpose of existence? What is the fundamental "problem" of human existence? What is the solution, or overcoming, of the problem of human existence? What is the method for attaining the "solution" to the problem?

Therefore, the second objective of this volume is to present students with examples of religious texts in which some or all of these questions are addressed, either explicitly or implicitly. Students should be encouraged to discuss these fundamental questions using the language and assumptions internal to the particular religion being studied. Issues of interpretation, meaning, and orthodoxy will arise, and secondary source material will be necessary for both student and teacher so that the development of religious terms and their usage (e.g., "heaven," "God") are understood in their proper context. Students should be able to notice similarities of structures or beliefs in different religions as well as profound and subtle distinctions that have been important in the self-definition of religious communities. To summarize this approach, the goal is to develop the capacity for engaging in, or at least imagining, serious reflection on fundamental religious/ existential questions from within the historical, conceptual, and image-world of the particular religions being studied.

Sensitizing the Student to What is and What Is *Not* in the Selected Readings.

No introductory course can include representative works of all groups and all perspectives of all religious traditions. The students should come to see each selection as representing a particular expression of a particular line of thought of a particular time period of a particular religion. The *Katha Upanishad* represents a relatively late development in the history of Hinduism's sacred literature, but it is an example of the "classical" formulation of "monistic" Hinduism. The two Buddhist selections reflect the particular emphases of the two major historical strands of Buddhism, Theravada and

Mahayana. Confucius and Lao Tzu were extremely influential in the emergence of certain cultural values in China, but their works have undergone a number of interpretations and uses by their commentators. Certainly the Biblical selections need to be seen as representing different genres of literature, different time periods, and different histories of interpretation. Just knowing that fact about the Bible is a major eye-opener for most undergraduates. *The Koran* (or *Quran*) selections ought to be seen as reflecting particular "inspired" receivings (*wahy*) that Muhammad "experienced" at different periods of his prophetic mission. The content and organization of the Islamic materials were chosen in light of Islam's current situation of being perhaps the fastest growing religion, but also the most unfamiliar religion to Western audiences. In the cases of Hinduism and Islam, I have included contemporary expositions of traditional doctrine, "The Seven Centers of Consciousness" and "Everyone is Speaking of Peace," in order to point out the ongoing nature of interpretation and transmission of religious ideas in light of the language and concerns of contemporary culture.

It is instructive to point out things said and left unsaid about women in the texts, so that students may see the pervasiveness of assumptions about gender roles in all cultures and, thus, the difficulty and time involved in modifying these views—of reinterpreting the texts—in a way that accommodates both "tradition" and "modernity."

Using the Texts Creatively and in Accordance with Students' Capacities.

I strongly recommend that teachers and students have in their school libraries the sources from which these selections are taken. They contain instructive footnotes and commentaries which I have not included in this volume. I also recommend as much exposure as possible to the arts that developed as forms of religious expression. Music and visual language provide not only additional sources of information about religions but also alternative modes for communicating ideas to students who learn more through the sensual, imaginative, and affective dimensions of cognition. There is much flexibility in the direction that teachers and students can take in utilizing these texts. In order to encourage thoughtfulness and to provide possible boundaries or points of departure for classroom discussion, some questions, themes, or clarifying remarks will be presented at the end of each selection.

I

Myth and Ritual in Traditional Cultures: A Point of Departure

The Myth of the Eternal Return: Eliade on "Archetypes and Repetition"

The Problem

This book undertakes to study certain aspects of archaic ontology—more precisely, the conceptions of being and reality that can be read from the behavior of the man of the premodern societies. The premodern or "traditional" societies include both the world usually known as "primitive" and the ancient cultures of Asia, Europe, and America. Obviously, the metaphysical concepts of the archaic world were not always formulated in theoretical language; but the symbol, the myth, the rite, express, on different planes and through the means proper to them, a complex system of coherent affirmations about the ultimate reality of things, a system that can be regarded as constituting a metaphysics. It is, however, essential to understand the deep meaning of all these symbols, myths, and rites, in order to succeed in translating them into our habitual language. If one goes to the trouble of penetrating the authentic meaning of an archaic myth or symbol, one cannot but observe that this meaning shows a recognition of a certain situation in the cosmos and that, consequently, it implies a metaphysical position. It is useless to search archaic languages for the terms so laboriously created by the great philosophical traditions: there is every likelihood that such words as "being," "nonbeing," "real," "unreal," "becoming," "illusory," are not to be found in the language of the Australians or of the ancient Mesopotamians. But if the word is lacking, the *thing* is present; only it is "said"—that is, revealed in a coherent fashion—through symbols and myths.

If we observe the general behavior of archaic man, we are struck by the following fact: neither the objects of the external world nor human acts, properly speaking, have any autonomous intrinsic value. Objects or acts acquire a value, and in so doing become real, because they participate, after one fashion or another, in a reality that transcends them. Among countless stones, one stone becomes sacred—and hence instantly becomes saturated with being—because it constitutes a hierophany, or possesses mana, or again because it commemorates a mythical act, and so on. The object appears as the receptacle of an exterior force that differentiates it from its milieu and gives it meaning and value. This force may reside in the substance of the object or in its form; a rock reveals itself to be sacred because its very existence is a hierophany: incompressible, invulnerable, it is that which man is not. It resists time; its reality is coupled with perenniality. Take the commonest of stones; it will be raised to the rank of "precious" that is, impregnated with a magical or religious power by virtue of its symbolic shape or its origin: thunderstone, held to have fallen from the sky: pearl, because it comes from the depths of the sea. Other stones will be sacred because they are the dwelling place of the souls of ancestors (India, Indonesia), or because they were once the scene of a theophany (as the *bethel* that served Jacob for a bed), or because a sacrifice or an oath has consecrated them.[1]

Now let us turn to human acts—those, of course, which do not arise from pure automatism. Their meaning, their value, are not connected with their crude physical datum but with their property of reproducing a primordial act, of repeating a mythical example. Nutrition is not a simple physiological operation; it renews a communion. Marriage and the collective orgy echo mythical prototypes; they are repeated because they were consecrated in the beginning ("in those days," *in illo tempore, ab origine*) by gods, ancestors, or heroes.

In the particulars of his conscious behavior the "primitive," the archaic man, acknowledges no act which has not been previously posited and lived by someone else, some other being who was not a man. What he does has been done before. His life is the ceaseless repetition of gestures initiated by others.

This conscious repetition of given paradigmatic gestures reveals an original ontology. The crude product of nature, the object fashioned by the industry of man, acquire their reality, their identity, only to the extent of their participation in a transcendent reality. The gesture acquires meaning, reality, solely to the extent to which it repeats a primordial act.

Various groups of facts, drawn here and there from different cultures, will help us to identify the structure of this archaic ontology. We have first sought out examples likely to show, as clearly as possible, the mechanism of traditional thought; in other words, facts which help us to understand how and why for the man of the premodern societies, certain things become real.

It is essential to understand this mechanism thoroughly, in order that we may afterward approach the problem of human existence and of history within the horizon of archaic spirituality.

We have distributed our collection of facts under several principal headings:

1. Facts which show us that, for archaic man, reality is a function of the imitation of a celestial archetype.

2. Facts which show us how reality is conferred through participation in the "symbolism of the Center": cities, temples, houses become real by the fact of being assimilated to the "center of the world."

3. Finally, rituals and significant profane gestures which acquire the meaning attributed to them, and materialize that meaning, only because they deliberately repeat such and such acts posited *ab origine* by gods, heroes, or ancestors.

The presentation of these facts will in itself lay the groundwork for a study and interpretation of the ontological conception underlying them.

Celestial Archetypes of Territories, Temples, and Cities

According to Mesopotamian beliefs, the Tigris has its model in the star Anunit and the Euphrates in the star of the Swallow.[2] A Sumerian text tells of the "place of the creation of the gods," where "the [divinity of] the flocks and grains" is to be found.[3] For the Ural–Altaic peoples the mountains, in the same way have an ideal prototype in the sky.[4] In Egypt, places and nomes were named after the celestial "fields": first the celestial fields were known, then they were identified in terrestrial geography.[5]

In Iranian cosmology of the Zarvanitic tradition, "every terrestrial phenomenon, whether abstract or concrete, corresponds to a celestial, transcendent invisible term, to an 'idea' in the Platonic sense. Each thing, each notion presents itself under a double aspect: that of *mēnōk* and that of *gētīk*. There is a visible sky: hence there is also a *mēnōk* sky which is invisible (*Bundahišn*, Ch. I). Our earth corresponds to a celestial earth. Each virtue practiced here below, in the *gētāh*, has a celestial counterpart which represents true reality....The year, prayer...in short, whatever is manifested in the *gētāh*, is at the same time *mēnōk*. The creation is simply duplicated. From the cosmogonic point of view the cosmic stage called *mēnōk* precedes the stage *gētīk*."[6]

The temple in particular—pre-eminently the sacred place—had a celestial prototype. On Mount Sinai, Jehovah shows Moses the "form" of the sanctuary that he is to build for him: "According to all that I shew thee, after the pattern of the tabernacle, and the pattern of all the instruments thereof, even so shall ye make it....And look that thou make them after their pattern, which was shewed thee in the mount" (Exodus 25:9,40). And when David gives his son Solomon the plan for the temple buildings, for the tabernacle, and for all their utensils, he assures him that "All this...the Lord made me understand in writing by his hand upon me, even all the works of this pattern" (I Chronicles 28:19). Hence he had seen the celestial model.[7]

The earliest document referring to the archetype of a sanctuary is Gudea's inscription concerning the temple he built at Lagash. In a dream the king sees the goddess Nidaba, who shows him a tablet on which the beneficent stars are named, and a god who reveals the plan of the temple to him.[8] Cities too have their divine prototypes. All the Babylonian cities had their archetypes in the constellations: Sippara in Cancer, Nineveh in Ursa Major, Assur in Arcturus, etc.[9] Sennacherib has Nineveh built according to the "form...delineated from distant ages by the writing of the heaven-of-stars." Not only does a model precede terrestrial architecture, but the model is also situated in an ideal (celestial) region of eternity. This is what Solomon announces: "Thou gavest command to build a sanctuary in thy holy mountain, And an altar in the city of thy habitation, A copy of the holy tabernacle which thou preparedst aforehand from the beginning."[10]

A celestial Jerusalem was created by God before the city was built by the hand of man; it is to the former that the prophet refers in the Syriac Apocalypse of Baruch II, 4:2–7: "'Dost thou think that this is that city of which I said: "On the palms of My hands have I graven thee"? This building now built in your midst is not that which is revealed with Me, that which was prepared beforehand here from the time when I took counsel to make Paradise, and showed it to Adam before he sinned...'"[11] The heavenly Jerusalem kindled the inspiration of all the Hebrew prophets: Tobias 13:16; Isaiah 59:11 ff.; Ezekiel 60, etc. To show him the city of Jerusalem, God lays hold of Ezekiel in an ecstatic vision and transports him to a very high mountain. And the *Sibylline Oracles* preserve the memory of the New Jerusalem in the center of which there shines "a temple... with a giant tower touching the very clouds and seen of all..."[12] But the most beautiful description of the heavenly Jerusalem occurs in the Apocalypse (21:2 ff.): "And I John saw the holy city, new Jerusalem, coming down from God out of heaven, prepared as a bride adorned for her husband."

We find the same theory in India: all the Indian royal cities, even the modern ones, are built after the mythical model of the celestial city where, in the age of gold (*in illo tempore*), the Universal Sovereign dwelt. And, like the latter, the king attempts to revive the age of gold, to make a perfect reign a present reality—an idea which we shall encounter again in the course of this study. Thus, for example, the palace-fortress of Sigiriya, in Ceylon, is built after the model of the celestial city Alakamanda and is "hard of ascent for human beings" (*Mahāvastu*, 39, 2). Plato's ideal city likewise has a celestial archetype (*Republic*, 592*b*; cf. 500*e*). The Platonic "forms" are not astral; yet their mythical region is situated on supraterrestrial planes (*Phaedrus*, 247, 250).

The world that surrounds us, then, the world in which the presence and the work of man are felt—the mountains that he climbs, populated and cultivated regions, navigable rivers, cities, sanctuaries—all these have an extraterrestrial archetype, be it conceived as a plan, as a form, or purely and simply as a "double" existing on a higher cosmic level. But everything in the world that surrounds us does not have a prototype of this kind. For example, desert regions inhabited by monsters, uncultivated lands, unknown seas on which no navigator has dared to venture do not share with the city of Babylon, or the Egyptian nome, the privilege of a differentiated prototype. They correspond to a mythical model, but of another nature: all these wild, uncultivated regions and the like are assimilated to chaos; they still participate in the undifferentiated, formless modality of pre-Creation. This is why, when possession is taken of a territory—that is, when its exploitation begins—rites are performed that symbolically repeat the act of Creation: the uncultivated zone is first "cosmicized," then inhabited. We shall presently return to the meaning of this ceremonial taking possession of newly discovered countries. For the moment, what we wish to emphasize is the fact that the world which surrounds us, civilized by the hand of man, is accorded no validity beyond that which is due to the extraterrestrial prototype that served as its model. Man constructs according to an archetype. Not only do his city or his temple have celestial models; the same is true of the entire region that he inhabits, with the rivers that water it, the fields that give him his food, etc. The map of Babylon shows the city at the center of a vast circular territory bordered by a river, precisely as the Sumerians envisioned Paradise. This participation by urban cultures in an archetypal model is what gives them their reality and their validity.

Settlement in a new, unknown, uncultivated country is equivalent to an act of Creation. When the Scandinavian colonists took possession of Iceland, *Landnāma*, and began to cultivate it, they regarded this act neither as an original undertaking nor as human and profane work. Their enterprise was for them only the repetition of a primordial act: the transformation of chaos into cosmos by the divine act of Creation. By cultivating the desert soil, they in fact repeated the act of the gods, who organized chaos by giving it forms and norms.[13] Better still, a territorial conquest does not become real until after—more precisely through—the ritual of taking possession, which is only a copy of the primordial act of the Creation of the World. In Vedic India the erection of an altar dedicated to Agni constituted legal taking possession of a territory.[14] "One settles (*avasyati*) when he builds the *gārhapatya*, and whoever are builders of fire-altars are 'settled' (*avasitāh*)," says the *Śatapatha Brāhmana* (VII, 1, 1–4). But the erection of an altar dedicated to Agni is merely the microcosmic imitation of the Creation. Furthermore, any sacrifice is, in turn, the repetition of the act of Creation, as Indian texts explicitly state.[15] It was in the name of Jesus Christ that the Spanish and Portuguese conquistadores took possession of the islands and continents that they had discovered and conquered. The setting up of the Cross was equivalent to a justification and to the consecration of the new country, to a "new birth," thus repeating baptism (act of Creation). In their turn the English navigators took possession of conquered countries in the name of the king of England, new Cosmocrator.

The importance of the Vedic, Scandinavian, or Roman ceremonials will appear more clearly when we devote a separate examination to the meaning of the repetition of the Creation, the pre-eminently divine act. For the moment, let us keep one fact in view: every territory occupied for the purpose of being inhabited or utilized as *Lebensraum* is first of all transformed from chaos into cosmos; that is, through the effect of ritual it is given a "form" which makes it become real. Evidently, for the archaic mentality, reality manifests itself as force, effectiveness, and duration. Hence the outstanding reality is the sacred; for only the sacred *is* in an absolute fashion, acts effectively, creates things and makes them endure. The innumerable gestures of consecration—of tracts and territories, of objects, of men, etc.—reveal the primitive's obsession with the real, his thirst for being.

The Symbolism of the Center

Paralleling the archaic belief in the celestial archetypes of cities and temples, and even more fully attested by documents, there is, we find, another series of beliefs, which refer to their being invested with the prestige of the Center. We examined this problem in an earlier work;[16] here we shall merely recapitulate our conclusions. The architectonic symbolism of the Center may be formulated as follows:

1. The Sacred Mountain—where heaven and earth meet—is situated at the center of the world.

2. Every temple or palace—and, by extension, every sacred city or royal residence—is a Sacred Mountain, thus becoming a Center.

3. Being an *axis mundi*, the sacred city or temple is regarded as the meeting point of heaven, earth, and hell.

A few examples will illustrate each of these symbols:

1. According to Indian beliefs, Mount Meru rises at the center of the world, and above it shines the polestar. The Ural–Altaic peoples also know of a central mountain, Sumeru, to whose summit the polestar is fixed. Iranian beliefs hold that the sacred mountain Haraberezaiti (Elburz) is situated at the center of the earth and is linked with heaven.[17] The Buddhist population of Laos, north of Siam, know of Mount Zinnalo, at the center of the world. In the *Edda*, Himinbjorg, as its name indicates, is a "celestial mountain"; it is here that the rainbow (Bifrost) reaches the dome of the sky. Similar beliefs are found among the Finns, the Japanese, and other peoples. We are reminded that for the Semangs of the Malay Peninsula an immense rock, Batu-Ribn, rises at the center of the world; above it is hell. In past times, a tree trunk on Batu—Ribn rose into the sky.[18] Hell, the center of the earth, and the "gate" of the sky are, then, situated on the same axis, and it is along this axis that passage from one cosmic region to another was effected. We should hesitate to credit the authenticity of this cosmological theory among the Semang pygmies if we did not have evidence that the same theory already existed in outline during the prehistoric period.[19] According to Mesopotamian beliefs, a central mountain joins heaven and earth; it is the Mount of the Lands,[20] the connection between territories. Properly speaking, the ziggurat was a cosmic mountain, i.e., a symbolic image of the cosmos, the seven stories representing the seven planetary heavens (as at Borsippa) or having the colors of the world (as at Ur).

Mount Tabor, in Palestine, could mean *tabbūr*, i.e., navel, *omphalos*. Mount Gerizim, in the center of Palestine, was undoubtedly invested with the prestige of the Center, for it is called "navel of the earth" (*tabbūr eres*; cf. Judges 9:37: "...See there come people down by the middle [Heb., navel] of the land..."). A tradition preserved by Peter Comestor relates that at the summer solstice the sun casts no shadow on the "Fountain of Jacob" (near Gerizim). And indeed, Peter continues, "sunt qui dicunt locum illum esse umbilicum terrae nostrae habitabilis." Palestine, being the highest country—because it was near to the summit of the cosmic mountain—was not covered by the Deluge. A rabbinic text says: "The land of Israel was not submerged by the deluge."[21] For

Christians, Golgotha was situated at the center of the world, since it was the summit of the cosmic mountain and at the same time the place where Adam had been created and buried. Thus the blood of the Saviour falls upon Adam's skull, buried precisely at the foot of the Cross, and redeems him. The belief that Golgotha is situated at the center of the world is preserved in the folklore of the Eastern Christians.[22]

2. The names of the Babylonian temples and sacred towers themselves testify to their assimilation to the cosmic mountain: "Mount of the House," "House of the Mount of All Lands," "Mount of Tempests," "Link Between Heaven and Earth."[23] A cylinder from the period of King Gudea says that "The bed-chamber [of the god] which he built was [like] the cosmic mountain..."[24] Every Oriental city was situated at the center of the world. Babylon was a *Bāb-ilāni*, a "gate of the gods," for it was there that the gods descended to earth. In the capital of the Chinese sovereign, the gnomon must cast no shadow at noon on the day of the summer solstice. Such a capital is, in effect, at the center of the universe, close to the miraculous tree (*kien-mu*), at the meeting place of the three cosmic zones: heaven, earth, and hell.[25] The Javanese temple of Borobudur is itself an image of the cosmos, and is built like an artificial mountain (as were the ziggurats). Ascending it, the pilgrim approaches the center of the world, and, on the highest terrace, breaks from one plane to another, transcending profane, heterogeneous space and entering a "pure region." Cities and sacred places are assimilated to the summits of cosmic mountains. This is why Jerusalem and Zion were not submerged by the Deluge. According to Islamic tradition, the highest point on earth is the Kaaba, because "the polestar proves that...it lies over against the center of heaven."[26]

3. Finally, because of its situation at the center of the cosmos, the temple or the sacred city is always the meeting point of the three cosmic regions: heaven, earth, and hell. *Dur-an-ki*, "Bond of Heaven and Earth," was the name given to the sanctuaries of Nippur and Larsa, and doubtless to that of Sippara. Babylon had many names, among them "House of the Base of Heaven and Earth," "Bond of Heaven and Earth." But it is always Babylon that is the scene of the connection between the earth and the lower regions, for the city had been built upon *bāb apsī*, the "Gate of the Apsu"[27]—*apsu* designating the waters of chaos before the Creation. We find the same tradition among the Hebrews. The rock of Jerusalem reached deep into the subterranean waters (*tehōm*). The Mishnah says that the Temple is situated exactly above the *tehōm* (Hebrew equivalent of *apsu*). And just as in Babylon there as the "gate of the *apsu*," the rock of the Temple in Jerusalem contained the "mouth of the *tehōm*."[28] We find similar conceptions in the Indo-European world. Among the Romans, for example, the *mundus*—that is, the trench dug around the place where a city was to be founded—constitutes the point where the lower regions and the terrestrial world meet. "When the *mundus* is open it is as if the gates of the gloomy infernal gods were open," says Varro (cited by Macrobius, *Saturnalia*, I, 16, 18). The

Italic temple was the zone where the upper (divine), terrestrial, and subterranean worlds intersected.

The summit of the cosmic mountain is not only the highest point of the earth: it is also the earth's navel, the point at which the Creation began. There are even instances in which cosmological traditions explain the symbolism of the Center in terms which might well have been borrowed from embryology. "The Holy One created the world like an embryo. As the embryo proceeds from the navel onwards, so God began to create the world from its navel onwards and from there it was spread out in different directions." The *Yoma* affirms: "The world has been created beginning from Zion."[29] In the *Rg-Veda* (for example X, 149), the universe is conceived as spreading from a central point.[30] The creation of man, which answers to the cosmogony, likewise took place at a central point, at the center of the world. According to Mesopotamian tradition, man was formed at the "navel of the earth" in *uzu* (flesh), *sar* (bond), *ki* (place, earth), where *Dur-an-ki*, the "Bond of Heaven and Earth," is also situated. Ormazd creates the primordial ox Evagdāth, and the primordial man, Gajōmard, at the center of the earth.[31] Paradise, where Adam was created from clay, is, of course, situated at the center of the cosmos. Paradise was the navel of the Earth and, according to a Syrian tradition, was established on a mountain higher than all others. According to the Syrian *Book of the Cave of Treasures*, Adam was created at the center of the earth, at the same spot where the Cross of Christ was later to be set up. The same traditions have been preserved by Judaism. The Jewish apocalypse and a midrash state that Adam was formed in Jerusalem.[32] Adam being buried at the very spot where he was created, i.e., at the center of the world, on Golgotha, the blood of the Saviour—as we have seen—will redeem him too.

The symbolism of the Center is considerably more complex, but the few aspects to which we have referred will suffice for our purpose. We may add that the same symbolism survived in the Western world down to the threshold of modern times. The very ancient conception of the temple as the *imago mundi*, the idea that the sanctuary reproduces the universe in its essence, passed into the religious architecture of Christian Europe: the basilica of the first centuries of our era, like the medieval cathedral, symbolically reproduces the Celestial Jerusalem.[33] As to the symbolism of the mountain, of the Ascension, and of the "Quest for the Center," they are clearly attested in medieval literature, and appear, though only by allusion, in certain literary works of recent centuries.[34]

Repetition of the Cosmogony

The center, then, is pre-eminently the zone of the sacred, the zone of absolute reality. Similarly, all the other symbols of absolute reality (trees of life and immortality, Fountain of Youth, etc.) are also situated at a center. The road leading to the center is a "difficult road" (*dūrohana*), and this is verified at every level of reality: difficult convolutions of a temple (as at Borobudur); pilgrimage to sacred places (Mecca, Hardwar, Jerusalem); danger–ridden voyages of the heroic expeditions in search of the Golden Fleece, the Golden Apples, the Herb of Life; wanderings in labyrinths; difficulties of the seeker for the road to the self, to the "center" of his being, and so on. The road is arduous, fraught with perils, because it is, in fact, a rite of the passage from the profane to the sacred, from the ephemeral and illusory to reality and eternity, from death to life, from man to the divinity. Attaining the center is equivalent to a consecration, an initiation; yesterday's profane and illusory existence gives place to a new, to a life that is real, enduring, and effective.

If the act of the Creation realizes the passage from the nonmanifest to the manifest or, to speak cosmologically, from chaos to cosmos; if the Creation took place from a center; if, consequently, all the varieties of being, from the inanimate to the living, can attain existence only in an area dominantly sacred—all this beautifully illuminates for us the symbolism of sacred cities (centers of the world), the geomantic theories that govern the foundation of towns, the conceptions that justify the rites accompanying their building. We studied these construction rites, and the theories which they imply, in an earlier work,[35] and to this we refer the reader. Here we shall only emphasize two important propositions:

1. Every creation repeats the pre-eminent cosmogonic act, the Creation of the world.

2. Consequently, whatever is founded has its foundation at the center of the world (since, as we know, the Creation itself took place from a center).

Among the many examples at hand, we shall choose only one, which, as it is interesting in other respects too will reappear later in our exposition. In India, before a single stone is laid, "The astrologer shows what spot in the foundation is exactly above the head of the snake that supports the world. The mason fashions a little wooden peg from the wood of the Khadira tree, and with a coconut drives the peg into the ground at this particular spot, in such a way as to peg the head of the snake securely down....If this snake should ever shake its head really violently, it would shake the world to pieces."[36] A foundation stone is placed above the peg. The cornerstone is thus situated exactly at the "center of the world." But the act of foundation at the same time repeats the cosmogonic act, for to "secure" the snake's head, to drive the peg into it, is to imitate the primordial gesture of Soma (*Rg-Veda*, II, 12, 1) or of Indra when the latter "smote the Serpent in his lair" (VI, 17, 9), when his thunderbolt "cut off its head" (I, 52, 10). The serpent symbolizes chaos, the formless and nonmanifested. Indra comes upon Vrtra (IV, 19, 3) undivided (*aparvan)*, unawakened (*abudhyam*), sleeping (*abudhyamānam*), sunk in deepest sleep (*susupanam*), outstretched (*aśayānam*). The hurling of the lightning and the decapitation are equivalent to the act of Creation, with passage from the nonmanifested to the manifested, from the formless to the formed. Vrtra had confiscated the waters and was keeping them in the hollows of the mountains. This means either that Vrtra was the absolute master—in the same manner as Tiamat or any serpent divinity—of all chaos before the Creation; or that the great serpent, keeping the waters for himself alone, had left the whole world ravaged by drought. Whether this confiscation occurred before the act of Creation or is to be placed after the foundation of the world, the meaning remains the same: Vrtra "hinders"[37] the world from being made, or from enduring. Symbol of the nonmanifested, of the latent, or of the formless, Vrtra represents the chaos which existed before the Creation.

In our commentaries on the legend of Master Manole (cf. note 35, above) we attempted to explain construction rites through imitation of the cosmogonic gesture. The theory that these rites imply comes down to this: nothing can endure if it is not "animated," if it is not, through a sacrifice, endowed with a "soul"; the prototype of the construction rite is the sacrifice that took place at the time of the foundation of the world. In fact, in certain archaic cosmogonies, the world was given existence through the sacrifice of a primordial monster, symbolizing chaos (Tiamat), or through that of a cosmic giant (Ymir, Pan-Ku, Purusa). To assure the reality and the enduringness of a construction, there is a repetition of the divine act of perfect construction: the Creation of the worlds and of man. As the first step, the "reality" of the site is secured through consecration of the ground, i.e., through its transformation into a center; then the validity of the act of construction is confirmed by repetition of the divine sacrifice. Naturally, the consecration of the center occurs in a space qualitatively different from profane space. Through the paradox of rite, every consecrated space coincides with the center of the world, just as the time of any ritual coincides with the mythical time of the "beginning." Through repetition of the cosmogonic act, concrete time, in which the construction takes place, is projected into mythical time, *in illo tempore*, when the foundation of the world occurred. Thus the reality and the enduringness of a construction are assured not only by the transformation of profane space into a transcendent space (the center) but also by the transformation of concrete time into mythical time. Any ritual whatever, as we shall see later, unfolds not only in a consecrated space (i.e., one different in essence from profane space) but also in a "sacred time," "once upon a time" (*in illo tempore, ab origine*), that is, when the ritual was performed for the first time by a god, an ancestor, or a hero.

Divine Models of Rituals

E very ritual has a divine model, an archetype; this fact is well enough known for us to confine ourselves to recalling a few examples. "We must do what the gods did in the beginning" (*Śatapatha Brāhmana*, VII, 2, 1, 4). "Thus the gods did; thus men do" (*Taittirīya Brāhmana*), I, 5, 9, 4). This Indian adage summarizes all the theory underlying rituals in all countries. We find the theory among so-called primitive peoples no less than we do in developed cultures. The aborigines of southeastern Australia, for example, practice circumcision with a stone knife because it was thus that their ancestors taught them to do; the Amazulu Negroes do likewise because Unkulunkulu (civilizing hero) decreed *in illo tempore*: "Let men circumcise, that they may not be boys."[38] The hako ceremony of the Pawnee Indians was revealed to the priests by Tirawa, the supreme God, at the beginning of time. Among the Sakalavas of Madagascar, "all domestic, social, national, and religious customs and ceremonies must be observed in conformity with the *lilin-draza*, i.e., with the established customs and unwritten laws inherited from the ancestors..."[39] It is useless to multiply examples; all religious acts are held to have been founded by gods, civilizing heroes, or mythical ancestors.[40] It may be mentioned in passing that, among primitives, not only do rituals have their mythical model but any human act whatever acquires effectiveness to the extent to which it exactly *repeats* an act performed at the beginning of time by a god, a hero, or an ancestor. We shall return at the end of this chapter to these model acts, which men only repeat again and again.

However, as we said, such a "theory" does not justify ritual only in primitive cultures. In the Egypt of the later centuries, for example, the power of rite and word possessed by the priests was due to imitation of the primordial gesture of the god Thoth, who had created the world by the force of his word. Iranian tradition knows that religious festivals were instituted by Ormazd to commemorate the stages of the cosmic Creation, which continued for a year. At the end of each period—representing respectively, the creation of the sky, the waters, the earth, plants, animals, and man—Ormazd rested for five days, thus instituting the principal Mazdean festivals (cf. *Bundahišn*, I, A 18ff). Man only repeats the act of the Creation; his religious calendar commemorates, in the space of a year, all the cosmogonic phases which took place *ab origine*. In fact, the sacred year ceaselessly repeats the Creation; man is contemporary with the cosmogony and with the anthropogony because ritual projects him into the mythical epoch of the beginning. A bacchant, through his orgiastic rites, imitates the drama of the suffering Dionysos; an Orphic, through his initiation ceremonial, repeats the original gestures of Orpheus.

The Judaeo-Christian Sabbath is also an *imitatio dei*. The Sabbath rest reproduces the primordial gesture of the Lord, for it was on the seventh day of the Creation that God "...rested...from all his work which he had made" (Genesis 2:2). The message of the Savior is first of all an example which demands imitation. After washing his disciples' feet, Jesus said to them: "For I have given you an example, that ye should do as I have done to you" (John 13:15). Humility is only a virtue; but humility practiced after the Saviour's example is a religious act and a means of salvation: "...as I have loved you, that ye also love one another" (John 13:34; 15:12). This Christian love is consecrated by the example of Jesus. Its actual practice annuls the sin of the human condition and makes man divine. He who believes in Jesus can do what He did; his limitations and impotence are abolished. "He that believeth on me, the works that I do shall he do also..." (John 14:12). The liturgy is precisely a commemoration of the life and Passion of the Saviour. We shall see later that this commemoration is in fact a reactualization of those days.

Marriage rites too have a divine model, and human marriage reproduces the hierogamy, more especially the union of heaven and earth. "I am Heaven," says the husband, "thou art Earth" (*dyaur aham, pritivī tvam; Brahadāranyaka Upanisad*, VI, 4, 20). Even in Vedic times, husband and bride are assimilated to heaven and earth (*Atharva-Veda*, XIV, 2, 71), while in another hymn (*Atharva-Veda*, XIV, 1) each nuptial gesture is justified by a prototype in mythical times: "Wherewith Agni grasped the right hand of this earth, therefore grasp I thy hand...Let god Savitar grasp thy hand...Tvashtar disposed the garment for beauty, by direction of Brhaspati, of the poets; therewith let Savitar and Bhaga envelop this woman, like Sūrya, with progeny (48, 49, 52)."[41] In the procreation ritual transmitted by the *Brhadāranyaka Upanisad*, the generative act becomes a hierogamy of cosmic proportions, mobilizing a whole group of gods: "Let Visnu make the womb prepared! Let Tvashtri shape the various forms! Prajāpati—let him pour in! Let Dhātri place the germ for thee!" (VI, 4, 21).[42] Dido celebrates her marriage with Aeneas in the midst of a violent storm (Virgil, *Aeneid*, VI, 160); their union coincides with that of the elements; heaven embraces its bride, dispensing fertilizing rain. In Greece, marriage rites imitated the example of Zeus secretly uniting himself with Hera (Pausanias, II, 36, 2). Diodorus Siculus tells us that the Cretan hierogamy was imitated by the inhabitants of that island; in other words, the ceremonial union found its justification in a primordial event which occurred *in illo tempore*.

What must be emphasized is the cosmogonic structure of all these matrimonial rites: it is not merely a question of imitating an exemplary model, the hierogamy between heaven and earth; the principal consideration is the result of that hierogamy, i.e., the cosmic

Creation. This is why, in Polynesia, when a sterile woman wants to be fecundated, she imitates the exemplary gesture of the Primordial Mother, who, *in illo tempore*, was laid on the ground by the great god, Io. And the cosmogonic myth is recited on the same occasion. In divorce proceedings, on the contrary, an incantation is chanted in which the "separation of heaven and earth" is invoked.[43] The ritual recitation of the cosmogonic myth on the occasion of marriages is current among numerous peoples; we shall return to it later. For the moment let us point out that cosmic myth serves as the exemplary model not only in the case of marriages but also in the case of any other ceremony whose end is the restoration of integral wholeness; this is why the myth of the Creation of the World is recited in connection with cures, fecundity, childbirth, agricultural activities, and so on. The cosmogony first of all represents Creation.

Demeter lay with Iasion on the newly sown ground, at the beginning of spring (*Odyssey*, V, 125). The meaning of this union is clear: it contributes to promoting the fertility of the soil, the prodigious surge of the forces of telluric creation. This practice was comparatively frequent, down to the last century, in northern and central Europe—witness the various customs of symbolic union between couples in the fields.[44] In China, young couples went out in spring and united on the grass in order to stimulate "cosmic regeneration" and "universal germination." In fact, every human union has its model and its justification in the hierogamy, the cosmic union of the elements. Book IV of the *Li Chi*, the "Yüeh Ling" (book of monthly regulations), specifies that his wives must present themselves to the emperor to cohabit with him in the first month of spring, when thunder is heard. Thus the cosmic example is followed by the sovereign and the whole people. Marital union is a rite integrated with the cosmic rhythm and validated by that integration.

The entire Paleo-Oriental symbolism of marriage can be explained through celestial models. The Sumerians celebrated the union of the elements on the day of the New Year; throughout the ancient East, the same day receives its luster not only from the hierogamy but also from the rites of the king's union with the goddess.[45] It is on New Year's day that Ishtar lies with Tammuz, and the king reproduces this mythical hierogamy by consummating ritual union with the goddess (i.e., with the hierodule who represents her on earth) in a secret chamber of the temple, where the nuptial bed of the goddess stands. The divine union assures terrestrial fecundity; when Ninlil lies with Enlil, rain begins to fall.[46] The same fecundity is assured by the ceremonial union of the king, that of couples on earth, and so on. The world is regenerated each time the hierogamy is imitated, i.e., each time matrimonial union is accomplished. The German *Hochzeit* is derived from *Hochgezît*, New Year festival. Marriage regenerates the "year" and consequently confers fecundity, wealth, and happiness.

The assimilation of the sexual act to agricultural work is frequent in numerous cultures.[47] In the *Śatapatha Brāhmana* (VII, 2, 2, 5) the earth is assimilated to the female organ of generation (*yoni*) and the seed to the *semen virile.* "Your women are your tilth, so come into your tillage how you choose" (Qur'ân, II, 223).[48] The majority of collective orgies find a ritual justification in fostering the forces of vegetation: they take place at certain critical periods of the year, e.g., when the seed sprouts or the harvests ripen, and always have a hierogamy as their mythical model. Such, for example, is the orgy practiced by the Ewe tribe (West Africa) at the time when the barley begins to sprout; the orgy is legitimized by a hierogamy (young girls are offered to the python god). We find this same legitimization among the Oraons: their orgy takes place in May, at the time of the union of the sun god with the earth goddess. All these orgiastic excesses find their justification, in one way or another, in a cosmic or biocosmic act: regeneration of the year, critical period of the harvest, and so forth. The boys who paraded naked through the streets of Rome at the Floralia (April 28) or who, at the Lupercalia, touched women to exorcise their sterility; the liberties permitted throughout India on the occasion of the Holi festival; the licentiousness which was the rule in central and northern Europe at the time of the harvest festival and against which the ecclesiastical authorities struggled so unavailingly[49]—all these manifestations also had a superhuman prototype and tended to institute universal fertility abundance.[50]

For the purpose of this study, it is of no concern that we should know to what extent marriage rites and the orgy created the myths which justify them. What is important is that both the orgy and marriage constituted rituals imitating divine gestures or certain episodes of the sacred drama of the cosmos—the legitimization of human acts through an extrahuman model. If the myth sometimes followed the rite—for example, preconjugal ceremonial unions preceded the appearance of the myth of the preconjugal relations between Hera and Zeus, the myth which served to justify them—the fact in no wise lessens the sacred character of the ritual. The myth is "late" only as a formulation; but its content is archaic and refers to sacraments—that is, to acts which presuppose an absolute reality, a reality which is extrahuman.

Archetypes of Profane Activities

T o summarize, we might say that the archaic world knows nothing of "profane" activities: every act which has a definite meaning—hunting, fishing, agriculture; games, conflicts, sexuality—in some way participates in the sacred. As we shall see more clearly later, the only profane activities are those which have no mythical meaning that is, which lack exemplary models. Thus we may say that every responsible activity in pursuit of a definite end is, for the archaic world, a ritual. But since the majority of these activities have undergone a long process of desacralization and have, in modern societies, become profane, we have thought it proper to group them separately.

Take the dance, for example. All dances were originally sacred; in other words, they had an extrahuman model. The model may in some cases have been a totemic or emblematic animal, whose motions were reproduced to conjure up its concrete presence through magic, to increase its numbers, to obtain incorporation into the animal on the part of man. In other cases the model may have been revealed by a divinity (for example the pyrrhic, the martial dance created by Athena) or by a hero (cf. Theseus' dance in the Labyrinth). The dance may be executed to acquire food, to honor the dead, or to assure good order in the cosmos. It may take place upon the occasion of initiations, of magico-religious ceremonies, of marriages, and so on. But all these details need not be discussed here. What is of interest to us is its presumed extrahuman origin (for every dance was created *in illo tempore*, in the mythical period, by an ancestor, a totemic animal, a god, or a hero). Choreographic rhythms have their model outside of the profane life of man; whether they reproduce the movements of the totemic or emblematic animal, or the motions of the stars; whether they themselves constitute rituals (labyrinthine steps, leaps, gestures performed with ceremonial instruments)—a dance always imitates an archetypal gesture or commemorates a mythical moment. In a word, it is a repetition, and consequently a reactualization, of *illud tempus*, "those days."

Struggles, conflicts, and wars for the most part have a ritual cause and function. They are a stimulating opposition between the two halves of a clan, or a struggle between the representatives of two divinities (for example, in Egypt, the combat between two groups representing Osiris and Set); but this always commemorates an episode of the divine and cosmic drama. War or the duel can in no case be explained through rationalistic motives. Hocart has very rightly brought out the ritual role of hostilities.[51] Each time the conflict is repeated, there is imitation of an archetypal model. In Nordic tradition, the first duel took place when Thor, provoked by the giant Hrungnir, met him at the "frontier" and conquered him in single combat. The motif is found again in Indo-European mythology, and Georges Dumézil[52] rightly regards it as a late but authentic version of the very ancient scenario of a military initiation. The young warrior had to reproduce the combat between Thor and Hrungnir: in fact, the military initiation consists in an act of daring whose mythical prototype is the slaying of a three-headed monster. The frenzied *berserkir*, ferocious warriors, realized precisely the state of sacred fury (*wut, menos, furor*) of the primordial world.

The Indian ceremony of the consecration of a king, the *rājasūya*, "is only the terrestrial reproduction of the ancient consecration which Varuna, the first Sovereign, performed for his own benefit—as the *Brāhmana* repeat again and again...All through the ritual exegeses, we find it tediously but instructively reiterated that if the king makes such and such a gesture, it is because in the dawn of time, on the day of his consecration, Varuna made it."[53] And this same mechanism can be shown to exist in all other traditions, so far as the available documentation permits.[54] Construction rituals repeat the primordial act of the cosmogonic construction. The sacrifice performed at the building of a house, church, bridge, is simply the imitation, on the human plane, of the sacrifice performed *in illo tempore* to give birth to the world.

As for the magical and pharmaceutical value of certain herbs, it too is due to a celestial prototope of the plant, or to the fact that it was first gathered by a god. No plant is precious in itself, but only through its participation in an archetype, or through the repetition of certain gestures and words which, by isolating it from profane space, consecrate it. Thus two formulas of incantation, used in England in the sixteenth century at the gathering of simples, state the origin of their therapeutic virtue: they grew for the first time (i.e., *ab origine*) on the sacred hill of Calvary, at the "center" of the Earth:

> Haile be thou, holie hearbe, growing on the ground;/all in the mount Caluarie first wert thou found./Thou art good for manie a sore, and healest manie a wound;/in the name of sweet Jesus, I take thee from the ground [1584].

> Hallowed be thou, Vervein [verbena], as thou growest on the ground,/for in the Mount of Calvary, there thou wast first found./Thou healedst our Saviour Jesus Christ, and staunchest his bleeding wound;/in the name of [Father, Son, Holy Ghost], I take thee from the ground [1608].

The effectiveness of these herbs is attributed to the fact that their prototypes were discovered at a decisive cosmic moment (*in illo tempore*) on Mount Calvary. They received their Consecration for having healed the Redeemer's wounds. The virtue of gathered herbs is effective only insofar as the person gathering them repeats this primordial gesture of cure. This is why an old formula of incantation says: "We go to gather herbs to put them on the wounds of the Lord..."[55]

These formulas of popular Christian magic continue an ancient tradition. In India, for example, the herb *Kapitthaka* (*Feronia elephantum*) cures sexual impotence because, *ab origine*, the Gandharva used it to restore the virility of Varuna. Hence the ritual gathering of this herb is, in effect, a repetition of the Gandharva's act. "Thee that the Gandharva dug for Varuna whose virility was dead, thee here do we dig, a penis-erecting herb" (*Atharva-Veda* IV, 4, 1).[56] A long invocation in the *Papyrus magique de Paris* indicates the exceptional status of the herb gathered:

> Thou wast sown by Cronos, received by Hera, preserved by Ammon, brought forth by
> Isis, nourished by rainy Zeus; thou grewest by grace of the Sun and dew...

For Christians, medicinal herbs owed their effectiveness to the fact that they were found for the first time on the mount of Calvary. For the ancients, herbs owed their curative virtues to the fact that they were first discovered by gods. "Betony, thou who wast first discovered by Aesculapius, or by the centaur Chiron..."—such is the invocation recommended by a treatise on herbs.[57]

It would be tedious, as well as purposeless, for this essay to mention the mythical prototypes of all human activities. The fact that human justice, for example which is founded upon the idea of "law," has a celestial and transcendent model in the cosmic norms (*tao, artha, rta, tzedek, themis,* etc.) is too well known for us to insist upon it. That "works of human art are imitations of those of divine art" (*Aitareya Brāhmana,* VI, 27)[58] is likewise a leitmotiv of archaic aesthetics, as Ananda K. Coomaraswamy's studies have admirably shown.[59] It is interesting to observe that the state of beatitude itself, *eudaimonia,* is an imitation of the divine condition, not to mention the various kinds of *enthousiasmos* created in the soul of man by the repetition of certain acts realized by the gods *in illo tempore* (Dionysiac orgy, etc.): "The Working of the Gods, eminent in blessedness, will be one apt for Contemplative Speculation: and of all human Workings that will have the greatest capacity for Happiness which is nearest akin to this" (Aristotle, *Nicomachean Ethics,* 1178*b,* 21);[60] "to become as like as possible to God" (Plato, *Theaetetus,* 176*e*); "haec hominis est perfectio, similitudo Dei" (St. Thomas Aquinas).

We must add that, for the traditional societies, all the important acts of life were revealed *ab origine* by gods or heroes. Men only repeat these exemplary and paradigmatic gestures *ad infinitum.* The Yuin tribe of Australia know that Daramulun, the "All Father," invented, for their especial benefit, all the utensils and arms that they have employed down to today. In the same way the Kurnai tribe know that Mungan-ngaua, the Supreme Being, lived among them, on earth, at the beginning of time, in order to teach them to make their implements, boats, weapons, "in fact, all the arts they know."[61] In New Guinea, many myths tell of long sea voyages, "and thus they provide exemplars for the modern voyagers," as well as for all other activities, "whether of love, or war, or rain-making, or fishing, or whatever else...[Myth] gives precedents for the construction, the tabu on sexual intercourse, etc." When a captain goes to sea, he personifies the mythical hero Aori. "He wears the costume which Aori is supposed to have worn, with a blackened face (and in a way prematurely) the same kind of *love* in his hair which Aori plucked from Iviri's head. He dances on the platform and extends his arms like Aori's wings...A man told me that when he went fish shooting (with bow and arrow) he pretended to be Kivavia himself."[62] He did not implore Kivavia's favor and help; he identified himself with the mythical hero.

This same symbolism of mythical precedents is to be found in other primitive cultures. In regard to the Karuk Indians of California, J. P. Harrington writes: "Everything that the Karuk did was enacted because the Ikxareyavs were believed to have set the example in story times. The Ikxareyavs were the people who were in America before the Indians came. Modern Karuks, in a quandary now to render the word, volunteer such translations as 'the princes,' 'the chiefs,' 'the angels'... [These Ikxareyavs...] remaining with the Karuk only long enough to state and start all customs, telling them in every instance, 'Humans will do the same.' These doings and sayings are still related and quoted in the medicine formulas of the Karuk."[63]

The curious system of ritual commerce—the potlatch—which is found in the American Northwest, and to which Marcel Mauss has devoted a well-known study,[64] is only the repetition of a practice introduced by the ancestors in mythical times. It would be easy to multiply examples.[65]

Myths and History

Each of the examples cited in the present chapter reveals the same "primitive" ontological conception: an object or an act becomes real only insofar as it imitates or repeats an archetype. Thus, reality is acquired solely through repetition or participation; everything which lacks an exemplary model is "meaningless," i.e., it lacks reality. Men would thus have a tendency to become archetypal and paradigmatic. This tendency may well appear paradoxical, in the sense that the man of a traditional culture sees himself as real only to the extent that he ceases to be himself (for a modern observer) and is satisfied with imitating and repeating the gestures of another. In other words, he sees himself as real, i.e., as "truly himself," only, and precisely, insofar as he ceases to be so. Hence it could be said that this "primitive" ontology has a Platonic structure; and in that case Plato could be regarded as the outstanding philosopher of "primitive mentality," that is, as the thinker who succeeded in giving philosophic currency and validity to the modes of life and behavior of archaic humanity. Obviously, this in no way lessens the originality of his philosophic genius; for his great title to our admiration remains his effort to justify this vision of archaic humanity theoretically, through the dialectic means which the spirituality of his age made available to him.

But our interest here is not in this aspect of Platonic philosophy; it is in archaic ontology. Recognizing the Platonic structure of that ontology would not take us very far. No less important is the second conclusion to be drawn from analyzing the facts cited in the foregoing pages—that is, the abolition of time through the imitation of archetypes and the repetition of paradigmatic gestures. A sacrifice, for example, not only exactly reproduces the initial sacrifice revealed by a god *ab origine*, at the beginning of time, it also takes place at that same primordial mythical moment; in other words, every sacrifice repeats the initial sacrifice and coincides with it. All sacrifices are performed at the same mythical instant of the beginning; through the paradox of rite, profane time and duration are suspended. And the same holds true for all repetitions, i.e., all imitations of archetypes; through such imitation, man is projected into the mythical epoch in which the archetypes were first revealed. Thus we perceive a second aspect of primitive ontology: insofar as an act (or an object) acquires a certain reality through the repetition of certain paradigmatic gestures, and acquires it through that alone, there is an implicit abolition of profane time, of duration, of "history"; and he who reproduces the exemplary gesture thus finds himself transported into the mythical epoch in which its revelation took place.

The abolition of profane time and the individual's projection into mythical time do not occur, of course, except at essential periods—those, that is, when the individual is truly himself: on the occasion of rituals or of important acts (alimentation, generation, ceremonies, hunting, fishing, war, work). The rest of his life is passed in profane time, which is without meaning: in the state of "becoming." Brahmanic tests clearly bring out the heterogeneity of these two times, the sacred and the profane, of the modality of the gods, which is coupled with immortality, and the modality of man, which is coupled with death. Insofar as he repeats the archetypal sacrifice, the sacrificer, in full ceremonial action, abandons the profane world of mortals and introduces himself into the divine world of the immortals. He himself, indeed, declares this, in the following terms: "I have attained Heaven, the gods; I am become immortal!" (*Taittirīya Samhitā*, I, 7, 9). Should he now descend once more to the profane world, which he has left during the rite, he would die instantly; hence various rites of desacralization are indispensable to restore the sacrificer to profane time. The same is true in the case of ceremonial sexual union: the individual ceases to live in profane and meaningless time, since he is imitating a divine archetype "I am Heaven, thou art Earth," etc.). The Melanesian fisherman, when he goes to sea, becomes the hero Aori and is projected into mythical time, into the moment when the paradigmatic voyage took place. Just as profane space is abolished by the symbolism of the Center, which projects any temple, palace, or building into the same central point of mythical space, so any meaningful act performed by archaic man, any real act, i.e., any repetition of an archetypal gesture, suspends duration, abolishes profane time, and participates in mythical time.

This suspension of profane time answers to a profound need on the part of primitive man, as we shall have occasion to observe in the next chapter when we examine a series of parallel conceptions relating to the regeneration of time and the symbolism of the New Year. We shall then understand the significance of this need, and we shall see that the man of archaic cultures tolerates "history" with difficulty and attempts periodically to abolish it. The facts that we have examined in the present chapter will then acquire other meanings. But before entering upon the problem of the regeneration of time, we must look from another point of view at the mechanism of the transformation of man into archetype through repetition. We shall examine a definite case: to what extent does collective memory preserve the recollection of a historic event? We have seen that the warrior, whoever he may be, imitates a hero and seeks to approach this archetypal model as closely as possible. Let us now see what the memory of the people retains concerning a well-documented historical personage. By attacking the problem from this angle, we advance a step because in this instance we are dealing with a society which, though "popular," cannot be called primitive.

Thus, to give only one example, a familiar paradigmatic myth recounts the combat between the hero and a gigantic serpent, often three-headed, sometimes replaced by a marine monster (Indra, Herakles, and others; Marduk). Where tradition is still more or less a living thing, great monarchs consider themselves imitators of the primordial hero: Darius saw himself as a new Thraetona, the mythical Iranian hero who was said to have slain a three-headed monster; for him—and through him—history was regenerated, for it was in fact the revivification, the reactualization, of a primordial heroic myth. The Pharaoh's adversaries were considered "sons of ruin, wolves, dogs," and so forth. In the *Book of Apophis* the enemies whom the Pharaoh fights are identified with the dragon Apophis, while the Pharaoh himself is assimilated with the god Re, conqueror of the dragon.[66] The same transfiguration of history into myth, but from another point of view, is found in the visions of the Hebrew poets. In order to "tolerate history," that is, to endure their military defeats and political humiliations, the Hebrews interpreted contemporary events by means of the very ancient cosmogonico-heroic myth, which, though it of course admitted the provisional victory of the dragon, above all implied the dragon's final extinction through a King-Messiah. Thus their imagination gives the Gentile kings (Zadokite Fragments, IX:19–20) the characteristics of the dragon: such is the Pompey described in the Psalms of Solomon (IX:29), the Nebuchadnezzar presented by Jeremiah (51:34). And in the Testament of Asher (VII:3) the Messiah kills the dragon under water (cf. Psalm 74:13).

In the case of Darius and the Pharaoh, as in that of the Hebrew Messianic tradition, we are dealing with the conception of an "elite" who interpret contemporary history by means of a myth. A series of contemporary events is given an articulation and an interpretation that conform with the atemporal model of the heroic myth. For a hyper-critical modern, Darius' pretention might signify boasting or political propaganda; the mythical transformation of the Gentile kings into dragons might represent a labored intention on the part of a Hebraic minority unable to tolerate "historical reality" and seeking to console themselves at any cost by taking refuge in myth and wishful thinking. That such an interpretation is erroneous, because it makes no allowance for the structure of archaic mentality, is shown, for one thing, by the fact that popular memory applies a strictly analogous process of articulation and interpretation to historical events and personages. If the transformation into myth of the biography of Alexander the Great may be suspected of having a literary origin, and consequently be accused of artificiality, the objection has no force in regard to the documents to which we shall now refer.

Dieudonné de Gozon, third Grand Master of the Knights of St. John at Rhodes, has remained famous for having slain the dragon of Malpasso. Legend, as was natural, bestowed on him the attributes of St. George, famed for his victorious fight with the monster. Needless to say, the documents of de Gozon's period make no reference to any such combat, and it does not begin to be mentioned until some two centuries after the hero's birth. In other words, by the simple fact that he was regarded as a hero, de Gozon was identified with a category, an archetype, which, entirely disregarding his real exploits, equipped him with a mythical biography from which it was *impossible* to omit combat with a reptilian monster.[67]

Petru Caraman, in a copiously documented study of the genesis of the historical ballad, shows that, of a definitely established historical event—the expedition against Poland by Malkoš Pasha in 1499, in an especially severe winter, which is mentioned in Leunclavius' chronicle as well as in other Polish sources, and during the course of which a whole Turkish army perished in Moldavia—the Romanian ballad that narrates the catastrophic Turkish expedition preserves almost nothing, the historical event having been completely translated into a mythical action (Malkoš Pasha fighting King Winter, etc.).[68]

This "mythicization" of historical personages appears in exactly the same way in Yugoslavian heroic poetry. Marko Kraljević, protagonist of the Yugoslavian epic, became famous for his courage during the second half of the fourteenth century. His historical existence is unquestionable, and we even know the date of his death (1394). But no sooner is Marko's historical personality received into the popular memory than it is abolished and his biography is reconstructed in accordance with the norms of myth. His mother is a *Vila*, a fairy, just as the Greek heroes were the sons of nymphs or naiads. His wife is also a *Vila*; he wins her through a ruse and takes great care to hide her wings lest she find them, take flight, and abandon him—as, by the way, in certain variants of the ballad, proves to be the case after the birth of their first child.[69] Marko fights a three-headed dragon and kills it, after the archetypal model of Indra, Thraetona, Herakles, and others.[70] In accordance with the myth of the enemy brothers, he too fights with his brother Andrija and kills him. Anachronisms abound in the cycle of Marko, as in all other archaic epic cycles. Marko, who died in 1394, is now the friend, now the enemy of John Hunyadi, who distinguished himself in the wars against the Turks *ca.* 1450.

It is interesting to note that these two heroes are brought together in the manuscripts of epic ballads of the seventeenth century; that is, two centuries after Hunyadi's death. In modern epic poems, anachronisms are far less frequent.[71] The personages celebrated in them have not yet had time to be transformed into mythical heroes.

The same mythical prestige glorifies other heroes of Yugoslavian epic poetry. Vukašin and Novak marry *Vila*. Vuk (the "Dragon Despot") fights the dragon of Jastrebac and can himself turn into a dragon. Vuk, who reigned in Syrmia between 1471 and 1485, comes to the rescue of Lazar and Milica, who died about a century earlier. In the poems whose action centers upon the first battle of Kossovo (1389), persons figure who had been dead for twenty years (e.g., Vukašin) or who were not to die until a century later (Erceg Stjepan). Fairies (*Vila*) cure wounded heroes, resuscitate them, foretell the future to them, warn them of imminent dangers, just as in myth a female being aids and protects the hero. No heroic "ordeal" is omitted: shooting an arrow through an apple, jumping over several horses, recognizing a girl among a group of youths dressed alike, and so on.[72]

Certain heroes of the Russian *byliny* are most probably connected with historical prototypes. A number of the heroes of the Kiev cycle are mentioned in the chronicles. But with this their historicity ends. We cannot even determine whether the Prince Vladimir who forms the center of the Kiev cycle is Vladimir I, who died in 1015, or Vladimir II, who reigned from 1113 to 1125. As for the great heroes of the *byliny* of this cycle, Svyatogor, Mikula, and Volga, the historic elements preserved in their persons and adventures amount to almost nothing. They end by becoming indistinguishable from the heroes of myths and folk tales. One of the protagonists of the Kiev cycle, Dobrynya Nikitich, who sometimes appears in the *byliny* as Vladimir's nephew, owes his principal fame to a purely mythical exploit: he kills a twelve-headed dragon. Another hero of the *byliny*, St. Michael of Potuka, kills a dragon that is on the point of devouring a girl brought to it as an offering.

To a certain extent, we witness the metamorphosis of a historical figure into a mythical hero. We are not referring merely to the supernatural elements summoned to reinforce their legends: for example the hero Volga, of the Kiev cycle, changes into a bird or a wolf, exactly like a shaman or a figure of ancient legend; Egori is born with silver feet, golden arms, and his head covered with pearls; Ilya of Murom resembles a giant of folklore—he boasts that he can make heaven and earth touch. But there is something else: this mythicization of the historical prototypes who gave the popular epic songs their heroes takes place in accordance with an exemplary standard; they are "formed after the image" of the heroes of ancient myth. They all resemble one another in the fact of their miraculous birth; and, just as in the *Mahābhārata* and the Homeric poems, at least one of their parents is divine. As in the epic songs of the Tatars and the Polynesians, these heroes undertake a journey to heaven or descend into hell.

To repeat, the historical character of the persons celebrated in epic poetry is not in question. But their historicity does not long resist the corrosive action of mythicization. The historical event in itself, however important, does not remain in the popular memory, nor does its recollection kindle the poetic imagination save insofar as the particular historical event closely approaches a mythical model. In the *bylina* devoted to the catastrophes of the Napoleonic invasion of 1812, the role of Czar Alexander I as head of the army has been forgotten, as have the name and the importance of Borodino; all that survives is the figure of Kutusov in the guise of a popular hero. In 1912, an entire Serbian brigade saw Marko Kraljević lead the charge against the castle of Prilep, which, centuries earlier, had been that popular hero's fief: a particularly heroic exploit provided sufficient occasion for the popular imagination to seize upon it and assimilate it to the traditional archetype of Marko's exploits, the more so because his own castle was at stake.

"Myth is the last—not first—stage in the development of a hero."[73] But this only confirms the conclusion reached by many investigators (Caraman and others): the recollection of a historical event or a real personage survives in popular memory for two or three centuries at the utmost. This is because popular memory finds difficulty in retaining individual events and real figures. The structures by means of which it functions are different: categories instead of events, archetypes instead of historical personages. The historical personage is assimilated to his mythical model (hero, etc.), while the event is identified with the category of mythical actions (fight with a monsters, enemy brothers, etc.). If certain epic poems preserve what is called "historical truth," this truth almost never has to do with definite persons and events, but with institutions, customs, landscapes. Thus, for example, as Murko observes, the Serbian epic poems quite accurately describe life on the Austrian-Turkish and Turkish-Venetian frontier before the Peace of Karlowitz in 1699.[74] But such "historical truths" are not concerned with personalities or events, but with traditional forms of social and political life (the "becoming" of which is slower than the "becoming" of the individual)—in a word, with archetypes.

The memory of the collectivity is anhistorical. This statement implies neither a popular origin for folklore nor a collective creation for epic poetry. Murko, Chadwick, and other investigators have brought out the role of the creative personality, of the "artist," in the invention and development of epic poetry. We wish to say no more than that—quite apart from the origin of folklore themes and from the greater or lesser degree of talent in the creators of epic poetry—the memory of historical events is modified, after two or three centuries, in such a way that it can enter into the mold of the archaic mentality, which cannot accept what is individual and preserves only what is exemplary. This reduction of events to categories and of individuals to archetypes, carried out by the consciousness of the popular strata in Europe almost down to our day, is performed in conformity with archaic ontology. We might say that popular memory restores to the historical personage of modern times its meaning as imitator of the archetype and reproducer of archetypal gestures—a meaning of which the members of archaic societies have always been, and continue to be, conscious (as the examples cited in this chapter show), but which has been forgotten by such personages as Dieudonné de Gozon or Marko Kraljević.

Sometimes, though very rarely, an investigator chances to come upon the actual transformation of an event into myth. Just before the last war, the Romanian folklorist Constantin Brailoiu had occasion to record an admirable ballad in a village in Maramures. Its subject was a tragedy of love: the young suitor had been bewitched by a mountain fairy, and a few days before he was to be married, the fairy, driven by jealousy, had flung him from a cliff. The next day, shepherds found his body and, caught in a tree, his hat. They carried the body back to the village and his fiancée came to meet them; upon seeing her lover dead, she poured out a funeral lament, full of mythological allusions, a liturgical text of rustic beauty. Such was the content of the ballad. In the course of recording the variant that he was able to collect, the folklorist tried to learn the period when the tragedy had occurred; he was told that it was a very old story, which had happened "long ago." Pursuing his inquiries, however he learned that the event had taken place not quite forty years earlier. He finally even discovered that the heroine was still alive. He went to see her and heard the story from her own lips. It was a quite commonplace tragedy: one evening her lover had slipped and fallen over a cliff; he had not died instantly; his cries had been heard by mountaineers; he had been carried to the village, where he had died soon after. At the funeral, his fiancée, with the other women of the village, had repeated the customary ritual lamentations, without the slightest allusion to the mountain fairy.

Thus, despite the presence of the principal witness, a few years had sufficed to strip the event of all historical authenticity, to transform it into a legendary tale: the jealous fairy, the murder of the young man, the discovery of the dead body, the lament, rich in mythological themes, chanted by the fiancée. Almost all the people of the village had been contemporaries of the authentic historical fact; but this fact, as such, could not satisfy them: the tragic death of a young man on the eve of his marriage was something different from a simple death by accident; it had an occult meaning that could only be revealed by its identification with the category of myth. The mythicization of the accident had not stopped at the creation of a ballad; people told the story of the jealous fairy even when they were talking freely, "prosaically," of the young man's death. When the folklorist drew the villagers' attention to the authentic version, they replied that the old woman had forgotten; that her great grief had almost destroyed her mind. It was the myth that told the truth: the real story was already only a falsification. Besides, was not the myth truer by the fact that it made the real story yield a deeper and richer meaning, revealing a tragic destiny?

The anhistorical character of popular memory, the inability of collective memory to retain historical events and individuals except insofar as it transforms then into archetypes—that is, insofar as it annuls all their historical and personal peculiarities—pose a series of new problems, which we are obliged to set aside for the moment. But at this point we have the right to ask ourselves if the importance of archetypes for the consciousness of archaic man, and the inability of popular memory to retain anything but archetypes; do not reveal to us something more than the resistance to history exhibited by traditional spirituality; if this mnemonic lacuna does not reveal the transitoriness, or at least the secondary character, of human individuality as such—that individuality whose creative spontaneity, in the last analysis, constitutes the authenticity and irreversibility of history. In any case, it is remarkable that, on the one hand, popular memory refuses to preserve the personal, historical elements of a hero's biography while, on the other hand, higher mystical experiences imply a final elevation of the personal God to the transpersonal God. It would also be instructive to compare, from this point of view, the conceptions of life after death that have been elaborated by various traditions. The transformation of the dead person into an "ancestor" corresponds to the fusion of the individual into an archetypal category. In numerous traditions (in Greece for example) the souls of the common dead no longer possess a "memory"; that is, they lose what may be called their historical individuality. The transformation of the dead into ghosts, and so on, in a certain sense signifies their reidentification with the impersonal archetype of the ancestor. The fact that in the Greek tradition only heroes preserve their personality (i.e., their memory) after death, is easy to understand: having, in his life on earth, performed no actions which were not exemplary, the hero retains the memory of them, since from a certain point of view, these acts were impersonal.

Leaving aside the conceptions of the transformation of the dead into "ancestors," and regarding the fact of death as a concluding of the "history" of the individual, it still seems very natural that the post-mortem memory of that history should be limited or, in other words, that the memory of passions, of events, of all that is connected with the individual strictly speaking, comes to an end at a certain moment of his existence after death. As for the objection that an impersonal survival is equivalent to a real death (inasmuch as only the personality and the memory that are connected with duration and history can be called a survival), it is valid only from the point of view of a "historical consciousness," in other words, from the point of view of modern man, for archaic consciousness accords no importance to personal memories. It is not easy to define what such a "survival of impersonal consciousness" might mean, although certain spiritual experiences afford a glimpse. What is personal and historical in the emotion we feel when we listen to the music of Bach, in the attention necessary for the solution of a mathematical problem, in the concentrated lucidity presupposed by the examination of any philosophical question? Insofar as he allows himself to be influenced by history, modern man feels himself diminished by the possibility of this impersonal survival. But interest in the "irreversible" and the "new" in history is a recent discovery in the life of humanity. On the contrary, archaic humanity, as we shall presently see, defended itself to the utmost of its powers, against all the novelty and irreversibility which history entails.

Reflections

Mircea Eliade is one of the twentieth century's most well-known historians of religions. Born in Romania in 1907, his own special interests were in the areas of shamanism and Asian religions. From 1980 until his death in 1986, he was the editor-in-chief of the sixteen-volume *Encyclopedia of Religion*. In 1978, he was nominated for the Nobel literature prize. His most famous book is entitled *The Sacred and the Profane*. Eliade's studies of thousands of the world's religious traditions, including many that existed in the "pre-literate" period, led him to the conclusion that there was a distinction between "traditional," or "archaic" persons and cultures and those of the "modern" or "historical" era. He proposed certain structures common to all "traditional" religion, namely the categories of the sacred and the profane as well as the universality of myths and rituals which allowed "entrance" into "sacred time and space."

According to Eliade, how do objects or people acquire "meaning" in traditional or "archaic" culture? What does Eliade say happens in a "traditional" religious ritual, and what are the underlying assumptions about reality that are implied in this concept? How does he use the terms myth and history? How would members of religious communities you know (perhaps including yourself) describe the origin and function of their myths and rituals? Do you know "modern" people who fall into the category of "archaic" consciousness? Define the vocabulary words you do not know.

Notes

1. Cf. our *Patterns in Comparative Religion* (English trans., London and New York, 1958), pp. 216 ff.

2. Our *Cosmologie şi alchimie babiloniana* (Bucharest, 1937), pp. 21 ff.

3. Edward Chiera, *Sumerian Religious Texts*, I (Upland, 1924), p. 29.

4. Uno Harva (formerly Holmberg), *Der Baum des Lebens* (Annales Accademiae Scientiarum Fennicae, Helsinki, 1923), p. 39.

5. Raymond Weill, *Le Champs des roseaux et le champs des offrandes dans la religion funéraire et la religion générale* (Paris, 1936), pp. 62 ff.

6. H. S. Nyberg, "Questions de cosmogonie et de cosmologie mazdéennes," *Journal Asiatique* (Paris), CCXIX (July–Sept., 1931), pp. 35–36. But, as Henry Corbin rightly remarks, "we must take care not to reduce the contrast they [the *mēnōk* and the *gētīk*] express to a Platonic schema pure and simple. We are not dealing precisely with an opposition between idea and matter, or between the universal and the perceptible. *Mēnōk* should, rather, be translated by a celestial, invisible, spiritual, but perfectly concrete state. *Gētīk* designates an earthly visible, material state, but of a matter which is in itself wholly luminous, a matter immaterial in relation to the matter that we actually know." Corbin, "Cyclical Time in Mazdaism and Ismailism," in *Man and Time* (New York and London, 1957), p. 118.

7. Cf. the rabbinical traditions in Raphael Patai, *Man and Temple* (London, 1947), pp. 130 ff.

8. E. Burrows, "Some Cosmological Patterns in Babylonian Religion," in *The Labyrinth*, ed. S. H. Hooke (London, 1935), pp. 65 ff.

9. Cf. our *Cosmologie*, p. 22; Burrows, pp. 60 ff.

10. Wisdom of Solomon 9:8; trans. in R. H. Charles, *The Apocrypha and Pseudepigrapha of the Old Testament in English* (Oxford, 1913), I, p. 549.

11. Charles, II, p. 482.

12. Charles, II, p. 405; Alberto Pincherle, *Gli Oracoli Sibillini giudaici* (Rome, 1922), pp. 95–96.

13. Cf. van Hamel, cited by Gerardus van der Leeuw, *L'Homme primitif et la religion* (French trans., Paris, 1940), p. 110.

14. Ananda K. Coomaraswamy, *The Rg Veda as Land-náma-bók* (London, 1935), p. 16, etc.

15. For example, *Śatapatha Brāhmana*, XIV, 1, 2, 26, etc.; see below, Ch. II.

16. See our *Cosmologie*, pp. 26–50; cf. also our *Images and Symbols: Studies in Religious Symbolism* (English trans., London and New York, 1961), Ch. I.

17. Willibald Kirfel, *Die Kosmographie der Inder* (Bonn, 1920), p. 15; Harva, p. 41; Arthur Christensen, *Les Types du premier homme et du premier roi dans l'historie légendaire des Iraniens*, II (Stockholm, 1917), p. 42; our *Shamanism: Archaic Techniques of Ecstasy* (English trans., New York and London, 1964), pp. 259 ff.

18. Cf. Paul Schebesta, *Les Pygmées* (French trans., Paris, 1940), pp. 156 ff.; other examples in our *Shamanism*, pp. 280 ff.

19. Cf., for example, W. Gaerte, "Kosmische Vorstellungen im Bilde prähistorischer Zeit: Erdberg, Himmelsberg, Erdnabel und Welströme," *Anthropos* (Salzburg), IX (1914), pp. 956–79.

20. Alfred Jeremias, *Handbuch der altorientalischen Geistekultur* (2nd edn., Berlin and Leipzig, 1929), p. 130.

21. Cf. Burrows, pp. 51, 54, 68, note 1; A. J. Wensinck, *The Ideas of the Western Semites Concerning the Navel of the Earth* (Amsterdam, 1916), p. 15; Patai, p. 85. The same symbolism in Egypt: cf. Patai, p. 101, note 100.

22. E.g., among the Little Russians; Mansikka, cited by Harva, p. 72.

23. Theodor Dombart, *Der Sakralturm*, Part I: *Zikkurrat* (Munich, 1920), p. 34; cf. A. Parrot, *Ziggurats et Tour de Babel* (Paris, 1949). Indian temples are also assimilated to mountains: cf. Willy Foy, "Indische Kultbauten als Symbole des Götterbergs," in *Festschrift Ernst Windisch zum siebzigsten Geburtstag... Dargebracht* (Leipzig, 1914), pp. 213–16. The same symbolism among the Aztecs: cf. Walter Krickeberg, "Bauform und Weltbild im alten Mexico," *Paideuma* (Bamberg), IV (1950), 295–333.

24. W. F. Albright, "The Mouth of the Rivers," *The American Journal of Semitic Languages and Literatures* (Chicago), XXXV (1919), p. 173.

25. Marcel Granet, *La Pensée chinoise* (Paris, 1934), p. 324; our *Le Chamanisme*, pp. 243 ff.

26. *Kisā'ī*, fol. 15; cited by Wensinck, p. 15.

27. Jeremias, p. 113; Burrows, pp. 46 ff., 50.

28. Texts in Burrows, p. 49; cf. also Patai, pp. 55 ff.

29. Texts cited by Wensinck, pp. 19, 16; cf. also W. H. Roscher, "Neue Omphalosstudien," *Abhandlungen der Königlich Sächsischen Gesellschaft der Wissenschaft* (Leipzig), *Phil.-hist. Klasse*, XXXI, 1 (1915), pp. 16 ff., 73 ff.; Burrows, p. 57; Patai, p. 85.

30. Cf. the commentary of Kirfel, p. 8.

31. Burrows, p. 49; Christensen, I, pp. 22 ff.

32. Wensinck, p. 14 Sir E. A. Wallis Budge, *The Book of the Cave of Treasures* (trans. from the Syriac, London, 1927), p. 53; Oskar Daehnhardt, *Natursagen*, I (Leipzig, 1909), p. 112 Burrows, p. 57.

33. On the cosmic symbolism of temples in the ancient East, cf. A. M. Hocart, *Kings and Councillors* (Cairo, 1936), pp. 220 ff.; Patai, pp. 106 ff. On the cosmic symbolism of basilicas and cathedrals, see Hans Sedlimayr, "Architectur als abbildende Kunst," *Österreichische Akademie der Wissenschaften, Sitzungberichte* (Vienna), *Phil.-hist. Klasse*, 225/3 (1948), and *Die Kathedrale* (Zurich, 1950).

34. See our *Images and Symbols*.

35. *Comentari: la legenda Meșterului Manole* (Bucharest, 1943).

36. Mrs. (Margaret) Sinclair Stevenson, *The Rites of the Twice-Born* (London, 1920), p. 354 and note.

37. Mephistopheles too was *der Vater aller Hindernisse*," "the father of all hindrances" (*Faust*, v. 6209).

38. A. W. Howitt, *The Native Tribes South-East Australia* (London, 1904), pp. 645 ff; Henry Callaway, *The Religious System of the Amazulu* (London, 1869), p. 58.

39. Arnold van Gennep, *Tabou et totémisme à Madagascar* (Paris, 1904), pp. 27 ff.

40. Cf. Gerardus van der Leeuw, *Phänomenologie der Religion* (Tübingen, 1933), pp. 349 ff., 360 ff.

41. W. D. Whitney and C. R. Lanman (trans.) *Atharva-Veda* (Harvard Oriental Series, VIII, Cambridge, Mass., 1905), pp. 750–51.

42. R. E. Hume (trans.), *The Thirteen Principal Upanishads* (Oxford, 1931).

43. Cf. E. S. C. Handy, *Polynesian Religion* (Honolulu, 1927), pp. 10 ff.; Raffaele Pettazzoni, "Io and Rangi," *Pro regno pro sanctuario* [in homage to G. van der Leeuw] (Nijkerk, 1950), pp. 359-60.

44. J. W. E. Mannhardt, *Wald- und Feldkulte*, I (2nd edn., Berlin, 1904–1905), pp. 169 ff., 180 ff.

45. Cf. S. H. Hooke, ed., *Myth and Ritual* (London, 1935), pp. 9, 19, 34 ff.

46. René Labat, *Le Caractère religieux de la royauté assyro-babylonienne* (Paris, 1939), pp. 247 ff.; cf. the traces of a similar mythico-ritual complex in Israel: Patai, pp. 90 ff.

47. See the chapter on agricultural mysticism in our *Patterns in Comparative Religion*, pp. 354 ff.

48. Trans. E. H. Palmer, *Sacred Books of the East*, VI, p. 33.

49. Cf., for example, the Council of Auxerre in 590.

50. On the cosmological significance of the orgy, see Ch. II.

51. A. M. Hocart, *Le Progrés de l'homme* (French trans., Paris, 1935), pp. 183 ff., 319 ff.; cf. also W. C. MacLeod, *The Origin and History of Politics* (New York, 1931), pp. 217 ff.

52. Cf. his *Mythes et dieux des Germains* (Paris, 1939), pp. 99 ff., and his *Horace et les Curiaces* (Paris, 1942), pp. 126 ff.

53. Dumézil, *Ouranós-Váruna* (Paris, 1934), pp. 42, 62.

54. Cf. Moret's classic studies of the scared character of royalty in Egypt, and Labat's of Assyro-Babylonian royalty.

55. Ferdinand Ohrt, "Herba, gratiâ plena," *FF Communications* (Helsinki), No. 82 (1929), 17, 18; our "La Mandrogore et le mythe de la 'naissance miraculeuse,'" *Zalmoxis* (Paris and Bucharest), III (1943), 1–52, particular pp. 23 ff., and *Patterns in Comparative Religion*, pp. 296 ff.

56. Trans. Whitney and Lanman, VII, p. 149.

57. Armand Delatte, *Herbarius* (2nd edn., Liége, 1938), pp. 100, 102.

58. Cf. Plato, *Laws*, 667–69; *Statesman*, 306d, etc.

59. See especially Coomaraswamy, "The Philosophy of Mediæval and Oriental Art," *Zalmoxis* (Paris and Bucharest), I (1938), 20–49), and *Figures of Speech or Figures of Thought* (London, 1946), pp. 29–96.

60. Trans. D. P. Chase, *The Ethics of Aristotle* (London, 1934).

61. Howitt, pp. 543, 630.

62. F. E. Williams, cited by Lucien Lévy-Bruhl, *La Mythologie primitive* (Paris, 1935), pp. 162, 163–64.

63. J. P. Harrington, cited by Lévy-Bruhl, p. 165.

64. Marcel Mauss, "Essai sur le don, forme archaïque de l'échange," *Année Sociologique* (Paris), I, 2nd series (1923–24).

65. See, among others, Coomaraswamy's studies, "Vedic Exemplarism," *Harvard Journal of Asiatic Studies*, I (1936), 44–64, and *The Rg Veda as Land-náma-bók* (London, 1935).

66. Günther Roeder (ed.), *Urkunden zur Religion des alten Ägypten* (Jena, 1915), pp. 98 ff.

67. Cf. the documentation in F. W. Hasluck, *Christianity and Islam under the Sultans*, II (Oxford, 1929), p. 649.

68. Petru Caraman, "Geneza baladei istorice," *Anuarul Arhivei de Folklor* (Bucharest), I–II (1933–34).

69. Cf. the myth of the Maori hero Tawhaki, whom his wife, a fairy come down to earth from heaven, abandons after giving him a child.

70. This not the place to enter upon the problem of the combat between monster and hero (cf. Bernhard Schweitzer, *Herakles*, Tübingen, 1922; A. Lods, *Comptes rendus de l' Académie des Inscriptions*, Paris, 1943, pp. 283 ff). It is highly probable, as Georges Dumézil suggests (*Horace et les Curiaces*, Paris, 1942, especially pp. 126 ff.), that the hero's combat with a three-headed monster is the transformation into myth of an archaic initiation ritual. That this initiation does not always belong to the "heroic" type, appears, among other things, from the British Columbian parallels mentioned by Dumézil (pp. 129–30), where shamanic initiation is also involved. If, in Christian mythology, St. George fights and kills the dragon "heroically," other saints achieve the same result without fighting (cf. the French legends of St. Samson, St. Marguerite, St. Bié, etc.; Paul

Sébillot, *Le Folk-lore de France*, I, (Paris, 1904), p. 468; III (Paris, 1906), 298, 299. On the other hand, we must not forget that, apart from its possible role in the rites and myths of heroic initiation, the dragon, in many other traditions (East Asiatic, Indian, African, and others) is given a cosmological symbolism: it symbolizes the involution, the preformal modality, of the undivided "One" of pre-Creation (cf. Ananda K. Coomaraswamy, *The Darker Side of Dawn*, Washington, 1935: "Sir Gawain and the Green Knight: Indra and Namuci," *Speculum* (Cambridge, Mass.), Jan., 1944, pp. 1–23). This is why snakes and dragons are nearly everywhere identified with the "masters of the ground," with the autochthons against whom the newcomers, the "conquerors," those who are to form (i.e., create) the occupied territories, must fight. (On the assimilation of snakes and autochthons, cf. Charles Autran, *L' Epopée indoue*, Paris, 1946, pp. 66 ff.).

71. H. Munro and N. (Kershaw) Chadwick, *The Growth of Literature*, II (Cambridge, 1932–40), pp. 375 ff.

72. See the texts and critical bibliography in Chadwick, II, pp. 309–42, 374–89, etc.

73. Chadwick, III, p. 762.

74. Matthias Murito, *La Poésie populaie épique en Yougoslavie au début du XX siècle* (Paris, 1929), p. 29. An examination of the historical and mythical elements in the Germanic, Celtic, Scandinavian, and other epic literatures does not fail within the scope of this study. On this subject, the reader may refer to the Chadwicks' three volumes.

II

A
Native American
Voice

Black Elk Speaks: "The Offering of the Pipe"

The Offering of the Pipe

My friend, I am going to tell you the story of my life, as you wish; and if it were only the story of my life I think I would not tell it; for what is one man that he should make much of his winters, even when they bend him like a heavy snow? So many other men have lived and shall live that story, to be grass upon the hills.

It is the story of all life that is holy and is good to tell, and of us two-leggeds sharing in it with the four-leggeds and the wings of the air and all green things; for these are children of one mother and their father is one Spirit.

This, then is not the tale of a great hunter or of a great warrior, or of a great traveler, although I have made much meat in my time and fought for my people both as boy and man, and have gone far and seen strange lands and men. So also have many others done, and better than I. These things I shall remember by the way, and often they may seem to be the very tale itself, as when I was living them in happiness and sorrow. But now that I can see it all as from a lonely hilltop, I know it was the story of a mighty vision given to a man too weak to use it; of a holy tree that should have flourished in a people's heart with flowers and singing birds, and now is withered; and of a people's dream that died in bloody snow.

Reprinted from BLACK ELK SPEAKS, by John G. Neihardt, by permission of the University of Nebraska Press. Copyright 1932, 1959, 1972, by John G. Neihardt. Copyright © by the John G. Neihardt Trust.

But if the vision was true and mighty, as I know, it is true and mighty yet; for such things are of the spirit, and it is in the darkness of their eyes that men get lost.

So I know that it is a good thing I am going to do; and because no good thing can be done by any man alone, I will first make an offering and send a voice to the Spirit of the World, that it may help me to be true. See, I fill this sacred pipe with the bark of the red willow; but before we smoke it, you must see how it is made and what it means. These four ribbons hanging here on the stem are the four quarters of the universe. The black one is for the west where the thunder beings live to send us rain; the white one for the north, whence comes the great white cleansing wind; the red one for the east, whence springs the light and where the morning star lives to give men wisdom; the yellow for the south, whence come the summer and the power to grow.

But these four spirits are only one Spirit after all, and this eagle feather here is for that One, which is like a father, and also it is for the thoughts of men that should rise high as eagles do. Is not the sky a father and the earth a mother, and are not all living things with feet or wings or roots their children? And this hide upon the mouthpiece here, which should be bison hide, is for the earth, from whence we came and at whose breast we suck as babies all our lives, along with all the animals and birds and trees and grasses. And because it means all this, and more than any man can understand, the pipe is holy.

There is a story about the way the pipe first came to us. A very long time ago, they say, two scouts were out looking for bison; and when they came to the top of a high hill and looked north, they saw something coming a long way off, and when it came closer they cried out, "It is a woman!," and it was. Then one of the scouts, being foolish, had bad thoughts and spoke them; but the other said: "That is a sacred woman; throw all bad thoughts away." When she came still closer, they saw that she wore a fine white buckskin dress, that her hair was very long and that she was young and very beautiful. And she knew their thoughts and said in a voice that was like singing; "You do not know me, but if you want to do as you think, you may come." And the foolish one went; but just as he stood before her, there was a white cloud that came and covered them. And the beautiful young woman came out of the cloud, and when it blew away the foolish man was a skeleton covered with worms.

Then the woman spoke to the one who was not foolish: "You shall go home and tell your people that I am coming and that a big tepee shall be built for me in the center of the nation." And the man, who was very much afraid, went quickly and told the people, who did at once as they were told; and there around the big tepee they waited for the sacred woman. And after a while she came, very beautiful and singing, and as she went into the tepee this is what she sang:

> With visible breath I am walking.
> A voice I am sending as I walk.
> In a sacred manner I am walking.
> With visible tracks I am walking.
> In a sacred manner I walk.

And as she sang, there came from her mouth a white cloud that was good to smell. Then she gave something to the chief, and it was a pipe with a bison calf carved on one side to mean the earth that bears and feeds us, and with twelve eagle feathers hanging from the stem to mean the sky and the twelve moons, and these were tied with a grass that never breaks. "Behold!" she said. "With this you shall multiply and be a good nation. Nothing but good shall come from it. Only the hands of the good shall take care of it and the bad shall not even see it." Then she sang again and went out of the tepee; and as the people watched her going, suddenly it was a white bison galloping away and snorting, and soon it was gone.

This they tell, and whether it happened so or not I do not know; but if you think about it, you can see that it is true.

Now I light the pipe, and after I have offered to the powers that are one Power, and sent forth a voice to them, we shall smoke together. Offering the mouthpiece first of all to the One above—so—I send a voice:

> Hey hey! hey hey! hey hey! hey hey!

Grandfather, Great Spirit, you have been always, and before you no one has been. There is no other one to pray to but you. You yourself, everything that you see, everything has been made by you. The star nations all over the universe you have finished. The four quarters of the earth you have finished. The day, and in that day, everything you have finished. Grandfather, Great Spirit, lean close to the earth that you may hear the voice I send. You towards where the sun goes down, behold me; Thunder Beings, behold me! You where the White Giant lies in power, behold me! You where the sun shines continually, whence come the day-break star and the day, behold me! You where the summer lives, behold me! You in the depths of the heavens, an eagle of power, behold! And you, Mother Earth, the only Mother, you who have shown mercy to your children!

Hear me, four quarters of the world—a relative I am! Give me the strength to walk the soft earth, a relative to all that is! Give me the eyes to see and the strength to understand, that I may be like you. With your power only can I face the winds.

Great Spirit, Great Spirit, my Grandfather, all over the earth the faces of living things are all alike. With tenderness have these come up out of the ground. Look upon these faces of children without number and with children in their arms, that they may face the winds and walk the good road to the day of quiet.

This is my prayer; hear me! The voice I have sent is weak, yet with earnestness I have sent it. Hear me!

It is finished. Hetchetu aloh!

Now, my friend, let us smoke together so that there may be only good between us.

Reflections

B *lack Elk Speaks* is "the Life Story of a Holy Man of the Oglala Sioux" as told through John G. Neihardt (Flaming Rainbow). There is power, pride, and sadness in this Native American's discussion about his visionary experiences and the meaning of the sacred pipe.

What is the setting of Black Elk's discourse? What is a visionary experience? What can be said about the origin and nature of the universe, and the creatures in it, as envisioned by the Sioux people? Discuss the origin, meaning, and function of the sacred pipe.

III

Hinduism

Upanisads:

"Katha"

Katha

Om...
May Brahman protect us,
May he guide us,
May he give us strength and right understanding.
May love and harmony be with us all.
OM...Peace—peace—peace.

On a certain occasion Vajasrabasa, hoping for divine favor, performed a rite which required that he should give away all his possessions. He was careful, however, to sacrifice only his cattle, and of these only such as were useless—the old, the barren, the blind, and the lame. Observing this niggardliness, Nachiketa, his young son, whose heart had received the truth taught in the scriptures thought to himself: "Surely a worshiper who dares bring such worthless gifts is doomed to utter darkness!" Thus reflecting, he came to his father, and cried:

"Father, I too belong to thee: to whom givest thou *me*?"

His father did not answer; but when Nachiketa asked the question again and yet again, he replied impatiently:

"Thee I give to Death!"

Then Nachiketa thought to himself: "Of my father's many sons and disciples I am indeed the best, or at least of the middle rank, not the worst; but of what good am I to the King of Death?" Yet, being determined to keep his father's word, he said:

"Father, do not repent thy vow! Consider how it has been with those that have gone before, and how it will be with those that now live. Like corn, a man ripens and falls to the ground; like come, he springs up again in his season."

Having thus spoken, the boy journeyed to the house of Death.

But the god was not at home, and for three nights Nachiketa waited. When at length the King of Death returned, he was met by his servants, who said to him:

"A Brahmin, like to a flame of fire, entered thy house as guest, and thou wast not there. Therefore must a peace offering be made to him. With all accustomed rites, O King, thou must receive thy guest, for if a householder show not due hospitality to a Brahmin, he will lose what he most desires—the merits of his good deeds, his righteousness, his sons, and his cattle."

Then the King of Death approached Nachiketa and welcomed him with courteous words.

"0 Brahmin," he said, "I salute thee. Thou art indeed a guest worthy of all reverence. Let, I pray thee, no harm befall me! Three nights hast thou passed in my house and hast not received my hospitality; ask of me, therefore, three boons—one for each night."

"0 Death," replied Nachiketa, "so let it be. And as the first of these boons I ask that my father be not anxious about me, that his anger be appeased, and that when thou sendest me back to him, he recognize me and welcome me."

"By my will," declared Death, "thy father shall recognize thee and love thee as heretofore; and seeing thee again alive, he shall be tranquil of mind, and he shall sleep in peace."

Then said Nachiketa: "In heaven there is no fear at all. Thou, O Death, art not there, nor in that place does the thought of growing old make one tremble. There, free from hunger and from thirst, and far from the reach of sorrow, all rejoice and are glad. Thou knowest, O King, the fire sacrifice that leads to heaven. Teach me that sacrifice, for I am full of faith. This is my second wish."

Whereupon, consenting, Death taught the boy the fire sacrifice, and all the rites and ceremonies attending it. Nachiketa repeated all that he had learned, and Death, well pleased with him, said:

"I grant thee an extra boon. Henceforth shall this sacrifice be called the Nachiketa Sacrifice, after thy name. Choose now thy third boon."

And then Nachiketa considered within himself, and said:

"When a man dies, there is this doubt: Some say, he is; others say, he is not. Taught by thee, I would know the truth. This is my third wish."

"Nay," replied Death, "even the gods were once puzzled by this mystery. Subtle indeed is the truth regarding it, not easy to understand. Choose thou some other boon, O Nachiketa."

But Nachiketa would not be denied.

"Thou sayest, O Death, that even the gods were once puzzled by this mystery, and that it is not easy to understand. Surely there is no teacher. better able to explain it than thou—and there is no other boon equal to this."

To which, trying Nachiketa again, the god replied:

"Ask for sons and grandsons who shall live a hundred years. Ask for cattle, elephants, horses, gold. Choose for thyself a mighty kingdom. Or if thou canst imagine aught better, ask for that—not for sweet pleasures only but for the power, beyond all thought, to taste their sweetness. Yea, verily, the supreme enjoyer will I make make thee of every good thing. Celestial maidens, beautiful to behold, such indeed as were not meant for mortals—even these, together with their bright chariots and their musical instruments, will I give unto thee, to serve thee. But for the secret of death, O Nachiketa, do not ask!"

But Nachiketa stood fast, and said: "These things endure only till the morrow, O Destroyer of Life, and the pleasures they give wear out the senses. Keep thou therefore horses and chariots, keep dance and song, for thyself! How shall he desire wealth, O Death, who once has seen thy face? Nay, only the boon that I have chosen—that only do I ask. Having found out the society of the imperishable and the immortal, as in knowing thee I have done, how shall I, subject to decay and death, and knowing well the vanity of the flesh—how all I wish for long life?

"Tell me, O King, the supreme secret regarding which men doubt. No other boon will I ask."

Whereupon the King of Death, well pleased at heart, began to teach Nachiketa the secret of immortality.

King of Death

The good is one thing; the pleasant is another. These two, differing in their ends, both prompt to action. Blessed are they that choose the good; they that choose the pleasant miss the goal.

Both the good and the pleasant present themselves to men. The wise, having examined both, distinguish the one from the other. The wise prefer the good to the pleasant; the foolish, driven by fleshly desires, prefer the pleasant to the good.

Thou, O Nachiketa, having looked upon fleshly desires, delightful to the senses, hast renounced them all. Thou hast turned from the miry way wherein many a man wallows.

Far from each other and leading to different ends, are ignorance and knowledge. Thee, O Nachiketa, I regard as one who aspires after knowledge, for a multitude of pleasant objects were unable to tempt thee.

Living in the abyss of ignorance yet wise in their own conceit, deluded fools go round and round, the blind led by the blind.

To the thoughtless youth, deceived by the vanity of earthly possessions, the path that leads to the eternal abode is not revealed. *This world alone is real; there is no hereafter—* thinking thus, he falls again and again, birth after birth, into my jaws.

To many it is not given to hear of the Self. Many, though they hear of it, do not understand it. Wonderful is he who speaks of it. Intelligent is he who learns of it. Blessed is he who, taught by a good teacher, is able to understand it.

The truth of the Self cannot be fully understood when taught by an ignorant man, for opinions regarding it, not founded in knowledge, vary one from another. Subtler than the subtlest is this Self, and beyond all logic. Taught by a teacher who knows the Self and Brahman as one, a man leaves vain theory behind and attains to truth.

The awakening which thou hast known does not come through the intellect, but rather, in fullest measure, from the lips of the wise. Beloved Nachiketa, blessed, blessed art thou, because thou seekest the Eternal. Would that I had more pupils like thee!

Well I know that earthly treasure lasts but till the morrow. For did not I myself, wishing to be King of Death, make sacrifice with fire? But the sacrifice was a fleeting thing, performed with fleeting objects, and small is my reward, seeing that only for a moment will my reign endure.

The goal of worldly desire, the glittering objects for which all men long, the celestial pleasures they hope to gain by religious rites, the most sought-after of miraculous powers—all these were within thy grasp. But all these with firm resolve, thou hast renounced.

The ancient, effulgent being, the indwelling Spirit, subtle, deep-hidden in the lotus of the heart, is hard to know. But the wise man following the path of meditation, knows him, and is freed alike from pleasure and from pain.

The man who has learned that the Self is separate from the body, the senses, and the mind, and has fully known him, the soul of truth, the subtle principle—such a man verily attains to him, and is exceedingly glad, because he has found the source and dwelling place of all felicity. Truly do I believe, O Nachiketa, that for thee the gates of joy stand open.

Nachiketa

Teach me, O King, I beseech thee, whatsoever thou knowest to be beyond right and wrong, beyond cause and effect, beyond past, present, and future.

King of Death

Of that goal which all the Vedas declare, which is implicit in all penances, and in pursuit of which men lead lives of continence and service, of that will I briefly speak.

It is—OM.

This syllable is Brahman. This syllable is indeed supreme. He who knows it obtains his desire.

It is the strongest support. It is the highest symbol. He who knows it is reverenced as a knower of Brahman.

The Self, whose symbol is OM, is the omniscient Lord. He is not born. He does not die. He is neither cause nor effect. This Ancient One is unborn, imperishable, eternal: though the body be destroyed, he is not killed.

If the slayer think that he slays, if the slain think that he is slain, neither of them knows the truth. The Self slays not, nor is he slain.

Smaller than the smallest, greater than the greatest, this Self forever dwells within the hearts of all. When a man is free from desire, his mind and senses purified, he beholds the glory of the Self and is without sorrow.

Though seated, he travels far; though at rest, he moves all things. Who but the purest of the pure can realize this Effulgent Being, who is joy and who is beyond joy.

Formless is he, though inhabiting form. In the midst of the fleeting he abides forever. All-pervading and supreme is the Self. The wise man, knowing him in his true nature, transcends all grief.

The Self is not known through study of the scriptures, nor through subtlety of the intellect, nor through much learning; but by him who longs for him is he known.[1] Verily unto him does the Self reveal his true being.

By learning, a man cannot know him, if he desist not from evil, if he control not his senses, if he quiet not his mind, and practice not meditation.

To him Brahmins and Kshatriyas are but food, and death itself a condiment.

Both the individual self and the Universal Self have entered the cave of the heart, the abode of the Most High, but the knowers and the householders who perform the fire sacrifices see a difference between them as between sunshine and shadow.

May we perform the Nachiketa Sacrifice, which bridges the world of suffering. May we know the imperishable Brahman, who is fearless, and who is the end and refuge of those who seek liberation.

Know that the Self is the rider, and the body the chariot, that the intellect is the charioteer, and the mind the reins.[2]

The senses, say the wise, are the horses; the roads they travel are the mazes of desire. The wise call the Self the enjoyer when he is united with the body, the senses, and the mind.

When a man lacks discrimination and his mind is uncontrolled, his senses are unmanageable, like the restive horses of a charioteer. But when a man has discrimination and his mind is controlled, his senses, like the well-broken horses of a charioteer, lightly obey the rein.

He who lacks discrimination, whose mind is unsteady and whose heart is impure, never reaches the goal, but is born again and again. But he who has discrimination, whose mind is steady and whose heart is pure, reaches the goal, and having reached it is born no more.

The man who has a sound understanding for charioteer, a controlled mind for reins—he it is that reaches the end of the journey, the supreme abode of Vishnu, the all-pervading.[3]

The senses derive from physical objects, physical objects from mind, mind from intellect, intellect from ego, ego from the unmanifested seed, and the unmanifested seed from Brahman—the Uncaused Cause.

Brahman is the end of the journey. Brahman is the supreme goal.

This Brahman, this Self, deep-hidden all beings, is not revealed to all; but to the seers, pure in heart, concentrated in mind—to them is he revealed.

The senses of the wise man obey his mind, his mind obeys his intellect, his intellect obeys his ego, and his ego obeys the Self.

Arise! Awake! Approach the feet of the master and know THAT. Like the sharp edge of a razor, the sages say, is the path. Narrow it is, and difficult to tread!

Soundless, formless, intangible, undying, tasteless, odorless, without beginning, without end, eternal, immutable, beyond nature, is the Self. Knowing him as such, one is freed from death.

The Narrator

The wise man, having heard and taught the eternal truth revealed by the King of Death to Nachiketa, is glorified in the heaven of Brahma.

He who sings with devotion this supreme secret in the assembly of the Brahmins, or at the rites in memory of is fathers, is rewarded with rewards immeasurable!

King of Death

The Self-Existent made the senses turn outward. Accordingly, man looks toward what is without, and sees not what is within. Rare is he who, longing for immortality, shuts his eyes to what is without and beholds the Self.

Fools follow the desires of the flesh and fall into the snare of all-encompassing death; but the wise, knowing the Self as eternal, seek not the things that pass away.

He through whom man sees, tastes, smells, hears, feels, and enjoys, is the omniscient Lord.

He, verily, is the immortal Self. Knowing him, one knows all things.

He through whom man experiences the sleeping or waking states is the all-pervading Self. Knowing him, one grieves no more.

He who knows that the individual soul, enjoyer of the fruits of action, is the Self—ever present within, lord of time, past and future—casts out all fear. For this Self is the immortal Self.

He who sees the First-Born—born of the mind of Brahma, born before the creation of waters—and sees him inhabiting the lotus of the heart, living among physical elements, sees Brahman indeed. For this First-Born is the immortal Self.

That being who is the power of all powers, and is born as such, who embodies himself in the elements and in them exists, and who has entered the lotus of the heart, is the immortal Self.[4]

Agni, the all-seeing, who lies hidden in fire sticks, like a child well guarded in the womb, who is worshiped day by day by awakened souls, and by those who offer oblations in sacrificial fire—he is the immortal Self.[5]

That in which the sun rises and in which it sets, that which is the source of all the powers of nature and of the senses, that which nothing can transcend—that is the immortal Self.

What is within us is also without. What is without is also within. He who sees difference between what is within and what is without goes evermore from death to death.

By the purified mind alone is the indivisible Brahman to be attained. Brahman alone is—nothing else is. He who sees the manifold universe, and not the one reality, goes evermore from death to death.

That being, of the size of a thumb, dwells deep within the heart.[6] He is the lord of time, past and future. Having attained him, one fears no more. He, verily, is the immortal Self.

That being, of the size of a thumb, is like a flame without smoke. He is the lord of time, past and future, the same today and tomorrow. He, verily, is the immortal Self.

As rain, fallen on a hill, streams down its side, so runs he after many births who sees manifoldness in the Self.

As pure water poured into pure water remains pure, so does the Self remain pure, O Nachiketa, uniting with Brahman.

To the Birthless, the light of whose consciousness forever shines, belongs the city of eleven gates.[7] He who meditates on the ruler of that city knows no more sorrow. He attains liberation, and for him there can no longer be birth or death. For the ruler of that city is the immortal Self.

The immortal Self is the sun shining in the sky, he is the breeze blowing in space, he is the fire burning on the altar, he is the guest dwelling in the house; he is in all men, he is in the gods, he is in the ether, he is wherever there is truth; he is the fish that is born in water, he is the plant that grows in the soil, he is the river that gushes from the mountain—he, the changeless reality, the illimitable!

He, the adorable one, seated in the heart, is the power that gives breath. Unto him all the senses do homage.

What can remain when the dweller in this body leaves the outgrown shell, since he is verily, the immortal Self?

Man does not live by breath alone, but by him in whom is the power of breath.

And now, O Nachiketa, will I tell thee of the unseen, the eternal Brahman, and of what befalls the Self after death.

Of those ignorant of the Self, some enter into beings possessed of wombs, others enter into plants—according to their deeds and the growth of their intelligence.

That which is awake in us even while we sleep, shaping in dream the objects of our desire—that indeed is pure, that is Brahman, and that verily is called the Immortal. All the worlds have their being in that, and no one can transcend it. That is the Self.

As fire, though one, takes the shape of every object which it consumes, so the Self, though one, takes the shape of every object in which it dwells.

As air, though one, takes the shape of every object which it enters, so the Self, though one, takes the shape of every object in which it dwells.

As the sun, revealer of all objects to the seer, is not harmed by the sinful eye, nor by the impurities of the objects it gazes on, so the one Self, dwelling in all, is not touched by the evils of the world. For he transcends all.

He is one, the lord and innermost Self of all; of one form, he makes of himself many forms. To him who sees the Self revealed in his own heart belongs eternal bliss—to none else, to none else!

Intelligence of the intelligent, eternal among the transient, he, though one, makes possible the desires of many. To him who sees the Self revealed in his own heart belongs eternal peace—to none else, to none else!

Nachiketa

How, O King, shall I find that blissful Self, supreme, ineffable, who is attained by the wise? Does he shine by himself, or does he reflect another's light?

King of Death

Him the sun does not illumine, nor the moon, nor the stars, nor the lightning—nor, verily, fires kindled upon the earth. He is the one light that gives light to all. He shining, everything shines.

This universe is a tree eternally existing, its root aloft, its branches spread below. The pure root of the tree is Brahman, the immortals in whom the three worlds have their being, whom none can transcend, who is verily the Self.[8]

The whole universe came forth from Brahman and moves in Brahman. Mighty and awful is he, like to a thunderbolt crashing loud through the heavens. For those who attain him death has no terror.

In fear of him fire burns, the sun shines, the rains fall, the winds blow, and death kills.

If a man fail to attain Brahman before he casts off his body, he must again put on a body in the world of created things.

In one's own soul Brahman is realized clearly, as if seen in a mirror. In the heaven of Brahma also is Brahman realized clearly, as one distinguishes light from darkness. In the world of the fathers he is beheld as in a dream.[9] In the world of angels he appears as if reflected in water.

The senses have separate origin in their several objects. They may be active, as in the waking state, or they may be inactive, as in sleep. He who knows them to be distinct from the changeless Self grieves no more.

Above the senses is the mind. Above the mind is the intellect. Above the intellect is the ego. Above the ego is the unmanifested seed, the Primal Cause.

And very beyond the unmanifested seed is Brahman, the all-pervading spirit, the unconditioned, knowing whom one attains to freedom and achieves immortality.

None beholds him with the eyes, for he is without visible form. Yet in the heart is he revealed, through self-control and meditation. Those who know him become immortal.

When all the senses are stilled, when the mind is at rest, when the intellect wavers not—then, say the wise, is reached the highest state.

This calm of the senses and the mind has been defined as yoga. He who attains it is freed from delusion.

In one not freed from delusion this calm is uncertain, unreal: it comes and goes. Brahman words cannot reveal, mind cannot reach, eyes cannot see. How then, save through those who know him, can he be known?

There are two selves, the apparent self and the real Self. Of these it is the real Self, and he alone, who must be felt as truly existing. To the man who has felt him as truly existing he reveals his innermost nature.

The mortal in whose heart desire is dead becomes immortal. The mortal in whose heart the knots of ignorance are untied becomes immortal. These are the highest truths taught in the scriptures.

Radiating from the lotus of the heart there are a hundred and one nerves. One of these ascends toward the thousand-petaled lotus in the brain. If, when a man comes to die, his vital force passes upward and out through this nerve, he attains immortality. But if his vital force passes out through another nerve, he goes to one or another plane of mortal existence and remains subject to birth and death.

The Supreme Person, of the size of a thumb, the innermost Self, dwells forever in the heart of all beings. As one draws the pith from a reed, so must the aspirant after truth, with great perseverance, separate the Self from the body. Know the Self to be pure and immortal—yea, pure and immortal!

The Narrator

Nachiketa, having learned from the god this knowledge and the whole process of yoga, was freed from impurities and from death, and was united with Brahman. Thus will it be with another also if he know the innermost Self.

OM... Peace-peace-peace.

Reflections

T he text is a story from the *Upanisads*, a collection of stories that form the latter portion of the Hindu sacred scriptures, the Vedas. In this short story of a boy's search for knowledge about death, we learn much about the Hindu conception of life. What is the nature of "God" and world from the Upanisad perspective? What is the conception of the "self"? Draw the different "parts" of the self based on the model of the chariot described in the "Katha." What is the cause and result of ignorance according to the Katha? What constitutes knowledge?

Notes

1. There is another interpretation of this sentence, involving the mystery of grace: "Whom the Self chooses, by him is he attained."

2. In Hindu psychology the mind is the organ of perception.

3. Vishnu is here equivalent to Brahman.

4. Brahman, the absolute, impersonal existence, when associated with the power called Maya—the power to evolve as the empirical universe—is known as Hiranyagarbha, the First-Born.

5. The reference is to the Vedic sacrifice. Agni, whose name means fire, is said to be all-seeing, the fire symbolizing Brahman, the Revealer; the two fire sticks, which being rubbed together produce the fire, represent the heart and the mind of man.

6. The sages ascribe a definite, minute size to the Self in order to assist the disciple in meditation.

7. The Birthless is the Self; the city of eleven gates is the body with its apertures—eyes, ears, etc.

8. The "three worlds" are the sky, the earth, and the nether world.

9. The fathers are the spirits of the meritorious dead, who dwell in another world, reaping the fruits of their good deeds, but subject to rebirth.

Yoga and Psychotherapy: "The Seven Centers of Consciousness"

The Chakras: The Inner Playroom

It should be clear by now that yoga science is very complex and extensive. It includes a science of the body, an understanding of the energy level which governs the body's functions, a study of the mind and higher states of consciousness, as well as a whole philosophy of the structure and nature of the universe. This would seem enough to occupy a whole faculty of university professors and medical school specialists. Yet we have said that the major asset of yoga is its ability too integrate all these various disciplines into one meaningful whole. Its beauty is really in its simplicity and accuracy.

But how is it possible to integrate so many diverse areas of science and philosophy? How can all these bits and pieces of understanding be pulled into a coordinated whole? It would seem that yoga, like modern science and psychology, would break down into a host of different specialties that couldn't communicate and had no common ground. The reason it does not is that its philosophy, its understanding of all these various aspects of the human being, are organized around one's inner experience. The many facets of oneself and his world are coordinated by means of bringing them together within the field of inner life. Here they find their focus and their unity.

If one is to explore the world of inner experiences, his thoughts, his emotions, and learn about himself, he must have some framework within which to do this. He must have a

Excerpt entitled "The Seven Centers of Consciousness" from YOGA AND PSYCHOTHERAPY "The Seven Centers of Consciousness" by Swami Rama, Rudolf M. Ballentine, and Swami Ajaya-Allan in YOGA AND PSYCHOTHERAPY. Pp. 216-272. Copyright © 1976 by Himalayan Publications. Reprinted by permission of the Himalayan International Institute of Yoga Science and Philosophy of the U.S.A.

"playroom"—a sort of workshop or laboratory within which he can experiment with experiencing and expressing different aspects of his being and different reactions to the world. The framework provided by the centers of consciousness gives him a place to do this. It provides the student with a structured inner space in which he can play.

The more one studies these centers, their nature, and their interrelationships, the more he comes to understand the difference between various psychologies and therapeutic points of view. He becomes more able to understand and put in perspective different aspects of personality and to grasp in a firsthand way what goes on during the evolution of consciousness. Many things can be simplified and understood in a coherent, orderly way by understanding the various centers of consciousness and how they function.

Throughout the course of this book, we have seen how the yoga concept of who and what we are is very comprehensive. It goes beyond the idea that we have only a physical body which is controlled by a vague and undefinable thing called the mind. We have seen how beyond the physical body there are other "bodies" which, though operating on levels different from it, are coordinated with it.

The first of these is the energy body, and beyond it lies what we have called the "mental body." In other words, part of us is physical, having to do with various systems, muscular, skeletal, circulatory, respiratory, and so forth. But also a part of us, in terms of our functional selves, is energy. When we take in food and digest it, we extract energy which allows us to move around and do things. It is also energy which allows us to think as well as perform actions. Though we may characterize energy as chemical, as electrical, or as something still more subtle, it is in any case always involved along with the material phenomena of our functioning. A third aspect of the system is thinking. Matter and energy alone do not complete the picture. Some mental action is always involved. You might say that there are at least these three obvious components to our experience.

But, underlying them is a more basic principle, that which we call consciousness. This is, of course, the basic phenomena in yoga psychology. Consciousness is sometimes compared to a light, and the different bodies to lamp shades which cover it. These shades surround the light, one inside the other, each of a different color and material. Each shade captures light to a certain degree and is illuminated by it. Each transforms the light and modifies it according to its properties. The outer shades are the densest and allow the least light through. If we remove each of them in turn, the light becomes brighter and brighter and is less and less obscured. The physical body, the energy or pranic body, the mental body, and those beyond, have each been described in the preceding chapters. Each fits inside the next and is like another shade illuminated by the light of consciousness.

Each is denser than the one just interior to it. Or, in the terms of yoga philosophy, each involves to a greater degree the principle of matter (*prakriti*). Because of the way these bodies cover up and conceal the underlying consciousness (*purusha*), they are often called in the ancient philosophical writings "sheaths."

These bodies or sheaths do not each function independently. There is a connection between them so that they are more or less coordinated. We have seen, for instance, how the mental body, the energy body, and the physical body interact: if one focuses his *thoughts* on the solar plexus, it increases the concentration of the *energy* in that level. This concentration of energy speeds up the action of the digestive organs and improves their ability to secrete enzymes and process food. The solar plexus serves here as a focal point for the interaction between three bodies or sheaths. The solar plexus is a point in the physical body, but it also corresponds to a point in the energy "body" and in the mental "body." This point is thus a center of activity in each of these bodies. It constitutes, then, a sort of nodal point, a point of connection through which the three can interact. It is one of the "centers of consciousness" which provide the links between the various sheaths. The correspondence among the three bodies is best understood by studying experientially these centers of consciousness that serve as points of interconnection between them.

These centers we will describe are seven in number.[1] They are called *chakras*. Their positions correspond, in the physical body, to points along the spinal cord. The first is located at the base of the spine near the tiny little bone that lies at the lowest extreme of the vertebral column (coccyx). The second center is just a few inches up above that at the level of the genitals (in the region of the sacrum). The third is located at the level of the navel and is associated with the solar plexus. The fourth center is near the area of the heart. It lies at a point of intersection between a line drawn through the arms and shoulders and one through the trunk. These centers are all in a vertical line when one is sitting erectly. This is one reason for sitting straight during meditation: the centers are aligned. The fifth center is at the base of the throat. The sixth center lies at the point between the two eyebrows, while the seventh and last is at the topmost point of the skull, at the "crown" of the head. The highest or "crown" chakra has to do with the highest state of consciousness—while the lowest chakras are much more closely tied to the animal or instinct-based side of human nature.[2] Developing the capacity to concentrate more energy, attention, and awareness at the higher centers is one aspect of what happens as one's growth proceeds and consciousness evolves.

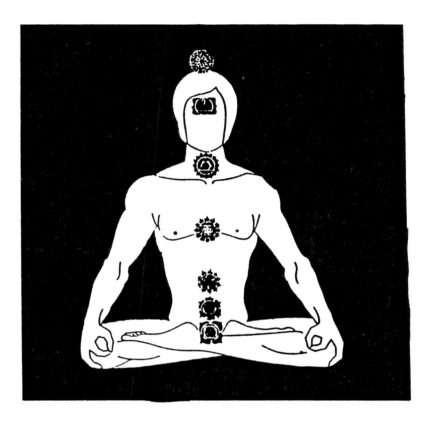

The Chakras: Centers of Integration

The word *chakra* itself means "wheel" in Sanskrit. At the outer circumference of a wheel there is more space, more material, more diversity, more movement. When one focuses on the rim of the wheel, it flies by in a blur, like the variegated world of material phenomena. This outermost aspect of the chakra relates to the grossest sheath, the physical body and material world. As one moves inward, the spokes of the wheel converge, and the dizzying movement slows. The inner aspects of the chakra correspond to the higher sheaths, energy, mental, etc. At the center is the center of consciousness—*purusha*, or Self.

Within each one of these dynamic centers can be seen, in condensed form, the relationship between certain aspects of the physical world, the energy system, the mind, and higher consciousness. For example, at the solar plexus, aggression, assertiveness, fire, heat, digestion, assimilation, and active metabolism, intermix in a way that cuts across our separate concepts of what is physical, what is physiological, and what is psychological.

Moreover, the interaction between the higher sheaths or levels of consciousness and the lower level of material phenomena and external events that is brought into awareness when one focuses his attention on one of the centers will reflect much about his particular circumstances, his peculiar place in the world, and the course of events that comprise his life. Traditionally, these centers are likened to wheels of fortune. In the carnival midway we find the wheel of fortune spinning constantly while people look on in fascination. We put our quarter on the numbered space and the wheel of fortune begins to turn. If it comes out in our favor, we win. We leave with our arms full. If not, we go away discouraged, or, maybe we try again. Our fate is decided by the spin of a wheel. Symbolically, then, the idea of the wheel of fortune has something to do with destiny, karma, and the spinning that unfolds the future. Thus, the term "chakras" or "wheels" for these centers of consciousness is apropos, for, like the wheel of fortune, they have a great deal to do with the shape and outcome of one's experience on its various levels. The spinning focus of energy and imagery experienced at each of these points reflects very concisely one's basic nature and contains the seeds of the fortune that awaits him.

Let's take the example of energy again. We each have available a certain amount of energy, and it can be directed within our systems in different ways. This energy can be focused in one place rather than another; it can be concentrated in one chakra or in another. The chakras are points where, on the pranic level, energy has its highest concentration and, anatomically, the nerves come together to form their most important centers or plexuses. In medicine it is recognized that within each system there are places where functioning is most vital, places which are most highly energized. This centralization of vital functioning is a characteristic of each of the different systems of the physical body. Moreover, these systems interact with each other at special points. Examples of system interaction points include the cardiac plexus, where a very important network of nerves surrounds the heart; and the solar plexus at the level of the navel, where the control functions of several systems that have to do with digestion and its regulation are more or less centered. Other chakras are associated with the major endocrine glands such as the thyroid, pineal, and pituitary. Modern medical research has established that the endocrine glands serve as strategic points of interaction between physiological, emotional, and psychological functioning.

From the point of view of yoga, one who is ill is unable to distribute his energy properly through the centers. Poor digestion may mean an inadequate focus of energy in the area of the solar plexus. This means improper control of the bodily functions governed here. Since the chakra is a point of intersection between the various sheaths, mental factors are obviously important, too. When there is a weakness at that center physically, pranically, psychologically, etc., one is susceptible to diseases of the digestive system.[3]

The Chakras and Symbolism

The chakras provide a sort of central point, an underlying framework, in which a multitude of factors intersect and interact. It should be clear that the experience of these centers is a highly intricate and complex affair. Any attempt to express it in words is certain to prove to be only partially successful. The experience of the centers of consciousness or chakras is a nonverbal one. Putting it into words is really difficult. It is for this reason that the chakras have been described symbolically. Even this, of course, presents problems, especially for the Westerner. The classic symbolic descriptions are framed in the terms of Eastern culture. For instance, one of the best known translations of the literature on the chakras bears the following description:

> ...at the center of the region of the naval, is the lotus Manipura...so called...because, owing to the presence of the fiery Tejas, it is lustrous as a gem...the triangular region of the Tejas-Tattva...has three Svastikas. The red Bija of fire, "Ram," is seated on a ram, the carrier of Agni, the lord of fire. Here is the old red Rudra, smeared with white ashes, and the Sakti Lakini who is Devata of this digestive center said to be "fond of animal food, and whose breasts are ruddy with the blood and fat which drop from Her mouth."

The intuitions and understandings of literature, of art, of mythology, of religious symbolism, of physiology, physics, and metaphysics all come together at a central focus in the centers of consciousness called the chakras. All understanding is distilled here. This is what is meant by saying that "the microcosm reflects the macrocosm." By immersing oneself in this inner experience, an understanding of the coordination between the various aspects of oneself and the universe begins to grow.

When one sits quietly, with his eyes closed, and focuses his attention on a particular center, he may catch a glimpse of a certain color, or he may have a fleeting impression of an inner sound, or he may observe that memories and thoughts of one particular type tend to bubble up into his awareness. If one focuses attention on the genital center, for example, sexual thoughts, memories, and fantasies begin to appear.

It becomes obvious, then, that each of the chakras has a rich meaning and is vast in its significance. Each center pulls together different aspects of the external and inner worlds into a coordinated, but difficult to describe, whole. Here the relationship between certain objects, colors, sounds, and certain inner states (the essence of what we call symbolism, poetry, music, and art) is clearly evident. Thus it is that at the solar plexus, where aggression is a central issue, the Ram figures as a prominent symbol, and the goddess is pictured as having blood dripping from her lips and lusting for flesh foods. The color is red and descriptions always include fire.

Traditional representation of
the manipura (solar plexus) chakra.

The descriptions of these centers are not limited to Eastern philosophy or psychology. Since they refer to underlying experiences in all human beings, we might expect similar descriptions in many cultures and historical periods wherever man's sensitivity and capacity for subtle inner exploration have been highly cultivated. Thus, for example, we find strikingly similar descriptions of such centers in the Hopi Indian culture. Here five of these seven centers have been identified. When the young Hopi child of seven or eight receives his first initiation into a religious society, he was taught that:

The living body of man and the living body of the earth were constructed in the same way. Through each ran an axis, man's axis being the backbone, the vertebral column....Along this axis were several vibratory centers....

The experience encountered at these focal points can be followed outward into any area of human thought or endeavor. We will focus here primarily on one limited aspects of their implications: We will attempt to present some aspects of their relation to psychology, psychopathology, and psychosomatic diseases.

The Root (Anal) Chakra: Fear and Paranoia

T he lowest center at the base of the spine is psychologically related to the most rudimentary survival instincts. It is connected with feelings of fear, the instinct for self-preservation, and a kind of jungle mentality. Here there is a great preoccupation with physical and bodily survival. This can be seen more clearly in the animal who lives in the wild. The most primitive responses to life-threatening situations involve energy at this point. This energy is not normally under conscious control and is to a great extent related to such autonomic responses as flight and fright. This can be observed in the squirrel, for instance, which is always on the lookout. It constantly looks around to see that nothing is going to attack. As soon as it sees another animal or a person, it scurries away. Such alertness and concern about self-preservation is a very common aspect of animal life. The first chakra is related to this very basic and primitive fear of being attacked or injured. On the other hand, it is also related to attacking, being aggressive, and searching out prey. The animal that hunts and kills another animal in order to eat it is also working at this level where the most basic survival instincts are focused.

Mentally, when a person has his energy centered here, he will be concerned about being hurt by others, not only psychologically but in a physical sense. One who has an unregulated focus of energy at the first chakra is constantly afraid of being injured or has a strong tendency to hurt and injure others, to attack another person in some way. The fear involved here is an intense, unreasonable fear of the magnitude that is associated with the role of the hunter and the hunted. It is a total and global sort of anxiety. Threats are not sensed so much as presenting the danger of loss, but rather as potential sources of total annihilation. The massive kind of terror associated with this chakra is seen in psychosis and in patients who are undergoing a paranoid episode.

The following statement about the nature and purpose of life from someone who looks at the world primarily from the perspective of this chakra is taken from an interview by one of the authors with a young man in his mid-twenties. He had been convicted of rape twice, and admitted to a number of brutal physical attacks upon others. At the time of the interview, he was a patient in a maximum security state mental hospital.

> You see, man is like an animal and like a hunter. He stalks the game he's going to kill...I feel that people are stalking me. So while they're stalking me, I'm stalking them. It's a cycle going round and round. It's survival of the fittest. I'm being stalked, so I stalk them, constantly. You see, I'm not going to let anyone mess me around. Like an animal—if he senses somebody's going to kill him, he's going to try to get you first. And that's how I feel. That's what life is, just a game of survival when you get downright basic about it. I do unto people what they would do unto me.

Each of the chakras is associated with a certain "element." These are not to be confused with the elements of modern chemistry which refer to *structure* on the atomic level. In Indian philosophy all the phenomenal universe is seen as made up of some combination of five basic ingredients or *bhutas*. These each contain different proportions of matter (*prakriti*) and consciousness (*purusha*). These proportions possess the quality of solidity (earth), that which is liquid (water), that which is combustive (fire), that which is like a gas (air), and that which constitutes the space in which the others exist (ether). These are neither literally earth, water, fire, etc., nor merely material, molecular substances. They are "elemental" in the sense that everything can be analyzed into some combination of them. They are practical and operational in that all the phenomenal world can be both understood in these terms and through them easily related to other aspects of our existence, such as energy, mind, and higher consciousness.

The first chakra is associated with the element of earth. It is associated with the denser levels of the being, that is, the physical body and awareness of and attention to the material plane. In this way it is easy to see how concerns about protection and preservation of the body and physical existence are involved when consciousness is centered at this chakra.

It is interesting that anatomically, this center is in the area of the anus and is associated with the excretion of solid matter from the body. When animals are observed in frightening situations, it will be seen that defecation is one of the main components of their fear response. If they are intensely frightened, they will defecate repeatedly. Persons who are subject to this primitive, basic fear may begin having bowel problems. If there is a strong underlying fear running through their emotional lives, they may develop such illnesses as ulcerative colitis or chronic diarrhea.

Emotionally and psychologically this chakra is concerned with the most primitive fears and the most extreme degrees of pathology. This dichotomy between the attacker and the attacked is related to the formation of the original categories of good and bad. It is at a time when one is beginning to experience these earliest primitive fears that he is beginning to organize his experience into the basic categories of what is pleasurable and what is painful or threatening. This lays the foundations for psychic organization. We have seen earlier how the bad or painful aspect of the infant's environment is what threatens his security. They threaten to overwhelm him and annihilate him. Later on, when his own negative or destructive impulses come up and he projects them out into the world, they also are sensed as threats, as potential attacks. This projection or attitude of paranoia often results when there is a habitual focus of energy at the first chakra. Classically, in psychoanalytic theory, paranoid thinking relates to a fear of attack from behind, which may in some cases be accompanied by fantasies of anal rape.

Becoming Conscious of Latent Fear and Paranoia

In many cases the energy focus at this center is not expressed in an obvious way. While most persons are not blatantly paranoid or consciously concerned with violence and attack, an undercurrent of paranoid functioning may color their emotional lives. Bringing this into awareness is often an important part of any successful process of growth.

As long as one operates from a predominantly paranoid stance, he remains unaware of much of himself. Everything that is negative or destructive is disowned and projected onto people around him. For this reason his destructive impulses are not really under his control. He is simply denying that they are part of him. He sees himself as very loving and kind. It is other people he has to watch out for. They want to hurt him, manipulate him or attack him. This attitude maintains a constant focus of energy at the first chakra. When too much of one's personality is not integrated, but projected out into the world, then he is constantly tossed about by fear and defensiveness. There is no feeling of solidity about him. In the ancient symbols of Indian thought it is said that the element of earth is deficient. He is flighty; he is jumpy; he is undependable. He vacillates from sweetness to viciousness or fearful defensiveness. Of course, the only way out of the dilemma is to bring into awareness the parts of himself that he really hasn't wanted to face.

The Buddhist scriptures tell the story of a farmer who grew the most spectacular crops year after year. He collected the manure from his animals and spread it over the land. Each year the soil was restored and the harvest once more came out to be rich and wonderful. The secret was the manure which fertilized the crops. The farmer's work was to dig out the manure and spread it over the field. A second farmer found such work unappealing. He didn't want to get involved in the dirty side of farm work, so he didn't collect the manure to spread on the fields. After a few years his harvest began to dwindle. His crops no longer grew well. The soil became sterile. Psychological growth is based on the process of continually bringing into awareness parts of oneself that were before regarded as repulsive and unsavory, so that they can become integrated and transmuted.

Though the experience of being contaminated by the consciousness and energies of the first chakra may sound rather strange to the average person, there are certain schools of psychology and psychiatry that have dealt with this area. The writings of Harry Stack Sullivan, for example, deal especially with psychotic experience and describe what it's like to see the world from the point of view of this first chakra, to be concerned constantly with the fear of annihilation, and to live in an intensely paranoid world.

Cultural Implications

We can characterize not only individuals and schools of psychology in terms of the chakra on which they focus but cultures as well. Primitive societies which are concerned primarily with hunting and basic survival in a natural environment, where survival of the fittest rules, reflect a domination of the anal chakra. In any social situation where law and order breaks down, there may occur a sort of cultural shift and predominant functioning may come to be oriented around survival and the fear of attack: a dramatic example is seen in the old Western movies where the vigilantes ran rampant. Toward the other extreme, an excessive or rigid emphasis on law and order can also betray a predominant influence by the first chakra. In a subtler way this influence can be seen in contemporary Western culture's exaggerated concern with dirt and "germs."

The Genital Chakra: Sensuality and Sexuality

The second center of consciousness is located near the genital organs, and physiologically this is where the output of fluids, i.e., control of urination and the expulsion of semen, takes place. Whereas the anal chakra was associated with the earth element, this center is connected with the element of water.

Psychologically, this center is concerned with sexual impulses, with lustful feelings, and with an emphasis on sensory pleasure. Whereas the first chakra is concerned with individual survival and self-preservation, the energies at this center concern the survival of the species. Though this is still a biological and instinctual urge, it is less primitive, a little beyond the more basic fear of being annihilated. Its purpose is something beyond simple defensiveness and self-protection. It is responsible for a kind of creativity, albeit one which is still operating on a gross biological level.

A person who has his energy centered in this second chakra will be someone who is preoccupied with sensual pleasures, especially sexual experience. When he meets another person, he will tend to regard that person as a sexual object rather than as a companion, friend, competitor, or as someone to be feared (as was the case when the first chakra was predominant).

Involvement in sexual acts, however, does not necessarily indicate a focus of energy at this center of consciousness. The young man described earlier who had raped a number of women and who had an extreme preoccupation with survival was asked: "What was on your mind during these attacks, physical pleasure or survival?" In recalling these experiences he said: "Sex is no big thing. It was just done for revenge. You've got to hurt someone once in a while to survive."

Certainly a person whose energy is centered at the second chakra is less crippled and more free than a person who is constantly preoccupied with the fear of annihilation that is associated with the focus of energy at the first chakra.

> When your consciousness is primarily directed toward providing you with the sensation patterns to which you are addicted, you will have more energy than when it was hung up on the Security Center of consciousness. You will usually be with more people and you will need to sleep less. An individual who is hunting for sex is definitely generating more energy than a person who is worried about his security. In fact, those whose consciousness is heavily addicted to the Security Level will probably have dropped off to sleep during the early part of the evening.

Freudian psychology takes its viewpoint about the nature of man from the orientation of this chakra. The basic theory of the psychological nature of man in the original orthodox Freudian system was derived from a study of sexual impulses. Sexuality was thought of as underlying all motivation. All conflict and discontent was initially thought to be associated with difficulties which were basically of a sexual nature. Freud's perspective on man seems to have been colored by the perspective of this chakra.

The energies available at this level are, of course, so potent that when one simply attempts to suppress them, they may continue to influence motivation and personality. In the tradition of yoga there are two methods of dealing with these energies. One can continue to channel energies through this chakra in an attempt to experience sex and sensuality in such a way that it contributes to his self-exploration and growth. Another possibility is to avoid focusing energy in this center and to concentrate on channeling or "raising" it to higher centers. This redirecting, which is called *sublimation* in psychoanalytic theory, allows the energy to be used for creative and productive purposes, such as art, or the self-exploration involved in meditation. This second path, that of sexual control or *brahmacharya*, is, therefore, not merely the outward suppression and avoidance of sexual activity, but rather an inner rechanneling of the energy that would be released sexually.

Sexual activity discharges a huge quantity of energy. Often we can tolerate only so much of the tension that results from the accumulation of energy in our systems. As energy builds up, we tend to become restless and look for some route of discharge. This may be in the form of emotional outbursts: "I've just got to let it all out." Then there is a sense of relief. Things calm down again. In other cases the release is accomplished through sexual activity. If this has become the customary method of relieving tension, then suppression of sex for a while is likely to result in a state of tension and restlessness. There will be not only a physical tension and the sense of unease, but a psychological discomfort as well. But with the proper training, the same energy can be refocused at other centers. This becomes increasingly possible as the process of personal growth and evolution proceeds. Gradually the energy can be tolerated and pleasurably employed in a variety of ways. It's as though one's "circuits" mature and come to be able to handle a higher voltage.

According to the ancient yogic manuals, in Vedic times there was a particular initiation which was given by the yogis to a few advanced disciples who practiced sexual control. This method, called *urdhvaretas* or "leading upward," helped to lead the energy (which normally goes into the creation of offspring) to ascend to the brain and recirculate it in the body. It channeled consciousness from lower to higher centers. This method of "upward traveling" is still known to a few yogis today. They report that the joy which is found in discharging sexual energy, or releasing sexual tension, cannot be compared with that joy which results from conserving that energy and leading it to focus at the higher chakras.

But not all schools of yoga deal with sexual and sensual energies by non-expression and sublimation. There are certain practices in a "leftist" branch of Tantra Yoga where the use of what would ordinarily be sensual objects of experiences, e.g., the taking of meat, alcohol, the practice of sexual intercourse, is part of the process of self-exploration and spiritual development. What some may view as sources of dissipation are utilized as means of growth. This is a tricky undertaking and can easily degenerate into a sort of depleting indulgence. But, when correctly done, one's involvement with the external object is a means toward transcending his attachment to it.

The successful use of these practices might be best understood by recalling that the higher and more transpersonal levels of consciousness can only be approached once the personal subconscious has been successfully explored and integrated. At the deeper levels of the subconscious one encounters the tendency within himself to become one with the objects of perception. Here one encounters the massive attachments and the feeling of total identification and absorption in another. Here where the higher, more developed levels of mental function are not in force, there is experienced a primitive, regressive merging. It is on this level where psychic phenomena can occur, where one *manas* becomes intermingled with the *manas* of another person. Here, from the point of view of ancient yoga psychology, even the basic psychic prana or *chitta* can come in contact with and mix with that of another person.

The Tantric practices of ritualized immersion in sensual experience are methods of experimenting with these phenomena. They are an approach to the experience of oneness and total identification. They bring up from the depths of the personal subconscious the tendency to fuse and merge with another. They provide a framework within which one can play with and explore the experience of becoming one with some other person or thing by bringing into behavior and awareness these most fundamental layers of mental life through rituals involving union with external objects. They bring the student to discover the inner dimensions of such experiences and to develop those levels of consciousness in themselves from which union is more transpersonal. Tantric techniques bring sensuality into awareness so that it can become a means of transcending itself.

In the practice of Tantra the student learns to redirect the urge to transcend himself and merge with another from the physical to the more subtle sheaths. At first he may regard an object or person in sensual terms and seek fusion at the physical level. But the ritualization of physical acts and the learning of observational skills in the midst of sensual activities leads one to see beyond the physical and sensory interaction and even beyond the fusion of personalities. Tantra teaches one to see the latent all-inclusive consciousness that exists within the other and to relate to and fuse with that innermost level of the other's being. Thus the intercourse between one and another becomes transformed. The male and female come to experience themselves as the male and female principle of the universe. In more advanced Tantric practices physical objects are no longer needed and the tendency toward fusion is brought into consciousness at a more abstract level than in external Tantric ritual.[4]

Of course, such techniques can only be successful if their practice is accompanied by at least some degree of non-attachment. Observation is necessary if learning is to occur. To play with these experiences means to not become caught up and lost in the pleasure itself. There must be a certain restraint, a certain distance, and in the case of sex, the sexual act an attitude of not being rushed to attain the climax itself. Openness and control, a sense of "foreplay" is necessary. In the words of one Western therapist who has tried to use sensuality to evolve a growth-promoting technique:

> If a person is living a sexual life and living out of his sexual feeling, then all of life is foreplay and one is ready to enter or be entered.

He says:

> Pleasure is not only gratification, it is not only satisfaction…it is that state of being which is itself gratifying…pleasure is really that state of feeling, acting which is truthful to one's becoming….Pleasure then is not the search for itself by avoiding pain or the pursuit of hedonistic goals. It is more a *unitary* movement toward contact, self-expression, toward becoming who we are.

Here pleasure becomes redefined. It is really what we can call "joy."

> Being who we are is pleasurable, self-revelation is pleasurable. It is the root of joy…*joy-pleasure is the feeling of our growth and aliveness.* We who think that we are gods because we have created a world are in our trap because we try to enjoy that which we have created, instead of really enjoying the creator in the act of creation.

The Solar Plexus Chakra:
Domination and Submission

Each of these chakras is experienced as being aligned along an axis. In the terms of the pranic sheath, this might be thought of as an "energy axis" that extends vertically through the center of the body from the base of the spine to the top of the skull. This axis runs centrally, not along the outer surface of the back. When one sits properly for meditation, the spinal column itself becomes aligned with this axis and the two are congruent. Under these conditions the experience of energy in the centers along the axis is easier to perceive.

The third center of consciousness is located at the level of the navel. This third center is associated with the element of fire. We often refer to this area of the body as the "solar plexus." It is a sort of internal sun produced by the oxidation or "burning" of food. In contrast to plants which can take their energy directly from the sun itself, animals must produce their own energy. They take that energy trapped in the plant matter and release it through the chemical processes of digestion. This creates an inner flame or fire which provides the energy for maintaining life. When this inner flame is properly regulated, it allows the person to be healthy, to digest his food properly, and to have a consistent energy level without being easily fatigued. If it is improperly regulated, it can lead to various disease states such as digestive problems like peptic ulcer. The flame may also, in other cases, be excessive but poorly centered so that one is red-faced, hot-tempered, and irritable. Energy is ordinarily stored at this solar plexus center. When the solar plexus chakra is energized, one has the quality of being dynamic and assertive.

When the psychological issues related to this chakra have not been brought into consciousness and resolved, then the resulting conflict will lead to a preoccupation with control and the exertion of power over other people. The issue becomes one of domination versus submission. Such a person may be given to a tyrannical kind of assertiveness, spending all his time and effort in extending his personal power. Or he may be just the opposite: submissive and cowed. More often, however, he will alternate between the two, depending on the situation. Such people are often labeled "authoritarian personalities." They are unable to see other people as peers, but judge everyone else as either superior or inferior. They cast others into the roles of either authority figures or underlings.

Other personality types may also reflect unresolved conflicts related to this center. Psychological studies of ulcer patients show that they are often the sort of people who force themselves to take on the responsibilities of a dominant, controlling position, although basically, underneath, they have a tendency to be passive, dependent, and submissive.

One school of psychology which has focused on this aspect of functioning was founded by Alfred Adler who coined the term "inferiority complex." He dealt extensively with the way we compensate for inferiority feelings by creating a false sense of superiority. Adler tended to see his patients as being preoccupied with concerns about adequacy, competition, power, and domination. He pointed out that even the sexual act can be experienced primarily in terms of conquest and domination rather than in terms of sexual pleasure. He felt that in childhood the feelings of inadequacy and inferiority experienced because of one's relative helplessness were very important and that much of human behavior could be explained in terms of an attempt to overcome this underlying feeling of inferiority and to gain a position of superiority. Out of this childhood experience, however, grew many of the positive aspects of control and autonomy that are necessary for mature functioning.

Although Freud did not approve of Adler's preoccupation with these issues, his own theory of psychology gradually developed in the direction of dealing with the more constructive aspects of ego-functioning. This grew into what is currently called "ego psychology." It is interesting to note the parallel between the psychoanalytic theory of development stages through which each person passes and the yogic hierarchy of chakras. Freud's anal and phallic stages seem closely related to the first two chakras.[5] Erik Erikson's extension of Freud's developmental model describes the next stage of development (corresponding to this third chakra) as centering on the issue of "industry vs. inferiority."

The first three centers or chakras which have been described thus far are related to basic instinctual urges and needs for self-maintenance. They are concerned with self-protection, with propagation of the species, and with functioning effectively in a competitive world. There is a progressive movement from the most basic concerns to those which are more refined. The first chakra is dominated by concern for self-preservation and the prevention of annihilation. The second center is associated with sensual gratification, especially sexuality. In a larger sense this relates to the maintenance of the species. The third center is concerned with effective and assertive individual behavior which will permit one to provide for his personal needs: clothing, shelter, and the securing and digestion of food.[6] As we move to the fourth chakra, however, we leave the field of domination by the instinctual and materially oriented aspects of life and move to a perspective that transcends the individual.

The Heart Chakra:
From Emotion to Empathy

The heart chakra corresponds to a point between the breasts and along the spine. It marks a sort of transition between those chakras below which are concerned with the more biological matters of self-maintenance and survival and the chakras above which are associated with a more evolved consciousness. The higher chakras, as we shall see, relate to a kind of awareness that is less tied down to the physical world, less bound up in attachments, and increasingly transpersonal in nature.

This chakra lies just above the diaphragm. The diaphragm is a dome-shaped muscular structure which separates the abdominal cavity from the chest cavity. Beneath the hollow of the dome lie the stomach, liver, duodenum, the major portion of the digestive apparatus, the solar plexus, and, as we have seen, the third chakra. Lying on top of the dome formed by the diaphragm is the heart. It is surrounded by the two lungs and

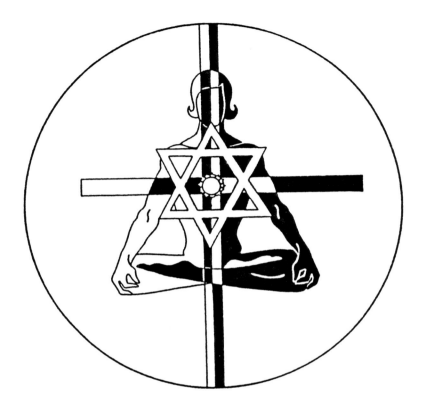

enmeshed in a network of nerves called the cardiac plexus. The center point of all this activity and energy is called the heart chakra, which is related to the element *air*.

This is the center of nurturance. The lungs are responsible for giving oxygen to the blood while the heart distributes this throughout the body, sending with it the nutrients that are necessary for growth and activity. It is at this level that the breasts are located. They are the only organs which are structured exclusively for the purpose of providing nourishment to another. Emotions and feelings for another person are often experienced as a welling up of energy in this region at the center of the chest. A feeling of going out toward, or relating strongly to, another person is traditionally expressed by the phrases "heartfelt," or "my heart went out to him." The heart is the symbol of emotion and feeling in the language of many cultures. Strong emotions are often accompanied by clearly identifiable physical sensations in the region of the heart and chest. For example, when ties to another are broken we often speak of "heartache" or "a broken heart." This sort of feeling and emotion marks a departure from the biological and survival concerns which are related to the lower three chakras. The diaphragm serves as a sort of boundary between the lower, more instinctual nature of man and the higher centers which become increasingly related to a more evolved consciousness.

In one American Indian tradition, the diaphragm is compared to the surface of the earth. Below this lies the subterranean level of instincts and man's animal nature. This is the realm of solid matter. Above this is the sky, the higher realms of man's more developed and evolved consciousness. Between heaven and earth lies the diaphragm. This body scheme is also echoed in the ancient symbols of Mexico, Egypt, and the Middle East.

The heart chakra is important because it represents the first dawning of consciousness above the horizon represented by the diaphragm. When the energy stored in the solar fire of the third chakra can be elevated to activate and bring to life the feelings and empathy which are the potential of the heart chakra, then the effect is, symbolically, likened to the rising sun. It radiates warmth. In biological evolution, the development of the capacity for feeling and compassion is a major step forward toward a higher consciousness.

Because this chakra is the center where our more basic impulses and our more evolved aspirations are integrated, the heart chakra is represented in many traditions by the six-pointed star. This symbol, which is found in ancient Indian writings as well as in the Hebrew tradition, is made up of two triangles, one pointing up, the other down. Their superimposition represents an integration of the higher and lower aspects of man's nature.

The heart chakra is of central importance in yoga theory because the heart is the meeting point between two separate polarities in the body's energy field. The first is that which exists between the chakras above and those below. The second is the polarity that exists between the right and left sides. As we have seen earlier, the right represents the active, the male, *yang* side of one's nature while the left corresponds to the passive, female, *yin* characteristics. A line drawn horizontally to represent this polarity between the right and left and one drawn vertically to represent the polarity between the higher and lower chakras forms a cross which has its point of intersection at the heart chakra. This cross is a symbol that appears almost universally, its form varying slightly from culture to culture. The heart chakra, then, represents a center of integration for these polarities. An outflow of energy or an interaction organized around this center potentially involves the whole of the person.

Breathing: Integration of Lower and Upper Chakras

A full use of the diaphragm is very important in creating the physiological conditions that promote the integration of the lower instinctual aspects of the system with the higher, more conscious ones. When the diaphragm moves rhythmically and naturally, there is a free interplay between the instinctual energies and the more evolved consciousness above which can coordinate and control them. The natural process of breathing is to inhale by contracting the diaphragm muscle, flattening out its dome shape. This act pushes the abdomen out a bit while it lowers the floor of the chest, increasing the space inside the rib cage and expanding the lungs. With exhalation, the diaphragm relaxes and allows the tightening abdominal muscles to force it upwards once more into its rounded, dome position. This decreases the space in the chest and collapses the lungs, forcing air outward. When breathing is carried out in this natural, relaxed way, very little effort is required. With a minimum of exertion by the diaphragm and the abdominal muscles, a great deal of air can be moved in and out. This creates an effortless, rhythmic sort of flow that promotes relaxation and a feeling of calmness. The chest and shoulder muscles are not used at all and the rib cage remains relaxed.

The use of the shoulder and chest muscles to assist in respiration is normally and naturally employed only when there is a great deal of exertion, in those situations, for example, where there is a necessity of flight or fight. In these cases, the lungs are filled to their full capacity by using not only the action of the diaphragm and abdominal muscles, but the chest and shoulder muscles are used also to expand the rib cage to its fullest. A maximum of air is brought in to provide the largest possible supply of oxygen so that one might defend himself or escape in the most effective possible way. These are situations associated with self-preservation, or, in some cases, with sexual or aggressive behavior.

Some people have been found to habitually breathe in a very awkward and uncoordinated way. When at rest, they use primarily chest and shoulder muscles which are normally employed only in emergency situations to supplement the action of the diaphragm. Yet the diaphragm itself is held in a fixed position and does not contribute to the respiratory movement at all.

Since respiratory movements by the chest are biologically and instinctually tied in with the emergency responses of self-defense or escape, their use tends to stir up these feelings. One who is feeling calm and has no reason for fear or anxiety will find that if he deliberately imitates these movements, his emotional state shifts. He soon begins to experience a state much like stress and alarm, a sort of feeling of anxiety.

Alexander Lowen has studied the relationship between respiration and personality disorders in some detail. He finds that the schizoid, the person who is withdrawn, who has hidden much of his personality from himself and the world, typically breathes in this shallow way, using mostly the chest muscles. He holds the diaphragm, stomach area, and lower part of the body in a tight, rigid position. In this way he tries to avoid the experience of feelings and impulses arising from the area of the first three chakras. Sexual and aggressive feelings are difficult for him to control or integrate. His solution to this problem is try, by keeping the diaphragm stationary, to prevent arousing such feelings and in this way keep them out of awareness.

Of course, the more primitive and biological impulses do not lose their potency or influence simply because they are kept out of awareness. In fact, providing for the needs they represent becomes even more difficult, causing increased tension and anxiety. In such a situation, they tend to operate outside awareness to push and pull one in directions he cannot fully understand. Reason and intellect are dragged along and do their best to justify the irrational behavior that results. Clarity of consciousness in the higher chakras is diminished, and what would be a higher mental activity comes to be instead a servant of distorted and twisted instinctual urges, justifying or denying them as best it can. Often, teaching diaphragmatic breathing to such persons can help bring back into awareness the impulses with which they are blindly wrestling. If they can overcome their aversion to these aspects of themselves, these can then be integrated and come under some reasonable control. The movement of the diaphragm is of central importance in providing a physiological basis for such integration.

Emotions: Effects of the Lower Chakras

Though emotions involve energy at the level of the heart chakra, instinctual influences from the lower chakras are also involved. The more feelings are dominated by fear, for example, or by sexual urges, the more the experience brings into play the lower chakras. According to yoga there are four basic well-springs from which emotion arises. These are the four instincts or primitive urges that serve as the foundation for all emotional experience. As mentioned earlier, these are: the push toward self-preservation or self-protection, which is related to the first chakra; the sexual urge related to the second; and the need for fuel or food which is in some respects related to the area of the third chakra, where food is digested and energy stored. These three instinctual urges serve as "automatic survival mechanisms" insuring that we don't neglect to provide for our basic needs. When the fuel in our system runs low, we get hungry. If we fail to provide ourselves with food, we're not allowed to forget. The fourth of these urges is that for sleep.[7] It's somewhat different form the first three. If one goes without sleep for long enough, he becomes disturbed and may develop behavior resembling a psychotic reaction. As we saw earlier, this urge to sleep represents the basic need for experiencing higher consciousness. When we sink into the deepest sleep, our awareness is allowed to escape the confines of its everyday, waking restrictions.

These four basic instincts or urges underlie all our emotions. The quality of the emotion varies, depending on how the instinctual urge is handled and how one reacts to it. Initially the satisfaction of these urges does not depend on specific objects. The need for food is merely a general urge to eat something and keep the body going. But in the course of one's life he learns to want not just food, but, for example, elaborate dishes or delicate pastries. Eventually, that's the only thing that will satisfy his craving. A plate of simple food is boring. The instinctual urge becomes *attached* to a specific object. These attachments are what lead us to become emotional in one way or another. Attachment or "addiction" is the basis of emotional experience. This is called *kama* in the yogic texts and is the fountain of all other emotions.

If the struggle to satisfy one's addictions is frustrated, he may become angry. For example:

> I arrive at the bakery to find that the last strawberry pie has just been sold. I become frustrated and angry: "I *called* you and told you to hold that pie for me and you sold it? What's the matter with you people here?!" There follows a justified rage, a fit of "righteous indignation."

In the terms of yoga psychology, anger comes from the frustration of a basic drive experienced in the form of an attachment to a specific object, goal, or idea. When such an attachment is thwarted, frustration and anger inevitably result. Or, on the other hand, if I see someone else walking out the door with the last pie, the emotional experience becomes envy or jealousy.

> Or, suppose I reach the store in time to buy my strawberry pie. But going out the door I trip and the pie flips out of my hand, landing upside-down on the ground. My beautiful strawberry pie is all squashed and dirty—and it was the last one! I become disappointed—even slightly depressed.

Our more profound depressions are over those losses where attachment was very strong.

Out of the permutations of what may happen to the object or person to which one is attached, each of the emotions arise. In each case there are two components to the emotion. There is the inherent urge from within and there is the learned experience of what specific object will satisfy that urge. All emotions can be understood as coming from one of the four instincts operating in combination with some particular object to which it has become attached.

Emotions and the Heart Chakra

When little energy is being elevated and experienced through the heart chakra, when there is little "feeling," one will appear emotionless and cold. This does not mean that he is not motivated by the most primitive instinctual urges. But we say of such a person that he "has no heart." He's ruthless and doesn't care about anyone else. He just forges ahead, walking over everyone in his way. In diagnostic terms, we refer to such a person as "psychopathic" or "sociopathic." His energy is channeled through the lower chakras in a manner that shows no concern for, or awareness of, others.

When a person has some energy focused at the heart center as well as at the third or solar plexus center, he may still be somewhat aggressive and egotistical, but his behavior will be at least partially tempered by some consideration for others, by some compassion and understanding. There will be a certain amount of integration. The influence of the heart chakra lends a feeling component to one's experience.

Sometimes in psychotherapy we see a patient who is beginning for the first time to experience some feeling for others. He's managed to free up some of the energy involved with the lower chakras and experience it at the level of the heart center. There begins to be an element of true "relatedness" in his interactions with others. But because of the contamination of this feeling with the drives related to the lower chakras, he gets himself in all sorts of predicaments. He may suddenly become absurdly romantic, for instance, spending all his money on expensive bouquets for his new-found love or squandering his savings on extravagant gifts. The therapist, however, may find himself reluctant to discourage such behavior, sensing that there is an element of something new here. From the therapist's perspective, the experience can be seen as a movement in the direction of growth although it still involves much pathology.

When the consciousness experienced at the heart chakra is not contaminated by influence from the instinctual urges, its quality is different. It would no longer be called, strictly speaking, emotion, but more simply "feeling," for example, "a feeling of compassion." The less attachments are involved, the more feeling is free from an emotional coloring.

Through concentration on this center during meditation, the experience associated with it is separated out in its purity. By focusing on and magnifying the consciousness here, the contaminants from other chakras can gradually be distinguished and come to fall away. It is then that one is able to experience less adulterated feelings which, in contrast to the turmoil of his previous emotions, are more joyful and peaceful. One is then experiencing the feeling that would usually accompany emotion without the coloration of attachment and addictions. He's then able to relate to others more fully, less hindered by instinct-dominated concerns for himself.

Unadulterated feeling and "pure compassion" or "selfless love" are not to be confused with the blissful state of oneness that will bee experienced toward the culmination of the evolution of consciousness. For there is still here a sense of separateness from others. But, there is no longer the same craving to possess or use them for the enhancement of personal power or sensual pleasure or to merge with them in an infantile manner. For the person whose life has never before been free from narrow self-concerns, the experience can be one of great freedom and joy. Though the "other" is still sensed as separate, he is no longer the object of frenetic attempts to possess, conquer, or defeat.

Compassion is possible only when there is a certain sense of fullness, when there is no longer so much outside oneself that is craved. This fullness implies some internal integration: internal schisms must have been healed to some significant extent. One's experience with people and objects is more from the point of view of relatedness and harmony rather than merely separation and conflict. Beginning to experience a true empathy through the heart chakra indicates that paranoid tendencies have been to some extent resolved. That is, there is no longer a drastic split between good and bad. There is less of a bad part of oneself which he must deny and project unto others. There remains some separateness between himself and those to whom he relates, but less of a schism between the parts of himself. This means that he is beginning to become whole, integrated, and full, and has less need to fuse with objects or people in the world to regain the projected parts of himself. There is no longer such a pressing need for attachment.

Rogerian therapy with its refusal to judge others and its emphasis on "unconditional positive regard" for another seems to promote empathy which is related to this chakra. The perspective of this chakra is also clearly elaborated in Erich Fromm's book, *The Art of Loving*. This is perhaps the most clear presentation of regarding the world from the point of view of the heart chakra in contemporary Western psychology. As Freud saw all motivation as primarily sexual, Fromm suggests that our various behaviors are based on the need for union.

> What Freud...ignores, is...the masculine-feminine polarity, and the desire to bridge this polarity by union...

> The sadistic person wants to escape from his aloneness and his sense of imprisonment by making another person part and parcel of himself.

According to him, this desire for self-transcendence is best expressed through loving. In defining love Fromm enumerates those qualities which characterize the heart chakra. They include giving, care, responsibility (responsiveness), respect, and knowing the other.

> The active character of love can be described by stating that love is primarily giving...
>
> The person whose character has not developed beyond the stage of the receptive, exploitative, or hoarding orientation experiences the act of giving...but only in exchange for receiving: giving without receiving for him is being cheated.

But of the more mature person, Fromm says:

> In thus giving of his life, he enriches the other person, he enhances the other's sense of aliveness....He does not give in order to receive: giving is in itself exquisite joy.

The Throat Chakra:
Nurturance and Creativity

T he fifth chakra is located in the area of the throat. It is through here that nurturance in the form of food and air area taken into the body. The thyroid gland which regulates the metabolism of food and oxygen is also situated here. Physiologically, then, this chakra has to do with being nurtured. Psychologically, too, energy focused in this area is related to receptivity, to taking in what is given. This area is very much related to the feeling of being cared for and experience here varies according to whether one feels open or closed to being nurtured. Learning to accept, to receive, is very much related to the throat chakra. It has to do with having a certain sense of trust, a sort of natural, comfortable connection with the source of nurturance.

Receiving Nurturance

The heart center has to do with being able to give nurturance as a mother gives to her child. But the throat center is more related to the role of the child, to receiving. This doesn't necessarily imply an infantile way of relating as we are prone to believe. Rather, we would see the child's way of relating as being an imitation of the mode of relating characteristic of this chakra. Both have to do with a feeling of being tied into a reliable source of nurturance, of feeling basically secure.

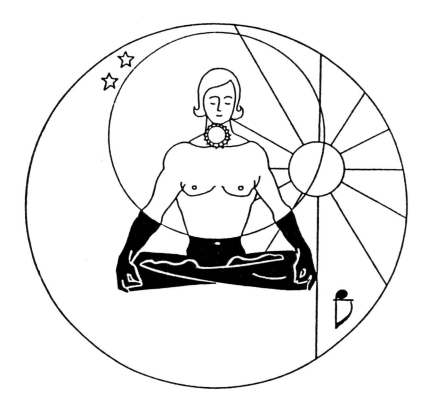

There is an interesting comparison here between yoga psychology and modern concepts of development. In modern psychology, the oral phase of development is the first. It's regarded as the most primitive mode of consciousness. It's thought to be predominant when the infant is born, as though, in terms of yoga psychology, there were another chakra below, and even prior to the anal one. Energy is said, at this earliest stage of development, to be concentrated around the mouth and involved with taking in nurturance. As we have noted earlier, with growth, the infant is thought to move through this oral stage to the next, which is called the anal stage, and which in the yoga system corresponds to the first chakra. In psychoanalytic theory there next comes a genital stage which is similar to the second chakra. Beyond that is the development of competence and effectiveness in the world which would be related in yogic theory to the third center of consciousness. The two theories show a striking correspondence except that what is considered the earliest and most primitive level of development in the psychoanalytic scheme and associated with orality and feeding is not parallel in the yogic conception of the evolution of consciousness. Instead, the issues related to receiving nurturance are thought to be resolved much further along in the developmental scheme. How can we understand or resolve such a major theoretical disparity?

In the psychoanalytic theory there is the tendency to move from the lower to the higher, from the pathological to the normal, seeing the more evolved state as built on the foundations of the more primitive—a sort of mimicry of earlier stages of development. In yogic theory, just the opposite is true. The most evolved states and the most subtle aspects of our being area seen as the center out of which more gross levels of our existence are manifest. In each case the outer sheath is a projection of the inner. Similarly, the more primitive, less conscious levels of development are seen as a weak and more or less distorted reflection of more evolved states. The primitive oral stage of human development is seen as a somewhat distorted *imitation* of the tendency toward trust and devotion that characterize the fifth chakra. In the infant, this attitude may be distorted by a lack of consciousness, an impulsiveness, a demandingness and an oscillation to states of distrust. In the mystic, as we have noted, such inconsistency and confusion is not likely to occur.

Both psychoanalysis and yoga psychology recognize that one level of development can "imitate" another, but the fundamental difference in the direction of imitation that is hypothesized has profound implications for our understanding of human nature. The psychoanalytic notion is more pessimistic. It remains anchored to the primitive, the primordial, and tends toward an emphasis in reduction to the infantile or pathological. The yogic approach, on the other hand, is somewhat more growth-oriented and leads the student toward a more evolved form of what he is currently experiencing.

Psychoanalytic theory grew largely out of studying people with severe emotional problems. Patients who are the most severely disturbed are often thought to have regressed to the most primitive levels of development. Severely paranoid and psychotic patients, for instance, may show a great deal of concern with being engulfed and annihilated. In psychoanalytic terms such a person is often thought of as having marked oral cravings which he projects unto those around him. In this way he comes to believe that others intend to get so close to him and take such control of his life that they will "swallow him up." This fear of being taken over or engulfed is understood by psychoanalysis as a projection of the patient's own extreme oral needs. Working with patients who remain preoccupied with unresolved infantile conflicts has often led to seeing all orality and longing for nurturance as a basically primitive and severely regressive phenomena.

However, this sort of psychological state is quite distinct from what is associated with the throat chakra in yoga psychology. The paranoid involves fear of the ego being lost or swallowed up in a regression to a more primitive undifferentiated stages of development; while in yoga, the longing and seeking associated with the throat chakra relates to the ego searching for some "nurturance from above," for some contact with a higher potential, some way to outgrow itself. The former is associated with the intense oral craving which leads to both the desire to engulf and the fear of engulfment. The latter is the search for guidance from a consciousness beyond one's present limits. Although both are related to having consciousness centered at the throat chakra, one is a higher step in the evolution of consciousness while the other is contaminated by the influence of the most primitive levels of development.

The distinction here is the one discussed earlier in relation to the mystic and the psychotic. It involves differentiating between two kinds of merging or oneness. What is longed for by the mystic is a sort of psychological nurturance from a transpersonal consciousness, sought out in an attempt to escape his present limitations and to grow. The psychotic, on the other hand, in becoming one with whatever is appearing on the screen of the lower mind, is often pulled toward stronger, more massive attachments and regression.

We saw earlier that many psychotherapists tended to explain the mystical experience in terms of the psychotic or tried to understand it by likening it to the primitive oral urges of the infant. The mapping of the centers of consciousness provided by yogic theory may help in clarifying the distinction between these two states. It suggests that the striving to contact a transpersonal source of nurturance is associated with the move toward higher levels of awareness and the uncontaminated experience of the fifth center of consciousness, whereas the fear of attack, penetration, and engulfment indicate that considerable energy is still bound up in the first chakra.

There are a number of techniques for resolving difficulties centered at the throat chakra. Alexander Lowen uses the initiation of the gag reflex to deal with muscular tensions in this area. It is interesting to note that in yoga training there is also an exercise which is called the "upper wash." This involves taking a large quantity of water in and repeatedly stimulating the gag reflex in order to throw it out. Although this serves in part to remove mucus from the esophagus and stomach, it has psychological effects as well. Some students experience great difficulty in performing the exercise because they are either unable to take the water in or unable to let it come out once it has been swallowed. Through repeated performance of the wash and the repetitive stimulation of the gag reflex, the student usually becomes able to comfortably take the water in and throw it out. This is often followed by an increased sense of well-being. In this way the physiological and psychological constriction related to fears of nurturance are partially worked through. As pointed out by Lowen, such exercises alone are not sufficient for creating a therapeutic effect. But in hatha yoga this exercise is part of a comprehensive program which leads, along with meditation and other practices, to a gradual transformation of the personality.

Creativity

The capacity to accept nurturance is a prominent theme in the psychology of religion. For example, the Madonna and Child occupies a central position in Christian art where there is an emphasis on raising consciousness to the heart and throat chakras. Moreover, the "prayer posture" (*mudra*) that is used in this and other traditions may also be related to working with these centers. When the hands are folded with palms together and held between the heart and throat, energy and awareness seem to be concentrated at these two chakras and a "devotional attitude" is created.

The yoga of devotion (*bhakti yogas*) and devotional practices in other religious traditions also emphasize ritual, worship, prayers, and the frequent use of chanting and sacred music. This may be related to the fact that in a certain psychological sense one's words, his utterances, create the universe within which he exists. The throat chakra is the focus of vocalization and singing, of verbalization and creativity. Traditionally in yoga, artists and musicians are said to have their energy concentrated here. It is through sound vibrations, words, and verbal symbols that we create our world.[8] By forming verbal concepts which structure our reality in a certain way, we determine which stimuli will be rejected, which accepted, and how they will be interpreted. Through the repetition of verbal ritual, one's reality can be restructured and recreated. New words and new thoughts create a new world, at least temporarily.[9]

The words that we say, the music that we sing, the artistic activities we undertake, these express the more inventive and creative aspects of our personality. So the throat chakra not only involves nurturance: it involves creation. Though the two seem on the surface to be two distinct functions, on closer examination they turn out to be two sides of the same coin.

The Hopi Indians say of man's relation to this center:

> It tied together those openings in his nose and mouth through which he received the breath of life and the vibratory organs that enabled him to give back his breath in sound....New and diverse sounds were given forth by these vocal organs in the forms of speech and song, their secondary function for man on this earth. But as he came to understand its primary function, he used this center to speak and sing praises to the Creator.

Historically, in both Eastern and Western culture, art and music developed out of expressions of such devotion. Historians of classical Western music trace its origins back to early Christian music, such as the Ambrosian and Gregorian chants, which survive today and are still sung in certain churches and monasteries. Even as music evolved it remained primarily a spiritual endeavor until after the time of Bach. The visual arts were also almost exclusively devoted to the depiction of spiritual themes until relatively recently in the history of Western art. Gradually, these forms of creative expression became secularized and were used to serve other diverse purposes. Nevertheless, art and music still remain a principal means of keeping alive the process of inner growth.

Art has often been used as a part of psychotherapy. It's often found that by means of painting or through music the patient is able to symbolize something important to him and to use this symbol in reintegrating himself. Carl Jung focused considerable attention on the way in which creative symbolization of the unconscious helped in the process of growth. Jung's extensive study of *mandala* and archetypal symbols in artistic expression and myth underscores the importance of the creative act in integrating the personality and expanding consciousness. Thus, it seems that in much of his work Jung was dealing with this, the creative aspect of the throat chakra, although he was not able to integrate it with the other, the devotional aspect of this center.

Art may be useful in the process of psychotherapy because it provides a symbolic expression of some aspect of the person that was previously unknown. But actually, on closer examination, all the symbolizations and formulations evolved during the course of the patient's free exploration of himself are no different. Work with dreams, for example, is basically the same thing: the dream symbols bring to consciousness something of importance that was outside the patient's awareness. The therapist takes hold of the dream symbol and helps the patient to use it inn conceptualizing and understanding himself. All of these processes involve using a symbol creatively to bring into awareness something which was before unknown. When the patient is able, from the point of view of a higher perspective (the "observing ego"), to formulate and bring to the verbal level some part of himself, he has, in fact, performed an artistic or creative task. This is more or less the basis of art. The artist is one who allows the better part of himself to have its say. He gives his underlying consciousness a means of expressing itself that is relatively uncontaminated by his ego-oriented thoughts and concerns. He stands aside, in other words, and lets the inner voice "speak."[10] Therefore, the artistic achievement is not merely to create art but to transform one's personality. For it is by the symbol that has been outwardly created that one is able to reintegrate and reach a new level of awareness. Hence, the act of creation and the act of being created are part and parcel of the same phenomenon. By contrast, when art becomes ego-entangled, creativity stagnates. It is then that an artist comes to "imitate himself"; his symbols no longer evolve and his personal growth ceases. In the act of being creative, one nurtures himself by giving himself and accepting for himself guidance from the higher consciousness that lies within. It is in this sense that we say that the act of nurturing and being nurtured are one and the same. A traditional yogic blessing at meal time says: "The food is Brahman (universal consciousness), the food is offered to Brahman and it is Brahman who offers the food." Similarly, the English word "grace" is used both for the words that are said before eating and also that which is given in the way of nurturance and sustenance as a gift from a more evolved level of consciousness.

When consciousness is first focused at the throat chakra, one's role is still that of the receiver of "grace." The ability to receive grace is a step above the capacities of the heart chakra where one is limited to being compassionate, to sharing as a separate being with a limited other. Now, instead, one is able to accept from an inner, unlimited source. Eventually, through the experience of receiving this grace, one's consciousness moves toward the next center (the one above the throat chakra) and the realization that giver and receiver are one and the same begins to dawn. The artist, for example, realizes through his art his essential identity with that inner voice which inspired him. At this point, the notion that "higher consciousness is within," that it is an underlying potential that can be increasingly developed, begins to make more sense.

The Third Eye:
The Seat of Intuitive Knowledge

T he next chakra is the *ajna* chakra which is located between the eyes and slightly above at the space between the two eyebrows.[11] This is sometimes called "the third ey" because it has to do with a certain kind of seeing. Behind the area of the "third eye" is located the pineal gland. There is a traditional relationship between this and the sixth chakra. The pineal gland was said by the ancients to be sensitive to "a light within." Centuries later, in his treatise on higher reason, Descartes included diagrams demonstrating rays of light entering the skull and affecting the pineal gland. He felt that somehow the most essential aspects of seeing were involved there. Though this was long discounted as a mere carryover from the prescientific era, recent research has begun to show that there may be some validity to this persistent belief. Although there is no direct connection of the pineal with the outside of the body, it has been shown in some animals to be sensitive to the level of light that exists in the environment. Its response varies according to seasonal and daily variations in light levels.

Consciousness that is centered at the ajna chakra involves "introspection" or "the ability to see within." In ancient times a "seer" was one who had focused his consciousness here and was able to see intuitively. The term "clairvoyance," though it has acquired "psychic" connotations, actually comes from the French which means "seeing clearly," and also refers to the centering of consciousness at this chakra. But the "third eye" has the ability to "see" in a way that the physical eyes cannot. This is a deeper vision or *intuitive* means of gaining knowledge.

In modern terms, "intuition" has also assumed a vaguely pejorative connotation. It is often used synonymously with the term "hunch." It is regarded as either unreliable or imaginary. It's certainly not considered something that a sensible person would rely on. If one had an intuitive feeling that the stock market were about to collapse, he probably would not hurriedly sell all his stock. Even if he became a bit concerned, most likely he'd simply reassure himself, "It's only a matter of superstition—a fantasy." In those cases where an intuition does turn out to be accurate, the tendency is to attribute it to coincidence. In modern psychology there is no systematic and scientific study of the intuitive faculty and how it may relate to and grow out of other psychological functions.

In Eastern psychology, by contrast, intuition is a clearly defined phenomenon. It is, moreover, something which can be distinguished from superstition and hunches. A "hunch" may involve an element of intuition, but it is one that is contaminated and confused with material from the personal unconscious. One's complexes and problems intermingle themselves with what little access he might have to something beyond his usual limited consciousness. His premonitions are, then, more often than not mistaken and, at best, unreliable. But "getting hunches" is a natural tendency of the human mind. When the mind spontaneously goes to a state of calmness and relaxation, one is likely to receive such an impression. But when he becomes aware of that potential, he more often than not begins to intervene in the process and intellectualize. Then, even the hunch, contaminated as it is, evaporates.

By contrast, true intuition is a stable, reliable function of the higher levels of consciousness and awareness from which a wider range of information is accessible. There intellect and emotion flow together and become integrated, permitting a new kind of knowing, a kind of knowing which both depends on and promotes self-realization. Intuition unquestionably comes from the highest source of knowledge. It dawns bit by bit with the growth of consciousness. Techniques of meditation provide one with the means through which he can discover and develop within himself that level from which intuition operates.

Intuition has two aspects: there is a difference between creative intuition and higher or inward-directed intuition. Examples of creative intuition are Newton's discovery of gravity or Kekule's discovery of the ring structure of benzene discussed earlier. It brings the super consciousness into productive contact with the outer world. The higher intuition, on the other hand, is not used for working with the more material, outer sheaths, but is used to grasp the innermost nature of our being. It is unalloyed and useful in helping one find his way deeper to even more advanced levels of consciousness.

In the advanced practice of meditation, a focusing of consciousness on the sixth center leads to gradually separating out the contaminants from the pure experience. Eventually, an accurate and reliable intuitive knowledge begins to dawn. We might say that the intuitive mode of consciousness that is associated with the left side is finally brought to its perfection. "Opening the third eye" means integrating the right and the left. It means bringing together the judgment and discrimination which characterize the right side of consciousness with the openness and access to the intuitive world that characterizes the left. It means putting an end both to dry, sterile intellectualization as well as to superstition and "hunches." It means bringing together these two partial, inaccurate ways of knowledge into an integrated whole that is more profound and penetrating.

A well-known symbol, which has survived in the West, portrays the integration that occurs between these two poles when consciousness is properly focused on this chakra. This is the Caduceus or medical symbol. Although it is commonly used in medicine, its origins and significance are not generally understood, even by physicians. It is apparently no accident[12] that this symbol is so strikingly similar to the traditional yogic way of depicting the relationship between consciousness, *prana* (energy) and the chakras. The central staff is analogous to the spinal cord, the coiled snakes as the left and right—*ida* and *pingala*, female and male, passive and active—aspects of human nature which we have discussed in Chapter Two. Like the *nadis* in yogic illustrations, the snakes of the Caduceus intertwine, finally meeting at the sixth center where two wings are depicted.[13]

Perhaps the Caduceus represents that ideal which should be attained by each person who seeks to heal others: his consciousness must be awakened to that deep intuition and understanding which characterizes this center, so that his efforts at healing come from the deep fountain of knowledge found here. This requires long and systematic training.

Even when preparation is not systematic, however, some fleeting contact with a more universal consciousness may be momentarily experienced. This may occur in people who have, through their life experience, reached a level of unusual maturity and personal evolution. Sudden flashes of an altered state of consciousness may be experienced and reported as overwhelming. Such experiences have been described by philosophers and poets through the ages, such as Spinoza, Walt Whitman, and William Blake. Their recollection may serve as a constant source of inspiration for years, but without any systematic preparation or well-designed discipline, such persons are usually unable to find their way back at will to these moments of illumination. They must wait for them to happen spontaneously. Their experience remains an important influence on their life and a crucial center of integration around which they can be creative, but it cannot grow into a completely integrated consciousness. It never develops into a constant, underlying awareness, but remains only an occasional, transient experience. However, through the practice of yoga, under the guidance of an accomplished teacher, the student is trained to systematically attain the highest states of consciousness at will.

Opening this inner vision means opening modes of awareness for which we have potential, but which we are at present not able to imagine. It means escaping the confines of our culturally endorsed everyday reality. It means escaping the limited concepts of a consciousness which is oriented around material, externally observable phenomena. It means moving beyond the limitations of time, space, and causality.

One who knows how to meditate on the space between the two eyebrows or ajna chakra gains a new perspective on the principles of time, space, and causality. The one-pointed inward focusing of awareness leads to a point from which the multiplicity of phenomena and events can be seen as one interrelated whole. The causal sequence of phenomena in the world is then transcended and "future" events can be apprehended. Though this may sound absurd to the hard-nosed, intellectualizing materialist, according to the exact and well-defined science of meditation, the network of past, present, and future is a flow of many events on the bed of time. And this entire bed can be visualized, with proper training.

Ramakrishna tried to describe to his close disciples the transcendent experience resulting when the mind is fully centered on this chakra. One day he said:

> I'll tell you everything today and will not keep anything secret." He described clearly the centers and the corresponding experiences up to the heart and throat, and then, pointing to the spot between the eyebrows, he said, "The supreme Self is directly known and the individual experiences *samadhi* when the mind comes here. There remains then but a thin transparent screen separating the supreme Self and the individual self. The *sadhaka* then experiences...," saying this, the moment he started to describe in detail the realization of the supreme Self, he was plunged in samadhi. When the samadhi came to an end, he tried again to describe it and was again in samadhi.

After repeated attempts, Ramakrishna breaks into tears and tells his disciples that, although he has a desire to tell them everything "without concealing anything whatsoever," he is unable to speak:

> Whenever I try to describe what kinds of visions I experience when it goes beyond this place (showing the throat) and think what kinds of visions I am witnessing, the mind rushes immediately up, and speaking becomes impossible.

Describing this state further, Ramakrishna says:

> If...anybody's mind reaches the spot between the eyebrows...He then has direct knowledge of the supreme Self....There is only a screen transparent like glass....The supreme Self is so near then that it seems as if one is merged in Him, identified with Him. But identification is yet to be.

When consciousness moves to the next and final center, however:

...the distinction between the subject of consciousness and the object of consciousness is destroyed. It is a state wherein self-identity and the field of consciousness are blended in one indissoluble whole.

The Crown Chakra:
The Highest State of Consciousness

T he seventh or highest center is located at the vertex or top of the head. It is called the "crown chakra." When consciousness is most evolved it comes to be focused primarily here. The custom of placing an ornate crown on the head of a monarch seems to be rooted in the idea that the person with the most evolved consciousness should be the one to lead the state. His understanding should be beyond that of his subjects. This is the concept of the "philosopher king."

A reverence for this center of consciousness is also seen in the symbology of certain religions. In the Christian tradition it has been customary for certain monks to shave the crown of the head and leave a bare circle there. In the Jewish tradition a skull cap is worn which covers that same area. Religious art often highlights the area of the crown chakra with a burst of light or a halo.

The Hopi Indians say of man's relationship to this center:

> Here, when he was born, was the soft spot...the "open door" through which he received his life and communicated with his Creator...At the time of...the last phase of his creation, the soft spot was hardened and the door was closed. It remained closed until his death, opening then for his life to depart as it had come.

The yogic tradition gives a similar significance to the soft spot of the infant, noting that it gradually hardens as the child's intuitive qualities are diminished during the development of rationality and ego functions. The yogic viewpoint, however, emphasizes that this door may be reopened through the attainment of the highest state of samadhi. It is said that highly evolved yogis have access to this center. These accomplished yogis become aware of the course future events will take. They have been known to announce and prepare for the exact date and time when their consciousness quietly and calmly, in the company of their closest students, abandons the physical body. Of course, the mastery, control, and highly evolved consciousness which this presupposes is rare.

At the level of this center, all the distinctions of ordinary consciousness break down. Awareness is expanded beyond the point that can be explained in verbal terms.

At this center there is a vast awareness that knows no limits. Even the differentiation between the experiencer and the experienced ceases. In the traditions of yoga this chakra is represented by a thousand-petaled lotus, and the experience is one comparable only to the dazzling light of countless suns. Any descriptions of the experience involved here must of necessity be couched in such highly symbolic terms that they are difficult to deal with in the context of psychological theory.

Though in a sense this experience lies beyond modern psychology, since it departs from the limitations of the psyche, it is obviously of vital importance to the subject. It offers the vantage point from which the mind can be most clearly appreciated. It serves as a crucial point of orientation. Through it lies beyond the realm of mental functioning, it provides the key to a framework in which the functioning of the mind becomes intelligible, and all the aspects of experience can be integrated into a unified theory.

Furthermore, the nature of this state is so fundamental to the nature of man's being that to be completely successful any psychological theory must at least be compatible with its existence.

Reflections

T his essay is a portion of a book entitled *Yoga and Psychotherapy* written by a team of Indian and American practitioners of yoga. The authors focus on the psychological dimension of yoga, offering useful comparisons to Western psychotherapeutic theories. The "Seven Centers of Consciousness" is an evocative discussion of the yogic theory of energy points in the body called the *chakras*, a system which provides a meditative tool for identifying areas of inner conflict or imbalance that need to be resolved before true "liberation" can take place.

NOTES

1. A number of "minor," less important centers have also been described elsewhere. To avoid too much complexity, however, they will not be discussed here.

2. Though the chakras serve to interconnect the sheaths, the higher chakras are more closely related to the innermost sheaths—higher (inward dwelling) levels of consciousness—and the lower chakras to the outermost sheaths—lower (outward-going) levels of consciousness.

3. Dr. Shafüa Karagulla studied several people whose awareness was developed to the point that they were able to "observe" the energy distribution in these centers. One of Dr. Karagulla's subjects, Diane, was able to use her awareness of the energy movement in these centers to accurately diagnose physical disorders.

4. Traditionally in yoga three classes of Tantric practices exist: 1) *kaula*—using externals and making physical acts as a means of worship; 2) *mishra*—a mixed form which uses external worship but also focuses on raising the energy through the chakras to develop one's creative potential; and 3) *samaya*—the most pure form of Tantra where the constituent principles from which the universe is manifest are merged with directly through the use of ritual mantram and visualization. Most Western conceptualizations of Tantra fall into the first or at best second category. The practice or understanding of the more pure and evolved Tantric practices are known only to a handful of individuals.

5. The issue of orality and trust which in the psychoanalytic model reflect the earliest stage in development are seen as being resolved at more advanced levels of development in the yogic system. See section on the fifth chakra.

6. As we shall see later, Abraham Maslow has proposed a motivational hierarchy similar to that suggested here. In Maslow's theory, however, physiological safety and security needs are seen as more "primary" and once they are fulfilled the individual is motivated by more self-actualizing tendencies.

7. Again note the similarity to Maslow's theory of motivation which suggests that "the most basic, the most powerful, the most obvious of all man's needs are his needs for food, liquid, shelter, sex, sleep, and oxygen."

8. The element associated with the throat chakra is *akasha*, usually translated "ether." The ether is sort of the underlying medium in which other things exist, the field in which things happen. The throat chakra involves creation within this field. It is the symbolizations mediated through this chakra that fill this field with the reality that we construct for ourselves.

9. Anthropologists have provided many examples of how linguistic concepts shape our concept of reality; see e.g. Benjamin Lee Whorf.

10. The use of the word or sound vibration to create an outward form is the very basis of psychotherapy. For it is around this outward form that one is able to integrate himself at a new and higher level. This is only useful and valuable, of course, when the outward form takes shape during a more evolved consciousness, i.e., from the point of view of detachment (observing ego).

11. There are no elements associated with the highest two chakras which lead one beyond even the most subtle forms of matter.

12. The Caduceus is a replica of the Staff of Mercury or Hermes, and the "Hermetic Science" of the Middle Ages was closely related to the practice of medicine, as taught by such Masters as Paracelsus (whose studies and wanderings are said to have taken him to Russia, the Near East, and eventually India). These medieval "alchemists," the forerunners of modern chemistry and medicine, were very much aware of the right-left polarity and its significance.

13. Here again the symbolism parallels that of the yogic chakras, for each chakra in traditional symbology is shown with its own particular number of subtle nerve currents depicted as lotus petals. The ajna chakra is shown with two such petals at a point corresponding to that where the wings of the Caduceus are found.

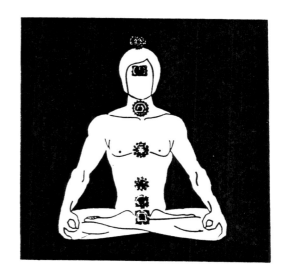

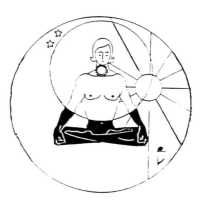

IV

Buddhism

The Teachings
of the
Compassionate Buddha

Buddha's Farewell Address

When the Blessed One had remained as long as he wished at Ambapali's grove, he went to Beluva, near Vaishali. There the Blessed One addressed the brethren, and said: "O mendicants, do you take up your abode for the rainy season roundabout Vaishali, each one according to the place where his friends and near companions may live. I shall enter upon the rainy season here at Beluva."

When the Blessed One had thus entered upon the rainy season there fell upon him a dire sickness, and sharp pains came upon him even unto death. But the Blessed One, mindful and self-possessed, bore them without complaint.

Then this thought occurred to the Blessed One,

"It would not be right for me to pass away from life without addressing the disciples, without taking leave of the order. Let me now, by a strong effort of will, bend this sickness down again, and keep my hold on life till the allotted time have come."

And the Blessed One, by a strong effort of the will, bent the sickness down, and kept his hold on life till the time he fixed upon should come. And the sickness abated.

Excerpt from THE TEACHINGS OF THE COMPASSIONATE BUDDHA, edited by E. A. Burtt. Pp. 48–50, 128–129. Copyright ©1982 by E. A. Burtt. Reprinted by permission of The Estate of E. A. Burtt.

Thus the Blessed One began to recover; and when he had quite got rid of the sickness, he went out from the monastery, and sat down on a seat spread out in the open air. And the venerable Ananda, accompanied by many other disciples, approached where the Blessed One was, saluted him, and taking a seat respectfully on one side, said: "I have beheld, Lord, how the Blessed One was in health, and I have beheld how the Blessed One had to suffer. And though at the sight of the sickness of the Blessed One my body became weak as a creeper, and the horizon became dim to me, and my faculties were no longer clear, yet notwithstanding I took some little comfort from the thought that the Blessed One would not pass away from existence until at least he had left instructions as touching the order."

And the Blessed One addressed Ananda for the sake of the order and said:

"What, then, Ananda, does the order expect of me? I have preached the truth without making any distinction between exoteric and esoteric doctrine; for in respect of the truth, Ananda, the Tathagata has no such thing as the closed fist of a teacher, who keeps some things back.

"Surely, Ananda, should there be any one who harbors the thought, 'It is I who will lead the brotherhood,' or, 'The order is dependent upon me,' he should lay down instructions in any matter concerning the order. Now the Tathagata, Ananda, thinks not that it is he who should lead the brotherhood, or that the order is dependent upon him.

"Why, then, should the Tathagata leave instructions in any matter concerning the order?

"I am now grown old, O Ananda, and full of years; my journey is drawing to its close, I have reached the sum of my days, I am turning eighty years of age.

"Just as a worn-out cart can only with much difficulty be made to move along, so the body of the Tathagata can only be kept going with much additional care.

"It is only, Ananda, when the Tathagata, ceasing to attend to any outward thing, becomes plunged in that devout meditation of heart which is concerned with no bodily object, it is only then that the body of the Tathagata is at ease.

"Therefore, O Ananda, be ye lamps unto yourselves. Rely on yourselves, and do not rely on external help.

"Hold fast to the truth as a lamp. Seek salvation alone in the truth. Look not for assistance to any one besides yourselves.

"And how, Ananda, can a brother be a lamp unto himself, rely on himself only and not on any external help, holding fast to the truth as his lamp and seeking salvation in the truth alone, looking not for assistance to any one besides himself?

"Herein, O Ananda, let a brother, as he dwells in the body, so regard the body that he, being strenuous, thoughtful, and mindful, may, whilst in the world, overcome the grief which arises from the body's cravings.

"While subject to sensations let him continue so to regard the sensations that he, being strenuous, thoughtful, and mindful, may, whilst in the world, overcome the grief which arises from the sensations.

"And so, also, when he thinks, or reasons, or feels, let him so regard his thought that being strenuous, thoughtful, and mindful he may, whilst in the world, overcome the grief which arises from the craving due to ideas, or to reasoning, or to feeling.

"Those who, either now or after I am dead, shall be a lamp unto themselves, relying upon themselves only and not relying upon any external help, but holding fast to the truth as their lamp, and seeking their salvation in the truth alone, shall not look for assistance to any one besides themselves, it is they, Ananda, among my bhikshus, who shall reach the very topmost height! But they must be anxious to learn....

> "My age is now full ripe, my life draws to its close:
> I leave you, I depart, relying on myself alone!
> Be earnest then, O brethren, holy, full of thought!
> Be steadfast in resolve! Keep watch o'er your own hearts!
> Who wearies not, but holds fast to his truth and law,
> Shall cross this sea of life, shall make an end of grief."

Hymn to the Buddha of Infinite Compassion and Wisdom

All the faults can never in any way be in him;
All the virtues are in every way in him established.

To go to him for refuge, to praise and honour him,
To abide in his religion, that is fit for those with sense....

Homage to the Self-Existent! Wonderful his many works,
Virtues potent and abundant, which refuse to be defined.

Any worldly thing one might compare can be damaged or obstructed,
Time and place set limits to it, to surpass it is not hard.

How can there be a likeness to your virtues, untouched by foe or obstacle,
Everlasting, unlimited, and which cannot be surpassed? ...

This form of yours, calm yet lovely, brilliant without dazzling,
Soft but mighty—whom would it not entrance?

Whether one has seen it a hundred times, or beholds it for the first time,
Your form gives the same pleasure to the eye....

Without distinction all this world was bound to the defilements,
That you might free it you were long in bondage to compassion.

Which shall I praise first, you or the great compassion by which
For so long you were held in Samsara, although you well knew its faults?

It was your compassion, given free course, which made you pass your time
Among the crowds, when the happiness of seclusion suited you so much better....

Your birth gives joy to people, and your growth delights them;
While you are there they benefit, on your departure they feel lost.

To praise you takes all guilt away, to recollect you lifts up the heart,
To seek you brings understanding, to comprehend you purity....

An island you are to those swept along by the flood, a shelter to the stricken,
A refuge to those terrified by becoming, the resource of those who desire release....

No matter by whom or where or how provoked,
Never do you transgress your own fair path of conduct.

Other men do not as much study the welfare of those who mean them well,
As you study that of those who seek your harm.

To an enemy intent on ill you are a good friend intent on good.
To one who constantly seeks for faults you respond by seeking for virtues....

Those who wish to benefit beings, and who are compassionate,
What can they do wherein you have not led the way?

Out of pity for the world you have promoted the good Dharma for a long time,
Many worthy disciples able to help the triple world have you raised....

What steadfastness! What conduct! What form! What virtues!
In Buddha's dharmas there is nothing that is not wonderful.

Reflections

Siddhartha Gautama, known as the Buddha, lived in northern India in the sixth century B.C. The story of his "Awakening" to the eternal truth and the exposition of the Buddha's doctrine of the Four Noble Truths are included in most world religion textbooks and should be referred to. One must see the Buddha's teachings as his reaction to certain developments in his native Hindu tradition. The Buddha preached intense self-effort, and the *Farewell Address* exemplifies this aspect of the Dhamma, the teaching. The Buddha taught that all mortal existence is characterized by *dukkha*, suffering, and that the root cause of suffering is desire, life's incessant craving. The overcoming of desire involves an "Eightfold Path": right understanding, right thought, right speech, right body action, right livelihood, right moral effort, right mindfulness, right concentration. Right understanding and thought may originate as faith, but ultimately must be experienced as wisdom. The cessation of desire is called Nirvana. While the Buddha maintained that he was only a pointer to the truth, he became the focus of devotion for many Buddhists, especially the Mahayana school, the larger of the two main groups of Buddhists. *The Hymn to the Buddha of Infinite Compassion and Wisdom* exemplifies the devotional character of Mahayana Buddhism. The smaller school, the

Theravada Buddhists, emphasize the attainment of wisdom; the Mahayana Buddhists emphasize the attainment of the compassion embodied in the Buddha's life.

V

Chinese Thought

The Analects of Confucius

1:1. Confucius said, "Is it not a pleasure to learn and to repeat or practice from time to time what has been learned? Is it not delightful to have friends coming from afar? Is one not a superior man if he does not feel hurt even though he is not recognized?"

Comment. Interpretations of Confucian teachings have differed radically in the last 2,000 years. Generally speaking, Han (206 B.C.-A.D. 220) scholars, represented in Ho Yen (d. 249), *Lun-yü chi-chieh* (Collected Explanations of the *Analects*), were inclined to be literal and interested in historical facts, whereas Neo-Confucianists, represented in Chu Hsi (1130–1200), *Lun-yü chi-chu* (Collected Commentaries on the *Analects*) were interpretative, philosophical, and often subjective. They almost invariably understand the Confucian Way (Tao) as principle (*li*), which is their cardinal concept, and frequently when they came to an undefined "this" or "it," they insisted that it meant principle. This divergency between the Han and Sung scholars has colored interpretations of this passage. To Wang Su (195–265), quoted in Ho, *hsi* (to learn) means to recite a lesson repeatedly. To Chu Hsi, however, *hsi* means to follow the examples of those who are first to understand, and therefore it does not mean recitation but practice. In revolt against both extremes, Ch'ing (1644–1912) scholars emphasized practical experience. In this case, *hsi* to them means both to repeat and to practice, as indicated in Liu Pao-nan (1791–1855), *Lun-yü cheng-i* (Correct Meanings of the *Analects*). Thus Ho Yen, Chu Hsi, and Liu Pao-nan neatly represent the three different approaches in the three different periods. Generally speaking, the dominant spirit of Confucian teaching is the equal emphasis on knowledge and action. This dual emphasis will be encountered again and again.

Translated by Chan, Wing-Tsit; A SOURCEBOOK IN CHINESE PHILOSOPHY. Copyright ©1969 by Princeton University Press. Reprinted by permission of Princeton University Press.

1:2. Yu Tzu said, "Few of those who are filial sons and respectful brothers will show disrespect to superiors, and there has never been a man who is not disrespectful to superiors and yet creates disorder. A superior man is devoted to the fundamentals (the root). When the root is firmly established, the moral law (Tao) will grow. Filial piety and brotherly respect are the root of humanity (*jen*)."

1:3. Confucius said, "A man with clever words and an ingratiating appearance is seldom a man of humanity."

1:4. Tseng-Tzu said, "Every day I examine myself on three points: whether in counseling others I have not been loyal; whether in intercourse with my friends I have not been faithful; and whether I have not repeated again and again and practiced the instructions of my teacher."

1:6. Young men should be filial when at home and respectful to their elders when away from home. They should be earnest and faithful. They should love all extensively and be intimate with men of humanity. When they have any energy to spare after the performance of moral duties, they should use it to study literature and the arts (*wen*).

1:8. Confucius said, "If the superior man is not grave, he will not inspire awe, and his learning will not be on a firm foundation." Hold loyalty and faithfulness to be fundamental. Have no friends who are not as good as yourself. When you have made mistakes, don't be afraid to correct them."

> *Comment*. The teaching about friendship here is clearly inconsistent with *Analects*, 8:5, where Confucius exhorts us to learn from inferiors. It is difficult to believe that Confucius taught people to be selfish. According to Hsing Ping (932–1010), Confucius meant people who are not equal to oneself in loyalty and faithfulness, assuming that one is or should be loyal and faithful; according to Hsü Kan (171–218), Confucius simply wanted us to be careful in choosing friends.

1:11. Confucius said, "When a man's father is alive, look at the bent of his will. When his father is dead, look at his conduct. If for three years [of mourning] he does not change from the way of his father, he may be called filial."

> *Comment*. Critics of Confucius have asserted that Confucian authoritarianism holds an oppressive weight on the son even after the father has passed away. Fan Tsu-yü (1041–1098) did understand the saying to mean that the son should observe the father's will and past conduct, but he was almost alone in this. All prominent commentators, from K'ung An-kuo to Cheng Hsüan (127–200), Chu Hsi, and Liu Pao-nan have interpreted the passage to mean that while one's father is alive, one's action is restricted, so that his

intention should be the criterion by which his character is to be judged. After his father's death, however, when he is completely autonomous, he should be judged by his conduct. In this interpretation, the way of the father is of course the moral principle which has guided or should have guided the son's conduct.

1:12. Yu Tzu said, "Among the functions of propriety (*li*) the most valuable is that it establishes harmony. The excellence of the ways of ancient kings consists of this. It is the guiding principle of all things great and small. If things go amiss, and you, understanding harmony, try to achieve it without regulating it by the rules of propriety, they will still go amiss."

1:14. Confucius said, "The superior man does not seek fulfillment of his appetite nor comfort in his lodging. He is diligent in his duties and careful in his speech. He associates with men of moral principles and thereby realizes himself. Such a person may be said to love learning."

1:15. Tzu-kung said, "What do you think of a man who is poor and yet does not flatter, and the rich man who is not proud?" Confucius replied, "They will do. But they are not as good as the poor man who is happy and the rich man who loves the rules of propriety (*li*)." Tzu-kung said, "*The Book of Odes* says:

> As a thing is cut and filed,
> As a thing is carved and polished....

Does that not mean what you have just said?"

Confucius said, "Ah! Tz'u. Now I can begin to talk about the odes with you. When I have told you what has gone before, you know what is to follow."

1:16. Confucius said, "[A good man] does not worry about not being known by others but rather worries about not knowing them."

2:1. Confucius said, "A ruler who governs his state by virtue is like the north polar star, which remains in its place while all the other stars revolve around it."

Comment. Two important principles are involved here. One is government by virtue, in which Confucianists stand directly opposed to the Legalists, who prefer law and force. The other is government through inaction, i.e., government in such excellent order that all things operate by themselves. This is the interpretation shared by Han and Sung Confucianists alike. In both cases, Confucianism and Taoism are in agreement.

2:2. Confucius said, "All three hundred odes can be covered by one of their sentences, and that is 'Have no depraved thoughts.'"

2:3. Confucius said, "Lead the people with governmental measures and regulate them by law and punishment, and they will avoid wrongdoing but will have no sense of honor and shame. Lead them with virtue and regulate them by the roles of propriety (*li*), and they will have a sense of shame and, moreover, set themselves right."

2:4. Confucius said, "At fifteen my mind was set on learning. At thirty my character had been formed. At forty I had no more perplexities. At fifty I knew the Mandate of Heaven (*T'ien-ming*). At sixty I was at ease with whatever I heard. At seventy I could follow my heart's desire without transgressing moral principles."

> *Comment.* What *T'ien-ming* is depends upon one's own philosophy. In general, Confucianists before the T'ang dynasty (618–907) understood it to mean either the decree of God, which determines the course of one's life, or the rise and fall of the moral order, whereas Sung scholars, especially Chu Hsi, took it to mean "the operation of Nature which is endowed in things and makes things be as they are." This latter interpretation has prevailed. The concept of *T'ien-ming* which can mean Mandate of Heaven, decree of God, personal destiny, and course of order, is extremely important in the history of Chinese thought. In religion it generally means fate or personal order of God, but in philosophy it is practically always understood as moral destiny, natural endowment, or moral order.

2:5. Meng I Tzu asked about filial piety. Confucius said: "Never disobey." [Later,] when Fan Ch'ih was driving him, Confucius told him, "Meng-sun asked me about filial piety, and I answered him, 'Never disobey.'" Fan Ch'ih said, "What does that mean?" Confucius said. "When parents are alive, serve them according to the rules of propriety. When they die, bury them according to the rules of propriety and sacrifice to them according to the rules of propriety."

2:6. Meng Wu-po asked about filial piety. Confucius said, "Especially be anxious lest parents should be sick."

2:7. Tzu-yu asked about filial piety. Confucius said, "Filial piety nowadays means to be able to support one's parents. But we support even dogs and horses. If there is no feeling of reverence, wherein lies the difference?"

2:11. Confucius said, "A man who reviews the old so as to find out the new is qualified to teach others."

2:12. Confucius said, "The superior man is not an implement (*ch'i*)."

Comment. A good and educated man should not be like an implement, which is intended only for a narrow and specific purpose. Instead, he should have broad vision, wide interests, and sufficient ability to do many things.

2:13. Tzu-kung asked about the superior man. Confucius said, "He acts before he speaks and then speaks according to his action."'

2:14. Confucius said, "The superior man is broadminded but not partisan; the inferior man is partisan but not broadminded."

2:15. Confucius said, "He who learns but does not think is lost; he who thinks but does not learn is in danger."

2:17. Confucius said, "Yu, shall I teach you [the way to acquire] knowledge? To say that you know when you do know and say that you do not know when you do not know—that is [the way to acquire] knowledge."

2:18. Tzu-chang was learning with a view to official emolument. Confucius said, "Hear much and put aside what's doubtful while you speak cautiously of the rest. Then few will blame you. See much and put aside what seems perilous while you are cautious in carrying the rest into practice. Then you will have few occasions for regret. When one's words give few occasions for blame and his acts give few occasions for repentance—there lies his emolument."

Comment. The equal emphasis on words and deeds has been a strong tradition in Confucianism. Eventually Wang Yang-ming identified them as one.

2:24. Confucius said, "It is flattery to offer sacrifice to ancestral spirits other than one's own. To see what is right and not to do it is cowardice."

3:3. Confucius said, "If a man is not humane (*jen*), what has he to do with ceremonies (*li*)? If he is not humane, what has he to do with music?"

3:4. Lin Fang asked about the foundation of ceremonies. Confucius said, "An important question indeed! In rituals or ceremonies, be thrifty rather than extravagant, and in funerals, be deeply sorrowful rather than shallow in sentiment."

3:12. When Confucius offered sacrifice to his ancestors, he felt as if his ancestral spirits were actually present. When he offered sacrifice to other spiritual beings, he felt as if they were actually present. He said, "If I do not participate in the sacrifice, it is as if I did not sacrifice at all."

3:13. Wang-sun Chia asked, "What is meant by the common saying, 'It is better to be on good terms with the God of the Kitchen [who cooks our food] than with the spirits of the shrine (ancestors) at the southwest corner of the house'?" Confucius said, "It is not true. He who commits a sin against Heaven has no god to pray to."

3:17. Tzu-kung wanted to do away with the sacrificing of a lamb at the ceremony in which the beginning of each month is reported to ancestors. Confucius said, "Tz'u! You love the lamb but I love the ceremony."

3:19. Duke Ting asked how the ruler should employ his ministers and how the ministers should serve their ruler. Confucius said, "A ruler should employ his ministers according to the principle of propriety, and ministers should serve their ruler with loyalty."

3:24. The guardian at I (a border post of the state of Wei) requested to be presented to Confucius, saying, "When gentlemen come here, I have never been prevented from seeing them." Confucius' followers introduced him. When he came out from the interview, he said, "Sirs, why are you disheartened by your master's loss of office? The Way has not prevailed in the world for a long time. Heaven is going to use your master as a bell with a wooden tongue [to awaken the people]."

4:2. Confucius said, "One who is not a man of humanity cannot endure adversity for long, nor can he enjoy prosperity for long. The man of humanity is naturally at ease with humanity. The man of wisdom cultivates humanity for its advantage."

4:3. Confucius said, "Only the man of humanity knows how to love people and hate people."

4:4. Confucius said, "If you set your mind on humanity, you will be free from evil."

4:5. Confucius said, "Wealth and honor are what every man desires. But if they have been obtained in violation of moral principles, they must not be kept. Poverty and humble station are what every man dislikes. But if they can be avoided only in violation of moral principles, they must not be avoided. If a superior man departs from humanity, how can he fulfill that name? A superior man never abandons humanity even for the lapse of a single meal. In moments of haste, he acts according to it. In times of difficulty or confusion, he acts according to it."

4:6. Confucius said, "I have never seen one who really loves humanity or one who really hates inhumanity. One who really loves humanity will not place anything above it. One who really hates inhumanity will practice humanity in such a way that inhumanity will have no chance to get at him. Is there any one who has devoted his strength to humanity for as long as a single day? I have not seen any one without sufficient strength to do so. Perhaps there is such a case, but I have never seen it."

4:8. Confucius said, "In the morning, hear the Way; in the evening, die content!"

4:10. Confucius said, "A superior man in dealing with the world is not for anything or against anything. He follows righteousness as the standard."

> *Comment*. This is a clear expression of both the flexibility and rigidity of Confucian eth-ics—flexibility in application but rigidity in standard. Here lies the basic idea of the Confucian doctrine of *ching-ch'üan*, or the standard and the exceptional, the absolute and the relative, or the permanent and the temporary. This explains why Confucius was not obstinate, had no predetermined course of action, was ready to serve or to withdraw whenever it was proper to do so, and, according to Mencius, was a sage who acted according to the circumstance of the time.
>
> The words *shih* and *mo* can be interpreted to mean being near to people and being distant from people, or opposing people and admiring people, respectively, and some commentators have adopted these interpretations. But the majority follow Chu Hsi, as I have done here. Chu Hsi was thinking about the superior man's dealing with things. Chang Shih (Chang Nan-hsien, 1133–1180), on the other hand, thought Confucius was talking about the superior man's state of mind. This difference reflects the opposition between the two wings of Neo-Confucianism, one inclining to activity, the other to the state of mind.

4:11. Confucius said, "The superior man thinks of virtue; the inferior man thinks of possessions. The superior man thinks of sanctions; the inferior man thinks of personal favors."

4:12. Confucius said, "If one's acts are motivated by profit, he will have many enemies."

4:15. Confucius said, "Shen, there is one thread that runs through my doctrines." Tseng Tzu said, "Yes." After Confucius had left, the disciples asked him, "What did he mean?" Tseng Tzu replied, "The Way of our Master is none other than conscientiousness (*chung*) and altruism (*shu*)."

Comment. Confucian teachings may be summed up in the phrase "one thread" (*i-kuan*), but Confucianists have not agreed on what it means. Generally, Confucianists of Han and T'ang times adhered to the basic meaning of "thread" and understood it in the sense of a system or a body of doctrines. Chu Hsi, true to the spirit of Neo-Confucian speculative philosophy, took it to mean that there is one mind to respond to all things. In the Ch'ing period, in revolt against speculation, scholars preferred to interpret *kuan* as action and affairs, that is, there is only one moral principle for all actions. All agree, however, on the meanings of *chung* and *shu*, which are best expressed by Chu Hsi, namely, *chung* means the full development of one's [originally good] mind and *shu* means the extension of that mind to others. As Ch'eng I (Ch'eng I-ch'uan, 1033–1107) put it, *chung* is the Way of Heaven, whereas *shu* is the way of man; the former is substance, while the latter is function. Liu Pao-nan is correct in equating *chung* with Confucius' saying, "Establish one's own character," and *shu* with "Also establish the character of others." Here is the positive version of the Confucian golden rule. The negative version is only one side of it.

4:16. Confucius said, "The superior man understands righteousness (*i*); the inferior man understands profit."

Comment. Confucius contrasted the superior man and the inferior in many ways, but this is the fundamental difference for Confucianism in general as well as for Confucius himself. Chu Hsi associated righteousness with the Principle of Nature (*T'ien-li*) and profit with the feelings of man, but later Neo-Confucianists strongly objected to his thus contrasting principle and feelings.

4:18. Confucius said, "In serving his parents, a son may gently remonstrate with them. When he sees that they are not inclined to listen to him, he should resume an attitude of reverence and not abandon his effort to serve them. He may feel worried, but does not complain."

4:19. Confucius said, "When his parents are alive, a son should not go far abroad; or if he does, he should let them know where he goes."

4:21. Confucius said, "A son should always keep in mind the age of his parents. It is an occasion for joy [that they are enjoying long life] and also an occasion for anxiety [that another year is gone]."

4:24. Confucius said, "The superior man wants to be slow in word but diligent in action."

5:11. Tzu-kung said, "What I do not want others to do to me, I do not want to do to them." Confucius said, "Ah Tz'u! That is beyond you."

5:12. Tzu-kung said, "We can hear our Master's [views] on culture and its manifestation, but we cannot hear his views on human nature and the Way of Heaven [because these subjects are beyond the comprehension of most people]."

5:25. Yen Yüan and Chi-lu were in attendance. Confucius said, "Why don't you each tell me your ambition in life?" Tzu-lu said, "I wish to have a horse, a carriage, and a light fur coat and share them with friends, and shall not regret if they are all worn out." Yen Yüan said, "I wish never to boast of my good qualities and never to brag about the trouble I have taken [for others]." Tzu-lu said, "I wish to hear your ambition." Confucius said, "It is my ambition to comfort the old, to be faithful to friends, and to cherish the young."

5:27. Confucius said, "In every hamlet of ten families, there are always some people as loyal and faithful as myself, but none who love learning as much as I do."

6:5. Confucius said, "About Hui (Yen Yüan), for three months there would be nothing in his mind contrary to humanity. The others could (or can) attain to this for a day or a month at the most."

> *Comment.* On the basis of this saying alone, some philosophers have concluded that Yen Yüan was a mystic and that Confucius praised mysticism!

6:16. Confucius said, "When substance exceeds refinement (*wen*), one becomes rude. When refinement exceeds substance, one becomes urbane. It is only when one's substance and refinement are properly blended that he becomes a superior man."

6:17. Confucius said, "Man is born with uprightness. If one loses it he will be lucky if he escapes with his life."

> *Comment.* Although the Confucian tradition in general holds that human nature is originally good, Confucius' own position is not clear. We have read that his doctrine of nature could not be heard, and we shall read his statement that by nature men are alike. But how they are alike is not clear. The saying here can be interpreted to mean that man can life throughout life because he is upright. This is the interpretation of Ma Jung (79–166) which is followed by Wang Ch'ung (27–100?). Most people followed Chu Hsi. He had the authority of Ch'eng Hao (Ch'eng Ming-tao, 1032–1085), who echoed Cheng Hsüan's interpretation that Confucius said that man is *born* upright. This means that Confucius was not only the first one in Chinese philosophy to assume a definite position about human nature, but also the first to teach that human nature is *originally* good.

6:18. Confucius said, "To know it [learning or the Way] is not as good as to love it, and to love it is not as good as to take delight in it."

6:19. Confucius said, "To those who are above average, one may talk of the higher things, but may not do so to those who are below average."

6:20. Fan Ch'ih asked about wisdom. Confucius said, "Devote yourself earnestly to the duties due to men, and respect spiritual beings but keep them at a distance. This may be called wisdom." Fan Ch'ih asked about humanity. Confucius said, "The man of humanity first of all considers what is difficult in the task and then thinks of success. Such a man may be called humane."

> *Comment.* Many people have been puzzled by this passage, some even doubting the sincerity of Confucius' religious attitude—all quite unnecessarily. The passage means either "do not become improperly informal with spiritual beings," or "emphasize the way of man rather than the way of spirits."

6:21. Confucius said, "The man of wisdom delights in water; the man of humanity delights in mountains. The man of wisdom is active; the man of humanity is tranquil. The man of wisdom enjoys happiness; the man of humanity enjoys long life."

> *Comment.* In the Confucian ethical system, humanity and vision are like two wings, one supporting the other. One is substance, the other is function. The dual emphasis has been maintained throughout history, especially in Tung Chung-shu (c.179–c.104 B.C.) and in a certain sense in K'anh Yu-wei (1858–1927). Elsewhere, courage is added as the third virtue, and Mencius grouped them with righteousness and propriety as the Four Beginnings.

6:23. Confucius said, "When a cornered vessel no longer has any corner, should it be called a cornered vessel? Should it?"

> *Comment.* Name must correspond to actuality.

6:25. Confucius said. "The superior man extensively studies literature (*wen*) and restrains himself with the rules of propriety. Thus he will not violate the Way."

6:26. When Confucius visited Nan-tzu (the wicked wife of Duke Ling of Wei, r. 533-490 B.C.) [in an attempt to influence her to persuade the duke to effect political reform], Tzu-lu was not pleased. Confucius swore an oath and said, "If I have said or done anything wrong, may Heaven forsake me! May Heaven forsake me!"

6:28. Tzu-kung said, "If a ruler extensively confers benefit on the people and can bring salvation to all, what do you think of him? Would you call him a man of humanity?" Confucius said, "Why only a man of humanity? He is without doubt a sage. Even (sage-emperors) Yao and Shun fell short of it. A man of humanity, wishing to establish his own character, also establishes the character of others, and wishing to be prominent himself, also helps others to be prominent. To be able to judge others by what is near to ourselves may be called the method of realizing humanity.""

Comment. The Confucian golden rule in a nutshell.

7:1. Confucius said, "I transmit but do not create. I believe in and love the ancients. I venture to compare myself to our old P'eng."

Comment. This is often cited to show that Confucius was not creative. We must not forget, however, that he "goes over the old so as to find out what is new." Nor must we overlook the fact that he was the first one to offer education to all. Moreover, his concepts of the superior man and of Heaven were at least partly new.

7:2. Confucius said, "To remember silently [what I have learned], to learn untiringly, and to teach others without being wearied–that is just natural with me."

7:6. Confucius said, "Set your will on the Way. Have a firm grasp on virtue. Rely on humanity. Find recreation in the arts."

7:7. Confucius said, "There has never been anyone who came with as little a present as dried meat (for tuition) that I have refused to teach him something."

7:8. Confucius said, "I do not enlighten those who are not eager to learn, nor arouse those who are not anxious to give an explanation themselves. If I have presented one corner of the square and they cannot come back to me with the other three, I should not go over the points again."

7:15. Confucius said, "With coarse rice to eat, with water to drink, and with a bent arm for a pillow there is still joy. Wealth and honor obtained through unrighteousness are but floating clouds to me."

7:16. Confucius said, "Give me a few more years so that I can devote fifty years to study Change. I may be free from great mistakes."

7:17. These were the things Confucius often talked about—poetry, history, and the performance of the rules of propriety. All these were what he often talked about.

7:18. The Duke of She asked Tzu-lu about Confucius, and Tzu-lu did not answer. Confucius said, "Why didn't you say that I am a person who forgets his food when engaged in vigorous pursuit of something, is so happy as to forget his worries, and is not aware that old age is coming on?"

7:19. Confucius said, "I am not one who was born with knowledge; I love ancient [teaching] and earnestly seek it."

7:20. Confucius never discussed strange phenomena, physical exploits, disorder, or spiritual beings.

7:22. Confucius said, "Heaven produced the virtue that is in me; what can Huan T'ui do to me?"

7:24. Confucius taught four things: culture (*wen*), conduct, loyalty, and faithfulness.

7:26. Confucius fished with a line but not a net. While shooting he would not shoot a bird at rest.

7:27. Confucius said. "There are those who act without knowing [what is right]. But I am not one of them. To hear much and select what is good and follow it, to see much and remember it, is the second type of knowledge (next to innate knowledge)."

7:29. Confucius said, "Is humanity far away? As soon as I want it, there it is right by me."

> *Comment.* This is simply emphasizing the ever-present opportunity to do good. There is nothing mystical about it. The practice of humanity starts with oneself.

7:34. Confucius was very ill. Tzu-lu asked that prayer be offered. Confucius said, "Is there such a thing?" Tzu-lu replied, "There is. A Eulogy says, 'Pray to the spiritual beings above and below.'" Confucius said, "My prayer has been for a long time [that is, what counts is the life that one leads]."

7:37. Confucius is affable but dignified, austere but not harsh, polite but completely at ease.

Comment. The Confucian Mean in practice.

8:5. Tseng Tzu said, "Gifted with ability, yet asking those without ability; possessing much, yet asking those who possess little; having, yet seeming to have none; full, yet seeming vacuous; offended, yet not contesting—long ago I had a friend [Confucius' most virtuous pupil Yen Yüan?] who devoted himself to these ways."

Comment. The similarity to Taoist teachings is striking.

8:6. Tseng Tzu said, "A man who can be entrusted with an orphaned child, delegated with the authority over a whole state of one hundred *li*, and whose integrity cannot be violated even in the face of a great emergency—is such a man a superior man? He is a superior man indeed!"

8:7. Tseng Tzu said, "An officer must be great and strong. His burden is heavy and his course is long. He has taken humanity to be his own burden—is that not heavy? Only with death does his course stop—is that not long?"

8:8. Confucius said, "Let a man be stimulated by poetry, established by the rules of propriety, and perfected by music."

8:9. Confucius said, "The common people may be made to follow it (the Way) but may not be made to understand it."

Comment. Confucianists have taken great pains to explain this saying. Cheng Hsüan said "the common people" refers to ignorant people and Chu Hsi said that ordinary people do things without understanding why. There can be no denial that Confucius reflected the feudal society in which it was the duty of ordinary people to follow the elite.

8:13. Confucius said, "Have sincere faith and love learning. Be not afraid to die for pursuing the good Way. Do not enter a tottering state nor stay in a chaotic one. When the Way prevails in the empire, then show yourself; when it does not prevail, then hide. When the Way prevails in your own state and you are poor and in a humble position, be ashamed of yourself. When the Way does not prevail in your state and you are wealthy and in an honorable position, be ashamed of yourself."

8:14. Confucius said, "A person not in a particular government position does not discuss its policies."

9:1. Confucius seldom talked about profit, destiny (*ming* or the Mandate of Heaven), and humanity.

> *Comment.* Few passages in the *Analects* have given commentators as much trouble as this one. It is true that the topic of profit is mentioned in the *Analects* only six times and destiny or fate only ten times, but fifty-eight of the 499 chapters of the *Analects* are devoted to humanity and the word *jen* occurs 105 times. Confucianists have tried their best to explain why Confucius can be said to have seldom talked about them. Huang K'an said these things are so serious that Confucius seldom expected people to live up to them. This line of thought was followed by Juan Yüan (1764–1849). Ho Yen thought that Confucius seldom talked about them because few people could reach those high levels. Hsing Ping, who commented on Ho's commentary, repeated it. Chu Hsi, quoting Ch'eng I, said that Confucius seldom talked about profit, for example, because it is injurious to righteousness, and seldom talked about the others because the principle of destiny is subtle and that of humanity is great.
>
> Other scholars have tried to change the meaning of the passage. Shih Sheng-tsu (fl. 1230) in his *Hsüeh-chai chan-pi* (Simple Observations) interpreted *yü* not as "and" but as "give forth," thus making the sentence say that Confucius seldom talked about profit but gave forth [instructions] on destiny and humanity. Bodde accepts this view. Laufer thinks it should be read: "The Master rarely discussed material gains compared with the will of Heaven and compared with humaneness." Chiao Hsün (1763–1820), in his *Lun-yü pu-shu* (Supplementary Commentary on the *Analects*) said that when Confucius occasionally talked about profit, he spoke of it together with destiny or humanity, that is, in the light of either of them. Han Yü (768-824) thought that what Confucius seldom talked about was the *men* of profit, destiny, or humanity, not the three subjects themselves (*Lun-yü pi-chieh*, or Explanations of the *Analects*). According to Huang Shih-nan's *Lun-yü hou-an* (Recent Examinations of the *Analects*, 1844) the word *han* does not mean "seldom," but is an alternate for *hsien* "elucidation." While this is possible, it seems to be going too far. Most scholars leave the difficulty alone. As K'ang Yu-wei, in his *Lun-yü chu*, says, Confucius talked about the three subjects a great deal, since they are inherently important subjects for discussion.

9:3. Confucius said, "The linen cap is prescribed by the rules of ceremony (*li*) but nowadays a silk one is worn. It is economical and I follow the common practice. Bowing below the hall is prescribed by the rules of ceremony, but nowadays people bow after ascending the hall. This is arrogant, and I follow the practice of bowing below the hall though that is opposed to the common practice."

9:4. Confucius was completely free from four things: He had no arbitrariness of opinion, no dogmatism, no obstinance, and no egotism.

9:5. When Confucius was in personal danger in K'uang, he said, "Since the death of King Wen, is not the course of culture (*wen*) in my keeping? If it had been the will of Heaven to destroy this culture, it would not have been given to a mortal [like me]. But if it is the will of Heaven that this culture should not perish, what can the people of K'uang do to me?"

9:6. A great official asked Tzu-kung, "Is the Master a sage? How is it that he has so much ability [in practical, specific things]?" Tzu-kung said, "Certainly Heaven has endowed him so liberally that he is to become a sage, and furthermore he has much ability. When Confucius heard this, he said, "Does the great official know me? When I was young, I was in humble circumstances, and therefore I acquired much ability to do the simple things of humble folk. Does a superior man need to have so much ability? He does not." His pupil Lao said, "The Master said, 'I have not been given official employment and therefore I [acquired the ability] for the simple arts.'"

9:13. Confucius wanted to live among the nine barbarous tribes of the East. Someone said, "They are rude. How can you do it?" Confucius said, "If a superior man lives there, what rudeness would there be?"

9:16. Confucius, standing by a stream, said, "It passes on like this, never ceasing day or night!"

> *Comment.* What was Confucius thinking about? Was he thinking of the unceasing operation of the universe (Chu Hsi and Ch'eng I)? Was he lamenting over the fact that the past cannot be recovered (Hsing Ping)? Was he comparing the untiring effort of a superior man's moral cultivation (Liu Pao-nan)? Was he praising water because its springs continuously gush out (Mencius and Tung Chung-shu)? Was he praising water because it has the qualities of virtue, righteousness, courage, and so forth (Hsün Tzu. fl. 298–238 B.C.)? One thing is fairly sure: water to him meant something quite different from what it meant to Indian and Western philosophers, and to some extent to Lao Tzu.

9:25. Confucius said, "The commander of three armies may be taken away, but the will of even a common man may not be taken way from him."

10:9. When his mat was not straight [Confucius] did not sit on it.

10:12. A certain stable was burned down. On returning from court, Confucius asked,"Was any man hurt?" He did not ask about the horses.

10:14. On entering the Ancestral Temple, he asked about everything.

11:8. When Yen Yüan died, Confucius said, "Alas, Heaven is destroying me! Heaven is destroying me!"

11:11. Cli-lu (Tzu-lu) asked about serving the spiritual beings. Confucius said, "If we are not yet able to serve man, how can we serve spiritual beings?" "I venture to ask about death," Confucius said. "If we do not yet know about life, how can we know about death?"

Comment. A most celebrated saying on humanism.

11:15. Tzu-kung asked who was the better man, Shih or Shang. Confucius said, "Shih goes too far and Shang does not go far enough." Tzu-kung said, "Then is Shih better?" Confucius said, "To go too far is the same as not to go far enough."

11:21. Tzu-lu asked, "Should one immediately practice what one has heard?" Confucius said, "There are father and elder brother [to be consulted]. Why immediately practice what one has heard?" Jan Yu (Jan Tzu) asked, "Should one immediately practice what one has heard?" Confucius said, "One should immediately practice what one has heard." Kung-hsi Hua said, "When Yu (Tzu-lu) asked you, 'Should one immediately practice what one has heard?' you said, 'There are father and elder brother.' When Ch'iu (Jan Yu) asked you, 'Should one immediately practice what he has heard?' you said, 'One should immediately practice what one has heard.' I am perplexed, and venture to ask you for an explanation." Confucius said, "Ch'iu is retiring; therefore I urged him forward. Yu has more than one man's energy; therefore I kept him back."

11:25. Tzu-lu, Tseng Hsi, Jan Yu, and Kung-hsi Hua were in attendance. Confucius said, "You think that I am a day or so older than you are. But do not think so. At present you are out of office and think that you are denied recognition. Suppose you were given recognition. What would you prefer?" Tzu-lu promptly replied, "Suppose there is a state of a thousand chariots, hemmed in by great powers, in addition invaded by armies, and as a result drought and famine prevail. Let me administer that state. In three years' time I can endow the people with courage and furthermore, enable them to know the correct principles." Confucius smiled at him [with disapproval].

"Ch'iu, how about you?" Jan Yu replied, "Suppose there is a state the sides of which are sixty or seventy *li* wide, or one of fifty or sixty *li*. Let me administer that state. In three years' time I can enable the people to be sufficient in their livelihood. As to the promotion of ceremonies and music, however, I shall have to wait for the superior man."

"How about you, Ch'ih?" Kung-hsi Hua replied, "I do not say I can do it but I should like to learn to do so. At the services of the royal ancestral temple, and at the conferences of the feudal lords, I should like to wear the dark robe and black cap (symbols of correctness) and be a junior assistant."

[Turning to Tsens Hsi,] Confucius said, "How about you, Tien?" Tseng Hsi was then softly playing the zither. With a bang he laid down the instrument, rose, and said, "My wishes are different from what the gentlemen want to do." Confucius said, "What harm is there? After all, we want each to tell his ambition." Tseng Hsi said, "In the late spring, when the spring dress is ready, I would like to go with five or six grown-ups and six or seven young boys to bathe in the I River, enjoy the breeze on the Rain Dance Altar, and then return home singing." Confucius heaved a sigh and said, "I agree with Tien."

> *Comment.* Why did Confucius agree with Tseng Hsi? The field is wide open for speculation, and most Confucianists have taken the best advantage of it. Thus it was variously explained that Tseng Hsi was enjoying the harmony of the universe (Wang Ch'ung), that he was following traditional cultural institutions (Liu Paonan), that he was wisely refraining from officialdom at the time of chaos (Huang K'an), that he was thinking of the "kingly way" whereas other pupils were thinking of the government of feudal states (Han Yü), that he was in the midst of the universal operation of the Principle of Nature (Chu Hsi), and that he was expressing freedom of the spirit (Wang Yang-ming, 1472–1529). It is to be noted that the last two interpretations reflect the different tendencies of the two wings of Neo-Confucianism, one emphasizing the objective operation of the Principle of Nature, the other emphasizing the state of mind.

12:1. Yen Yüan asked about humanity. Confucius said, "To master oneself and return to propriety is humanity. If a man (the ruler) can for one day master himself and return to propriety, all under heaven will return to humanity. To practice humanity depends on oneself. Does it depend on others?" Yen Yüan said, "May I ask for the detailed items?" Confucius said, "Do not look at what is contrary to propriety, do not listen to what is contrary to propriety, do not speak what is contrary to propriety, and do not make any movement which is contrary to propriety." Yen Yüan said, "Although I am not intelligent, may I put your saying into practice."

12:2. Chung-kung asked about humanity. Confucius said, "When you go abroad, behave to everyone as if you were receiving a great guest. Employ the people as if you were assisting at a great sacrifice. Do not do to others what you do not want them to do to you. Then there will be no complaint against you in the state or in the family (the ruling clan)." Chung-kung said, "Although I am not intelligent, may I put your saying into practice."

12:5. Ssu-ma Niu, worrying, said, "All people have brothers but I have none." Tzu-hsia said, "I have heard [from Confucius] this saying: 'Life and death are the decree of Heaven (*ming*); wealth and honor depend on Heaven. If a superior man is reverential (or serious) without fail, and is respectful in dealing with others and follows the rules of propriety, then all within the four seas (the world) are brothers." What does the superior man have to worry about having no brothers?"

12:7. Tzu-kung asked about government. Confucius said, "Sufficient food, sufficient armament, and sufficient confidence of the people." Tzu-kung said, "Forced to give up one of these, which would you abandon first?" Confucius said, I would abandon the armament." Tzu-kung said, "Forced to give up one of the remaining two, which would you abandon first?" Confucius said, "I would abandon food. There have been deaths from time immemorial, but no state can exist without the confidence of the people."

12:11. Duke Ching of Ch'i asked Confucius about government. Confucius replied, "Let the ruler *be* a ruler, the minister *be* a minister, the father *be* a father, and the son *be* a son." The duke said, "Excellent! Indeed when the ruler is not a ruler, the minister not a minister, the father not a father, and the son not a son, although I may have all the grain, shall I ever get to eat it?"

12:16. Confucius said, "The superior man brings the good things of others to completion and does not bring the bad things of others to completion. The inferior man does just the opposite."

12:17. Chi K'ang Tzu asked Confucius about government. Confucius replied, "To govern (*cheng*) is to rectify (*cheng*). If you lead the people by being rectified yourself, who will dare not be rectified?"

12:19. Chi K'ang Tzu asked Confucius about government, saying, "What do you think of killing the wicked and associating with the good?" Confucius replied, "In your government what is the need of killing? If you desire what is good, the people will be good. The character of a ruler is like wind and that of the people is like grass. In whatever direction the wind blows, the grass always bends."

12:22. Fan Ch'ih asked about humanity. Confucius said, "It is to love men." He asked about knowledge. Confucius said, "It is to know man."

Comment. As a general virtue, *jen* means humanity, that is, that which makes a man a moral being. As a particular virtue, it means love. This is the general interpretation during the Han and T'ang times. Later in Neo-Confucianism, it was modified to mean man and

Nature forming one body. The doctrine that knowledge of men is power has been maintained throughout the history of Confucianism. This humanistic interest has to a large degree prevented China from developing the tradition of knowledge for its own sake.

13:3. Tzu-lu said, "The ruler of Wei is waiting for you to serve in his administration. What will be your first measure?" Confucius said, "It will certainly concern the rectification of names." Tzu-lu said, "Is that so? You are wide of the mark. Why should there be such a rectification?" Confucius said, "Yu! How uncultivated you are! With regard to what he does not know, the superior man should maintain an attitude of reserve. If names are not rectified, then language will not be in accord with truth. If language is not in accord with truth, then things cannot be accomplished. If things cannot be accomplished, then ceremonies and music will not flourish. If ceremonies and music do not flourish, then punishment will not be just. If punishments are not just, then the people will not know how to move hand or foot. Therefore the superior man will give only names that can be described in speech and say only what can be carried out in practice. With regard to his speech, the superior man does not take it lightly. That is all."

Comment. Most ancient Chinese philosophical schools had a theory about names and actuality. In the Confucian school, however, it assumes special importance because its focus is not metaphysical as in Taoism, or logical as in the School of Logicians, or utilitarian as in the Legalist School, but ethical. This means not only that a name must correspond to its actuality, but also that rank, duties, and functions must be clearly defined and fully translated into action. Only then can a name be considered to be correct or rectified. With the ethical interest predominant, this is the nearest the ancient Confucianists came to a logical theory, except in the case of Hsün Tzu, who was the most logical of all ancient Confucianists.

13:6. Confucius said, "If a ruler sets himself right, he will be followed without his command. If he does not set himself right, even his commands will not be obeyed."

13:16. The Duke of She asked about government. Confucius said, "[There is good government] when those who are near are happy and those far away desire to come."

13:18. The Duke of She told Confucius, "In my country there is an upright man named Kung. When his father stole a sheep, he bore witness against him." Confucius said, "The upright men in my community are different from this. The father conceals the misconduct of the son and the son conceals the misconduct of the father. Uprightness is to be found in this."

13:19. Fan Ch'ih asked about humanity. Confucius said, "Be respectful in private life, be serious (*ching*) in handling affairs, and be loyal in dealing with others. Even if you are living amidst barbarians, these principles may never be forsaken."

13:23. Confucius said, "The superior man is conciliatory but does not identify himself with others; the inferior man identifies with others but is not conciliatory."

13:26. Confucius said. "The superior man is dignified but not proud; the inferior man is proud but not dignified."

13:27. Confucius said. "A man who is strong, resolute, simple, and slow to speak is near to humanity."

13:29. Confucius said, "When good men have instructed the people [in morals agriculture, military tactics] for seven years, they may be allowed to bear arms."

13:30. Confucius said, "To allow people to go to war without first instructing them is to betray them."

14:2. [Yüan Hsien] said, "When one has avoided aggressiveness, pride, resentment, and greed, he may be called a man of humanity." Confucius said, "This may be considered as having done what is difficult, but I do not know that it is to be regarded as humanity."

14:24. Confucius said, "The superior man understands the higher things [moral principles]; the inferior man understands the lower things [profit]."

14:29 Confucius said, "The superior man is ashamed that his words exceed his deeds."

14:30. Confucius said, "The way of the superior man is threefold, but I have not been able to attain it. The man of wisdom has no perplexities; the man of humanity has no worry; the man of courage has no fear." Tzu-kung said, "You are talking about yourself."

14:33. Confucius said, "He who does not anticipate attempts to deceive him nor predict his being distrusted, and yet is the first to know [when these things occur], is a worthy man."

14:36. Someone said, "What do you think of repaying hatred with virtue?" Confucius said, "In that case what are you going to repay virtue with? Rather, repay hatred with uprightness and repay virtue with virtue."

Comment. The word for uprightness, *chih*, is not to be understood as severity or justice, which would imply repaying evil with evil. The idea of repaying hatred with virtue is also found in the *Lao Tzu*, ch. 63, and some have therefore theorized that the questioner was a Taoist or that the saying was a prevalent one at the time. In any case, by uprightness Confucianists mean absolute impartiality, taking guidance from what is right instead of one's personal preference, however admirable. Obviously this does not satisfy followers of the Christian doctrine of loving one's enemy. As to the golden rule, see above, comment on 4:15.

14:37. Confucius said, "Alas! No one knows me!" Tzu-kung said, "Why is there no one that knows you?" Confucius said, "I do not complain against Heaven. I do not blame men. I study things on the lower level but my understanding penetrates the higher level. It is Heaven that knows me."

14:41. When Tzu-lu was stopping at the Stone Gate for the night, the gatekeeper asked him, "Where are you from?" Tzu-lu said, "From Confucius." "Oh, is he the one who knows a thing cannot be done and still wants to do it?"

14:45. Tzu-lu asked about the superior man. Confucius said, "The superior man is one who cultivates himself with seriousness (*ching*)." Tzu-lu said, "Is that all?" Confucius said, "He cultivates himself so as to give the common people security and peace." Tzu-lu said, "Is that all?" Confucius said, "He cultivates himself so as to give all people security and peace. To cultivate oneself so as to give all people security and peace, even Yao and Shun found it difficult to do."

15:2. Confucius said, "Tz'u (Tzu-kung), do you suppose that I am one who learns a great deal and remembers it?" Tzu-kung replied, "Yes. Is that not true?" Confucius said, "No. I have a thread (*i-kuan*) that runs through it all."

15:4. Confucius said. "To have taken no [unnatural] action and yet have the empire well governed, Shun was the man! What did he do? All he did was to make himself reverent and correctly face south [in his royal seat as the ruler]."

15:8. Confucius said, "A resolute scholar and a man of humanity will never seek to live at the expense of injuring humanity. He would rather sacrifice his life in order to realize humanity."

15:17. Confucius said, "The superior man regards righteousness (*i*) as the substance of everything. He practices it according to the principles of propriety. He brings it forth in modesty. And he carries it to its conclusion with faithfulness. He is indeed a superior man!"

15:20. Confucius said, "The superior man seeks [room for improvement or occasion to blame] in himself; the inferior man seeks it in others."

15:22. Confucius said, "The superior man (ruler) does not promote (put in office) a man on the basis of his words; nor does he reject his words because of the man."

15:23. Tzu-kung asked, "Is there one word which can serve as the guiding principle for conduct throughout life?" Confucius said, "It is the word altruism (*shu*). Do not do to others what you do not want them to do to you."

15:28. Confucius said, "It is man that can make the Way great, and not the Way that can make man great."

> *Comment*. Humanism in the extreme! Commentators from Huang. K'an to Chu Hsi said that the Way, because it is tranquil and quiet and lets things take their own course, does not make man great. A better explanation is found in the *Doctrine of the Mean*, where it is said, "Unless there is perfect virtue, the perfect Way cannot be materialized."

15:31. Confucius said, "The superior man seeks the Way and not a mere living. There may be starvation in farming, and there may be riches in the pursuit of studies. The superior man worries about the Way and not about poverty."

15:32. Confucius said "When a man's knowledge is sufficient for him to attain [his position] but his humanity is not sufficient for him to hold it, he will lose it again. When his knowledge is sufficient for him to attain it and his humanity is sufficient for him to hold it, if he does not approach the people with dignity, the people will not respect him. If his knowledge is sufficient for him to attain it, his humanity sufficient for him to hold it, and he approaches the people with dignity, yet does not influence them with the principle of propriety, it is still not good."

15:35. Confucius said, "When it comes to the practice of humanity, one should not defer even to his teacher."

15:38. Confucius said, "In education there should be no class distinction."

> *Comment*. Confucius was the first to pronounce this principle in Chinese history. Among his pupils there were commoners as well as nobles, and stupid people as well as intelligent ones.

15:40. Confucius said, "In words all that matters is to express the meaning."

16:1. Confucius said, "...I have heard that those who administer a state or a family do not worry about there being too few people, but worry about unequal distribution of wealth. They do not worry about poverty, but worry about the lack of security and peace on the part of the people. For when wealth is equally distributed, there will not be poverty; when there is harmony, there will be no problem of there being too few people; and when there are security and peace, there will be no danger to the state...."

16:4. Confucius said, "There are three kinds of friendship which are beneficial and three kinds which are harmful. Friendship with the upright, with the truthful, and with the well-informed is beneficial. Friendship with those who flatter, with those who are meek and who compromise with principles, and with those who talk cleverly is harmful."

16:8. Confucius said, "The superior man stands in awe of three things. He stands in awe of the Mandate of Heaven; he stands in awe of great men; and he stands in awe of the words of the sages. The inferior man is ignorant of the Mandate of Heaven and does not stand in awe of it. He is disrespectful to great men and is contemptuous toward the words of the sages."

16:9. Confucius said, "Those who are born with knowledge are the highest type of people. Those who learn through study are the next. Those who learn through hard work are still the next. Those who work hard and still do not learn are really the lowest type."'

16:10. Confucius said, "The superior man has nine wishes. In seeing, he wishes to see clearly. In hearing, he wishes to hear distinctly. In his expression, he wishes to be warm. In his appearance, he wishes to be respectful. In his speech, he wishes to be sincere. In handling affairs, he wishes to be serious. When in doubt, he wishes to ask. When he is angry, he wishes to think of the resultant difficulties. And when he sees an opportunity for a gain, he wishes to think of righteousness."

17:2. Confucius said, "By nature men are alike. Through practice they have become far apart."

> *Comment.* This is the classical Confucian dictum on human nature. Neo-Confucianists like Chu Hsi and Ch'eng I strongly argued that Confucius meant physical nature, which involves elements of evil, for since every man's original nature is good, men must be the *same* and therefore cannot be *alike*. Others, however, think that the word *chin* (near or alike) here has the same meaning as in Mencius' saying, "All things of the same kind are similar to one another." However, on the surface this saying is indisputably neutral, but all of Confucius' teachings imply the goodness of human nature.

17:3. Confucius said, "Only the most intelligent and the most stupid do not change."

> *Comment.* Advocates of the theory of three grades of nature, notably Wang Ch'ung, Chia I (201–169 B.C.), 88 and Han Yü, have drawn support from this saying by equating the most intelligent with those born good, the most stupid with those born evil, and the rest born neutral. They overlooked the fact that this passage has to do not with nature but only with intelligence. Practically all modern Confucianists are agreed on this point. As Ch'eng I, Wang Yang-Ming, Tai Chen (Tai Tung-yüan, 1723–1777), and Juan Yüan all pointed out, it is not that they cannot change. It is simply that they are too intelligent to change downward or too stupid to change upward.

17:4. Confucius went to the city of Wu [where his disciple Tzu-yu was the magistrate] and heard the sound of stringed instruments and singing. With a gentle smile, the Master said, "Why use an ox-knife to kill a chicken [that is, why employ a serious measure like music to rule such a small town]?" Tzu-yu replied, "Formerly I heard you say 'When the superior man has studied the Way, he loves men. When the inferior man has studied the Way, he is easy to employ.'" Confucius said, "My disciples, what I just said was only a joke."

17:6. Tzu-chang asked Confucius about humanity. Confucius said, "One who can practice five things wherever he may be is a man of humanity." Tzu-chang asked what the five are. Confucius said, "Earnestness, liberality, truthfulness, diligence, and generosity. If one is earnest, one will not be treated with disrespect. If one is liberal, one will win the hearts of all. If one is truthful, one will be trusted. If one is diligent, one will be successful. And if one is generous, one will be able to enjoy the service of others."

17:8. Confucius said, "Yu (Tzu-lu), have you heard about the six virtues and the six obscurations?" Tzu-lu replied, "I have not." Confucius said, "Sit down, then. I will tell you. One who loves humanity but not learning will be obscured by ignorance. One who loves wisdom but not learning will be obscured by lack of principle. One who loves faithfulness but not learning will be obscured by heartlessness. One who loves uprightness but not learning will be obscured by violence. One who loves strength of character but not learning will be obscured by recklessness."

17:9. Confucius said, "My young friends, why do you not study the odes? The odes can stimulate your emotions, broaden your observation, enlarge your fellowship, and express your grievances. They help you in your immediate service to your parents and in your more remote service to your rulers. They widen your acquaintance with the names of birds, animals, and plants."

17:19. Confucius said, "I do not wish to say anything." Tzu-kung said, "If you do not say anything, what can we little disciples ever learn to pass on to others?" Confucius said. "Does Heaven (*T'ien*, Nature) say anything? The four seasons run their course and all things are produced. Does Heaven say anything?"

> *Comment.* This is usually cited to support the contention that Confucius did not believe in an anthropomorphic God but in Heaven which reigns rather than rules. In Neo-Confucianism, Heaven came to be identified with principle (*li*).

17:23. Tzu-lu asked, "Does the superior man esteem courage?" Confucius said, "The superior man considers righteousness (*i*) as the most important. When the superior man has courage but no righteousness, he becomes turbulent. When the inferior man has courage but no righteousness, he becomes a thief."

17:25. Confucius said, "Women and servants are most difficult to deal with. If you are familiar with them, they cease to be humble. If you keep a distance from them, they resent it."

> *Comment.* From Confucius down, Confucianists have always considered women inferior.

18:6. Ch'ang-chü and Chieh-ni were cultivating their fields together. Confucius was passing that way and told Tzu-lu to ask them where the river could be forded. Ch'ang-chü said, "Who is the one holding the reins in the carriage?" Tzu-lu said, "It is K'ung Ch'iu (Confucius)." "Is he the K'ung Ch'iu of Lu?" "Yes." "Then he already knows where the river can be forded!" Tzu-lu asked Chieh-ni. Chieh-ni said, "Who are you, sir?" Tzu-lu replied, "I am Chung-yu (name of Tzu-lu)." "Are you a follower of K'ung Ch'iu of Lu?" "Yes." Chieh-ni said, "The whole world is swept as though by a torrential flood. Who can change it? As for you, instead of following one who flees from this man or that man, is it not better to follow those who flee the world altogether?" And with that he went on covering the seed without stopping. Tzu-lu went to Confucius and told him about their conversation. Confucius said ruefully, "One cannot herd with birds and beasts. If I do not associate with mankind, with whom shall I associate? If the Way prevailed in the world, there would be no need for me to change it."

19:6. Tzu-hsia said, "To study extensively, to be steadfast in one purpose, to inquire earnestly, and to reflect on what is at hand (that is, what one can put into practice) —humanity consists in these."

19:7. Confucius said, "The hundred artisans work in their works to perfect their craft. The superior man studies to reach to the utmost of the Way."

19:11. Tzu-hsia said, "So long as a man does not transgress the boundary line in the great virtues, he may pass and repass it in the small virtues."

> *Comment.* Even Chu Hsi quoted someone who pointed out that this passage is not free from defect.

19:13. Tzu-hsia said, "A man who has energy to spare after studying should serve his state. A man who has energy to spare after serving his state should study."

19:24. Shu-sun Wu-shu slandered Chung-ni (Confucius). Tzu-kung said, "It is no use. Chung-ni cannot be slandered. Other worthies are like mounds or small hills. You can still climb over them. Chung-ni, however, is like the sun and the moon that cannot be climbed over. Although a man may want to shut his eyes to the sun and the moon, what harm does it do to them? It would only show in large measure that he does not know his own limitations."

Reflections

Confucius (551–479 B.C.) had a profound and lasting impact on the development of Chinese culture. He was above all concerned with what constituted a good society and what it meant to be a perfected human being. In these verses, one notices his concept of *jen* or "humanity." The man of *jen* is the "chun-tzu," the "noble person," who is "noble," or superior, not by royal birth, but by virtue of character. There are a number of characteristics of the man of *jen*, including *li* (propriety, which means proper ritual and manners combined with "heart," or feeling), *wen* (the importance of learning, including the arts, poetry, and music), *te* (ruling by virtue, not by force), filial piety (reverence for parents and elders), altruism, simplicity, and modesty. Confucius also believed in the principle of "The Rectification of the Names," which states that there must be a correspondence between name and actuality (to be called a son, one must *be* a son), and the principle of "The Mean," that in all things, there ought to be balance, moderation, and action that is not in extremes. For Confucius, the concept nearest to a supreme being is the Mandate, or will, of Heaven, which is not a personal God who rules in the affairs of nature and humans, but, rather, "reigns." The concept of "the Way" was also an important concept for Confucius, referring to the natural moral law according to which society and individuals should develop. Choose analects to analyze and interpret in light of Confucius' world-view and in light of contemporary experience.

The Tao-te Ching
of Lao Tzu

1. The Tao (Way) that can be told of is not the eternal Tao;
   The name that can be named is not the eternal name.
   The Nameless is the origin of Heaven and Earth;
   The Named is the mother of all things.
   Therefore let there always be non-being so we may see their subtlety,
   And let there always be being so we may see their outcome.
   The two are the same,
   But after they are produced, they have different names.
   They both may be called deep and profound (*hsüan*).
   Deeper and more profound,
   The door of all subtleties!

   Comment. While ancient Chinese philosophical schools differed in many respects, most of them insisted on the correspondence of names and actualities. They all accepted names as necessary and good. Lao Tzu, however, rejected names in favor of the nameless. This, among other things, shows the radical and unique character of Taoism. To Lao Tzu, Tao is nameless and is the simplicity without names, and when names arise, that is, when the simple oneness of Tao is split up into individual things with names, it is time to stop.

2. When the people of the world all know beauty as beauty,
   There arises the recognition of ugliness.
   When they all know the good as good,
   There arises the recognition of evil.

Therefore:
> Being and non-being produce each other;
> Difficult and easy complete each other;
> Long and short contrast each other;
> High and low distinguish each other;
> Sound and voice harmonize with each other;
> Front and back follow each other.
> Therefore the sage manages affairs without action
>   (*wu-wei*)
> And spreads doctrines without words.
> All things arise, and he does not turn away from them.
> He produces them, but does not take possession of them.
> He acts, but does not rely on his own ability.
> He accomplishes his task, but does not claim credit for it.
> It is precisely because he does not claim credit that his accomplishment
>   remains with him.

Comment. The idea of teachings without words anticipated the Buddhist tradition of silent transmission of the mystic doctrine, especially in the Zen School. This is diametrically opposed to the Confucian ideal, according to which a superior man acts and "becomes the model of the world"; he speaks, and "becomes the pattern for the world." It is true that Confucianists say that a superior man "is truthful without any words," but they would never regard silence itself as virtue.

3. Do not exalt the worthy, so that the people shall not compete.
    Do not value rare treasures, so that the people shall not steal.
    Do not display objects of desire, so that the people's hearts
        shall not be disturbed.
    Therefore in the government of the sage,
>   He keeps their hearts vacuous (*hsu*),
>   Fills their bellies,
>   Weakens their ambitions,
>   And strengthens their bones,
    He always causes his people to be without knowledge (cunning) or desire,
    And the crafty to be afraid to act.
    By acting without action, all things will be in order.

4. Tao is empty (like a bowl),
    It may be used but its capacity is never exhausted.
    It is bottomless, perhaps the ancestor of all things.

It blunts its sharpness,
It unties its tangles.
It softens its light.
It becomes one with the dusty world.
Deep and still, it appears to exist forever.
I do not know whose son it is.
It seems to have existed before the Lord.

Comment. This chapter shows clearly that, in Taoism, function is no less important than substance. Substance is further described in *Lao Tzu*, chs. 14 and 21, but here, as in *Lao Tzu*, chs. 11 and 45, function (*yung*, also meaning use) is regarded with equal respect. There is no renunciation of phenomena as is the case with certain Buddhist schools.

5. Heaven and Earth are not humane (*jen*).
They regard all things as straw dogs.
The sage is not humane.
He regards all people as straw dogs.
How Heaven and Earth are like a bellows!
While vacuous, it is never exhausted.
When active, it produces even more.
Much talk will of course come to a dead end.
It is better to keep to the center (*chung*).

Comment. The term "not humane" is of course extremely provocative. It may be suggested that this is Lao Tzu's emphatic way of opposing the Confucian doctrine of humanity and righteousness. Actually, the Taoist idea here is not negative but positive, for it means that Heaven and Earth are impartial, have no favorites, and are not humane in a deliberate or artificial way. This is the understanding of practically all commentators and is abundantly supported by the *Chuang Tzu*. To translate it as unkind, as does Blakney, is grossly to misunderstand Taoist philosophy.

The two Taoist ideas, vacuity (*hsü*) and non-being (*wu*), later employed and elaborated by the Buddhists, were taboos to Confucianists. To them, these ideas are charged with a great danger of nihilism, even if Taoism is not. The Neo-Confucianist Chang Tsai (Chang Heng-ch'ü, 1020–1077) called Reality "Great Vacuity" (*T'ai-hsü*), Chu Hsi (1130–1200) characterized man's nature as *hsü* and intelligent, and Wang Yang-ming (Wang Shou-jen, 1472–1529) described the original mind of man in the same terms. But Chang's Vacuity is equivalent to material force (*ch'i*), which is real and active. To Chu and Wang, as to other Confucianists, vacuity means purity, being devoid of selfish desires, impartiality, and so forth. Even then, they used the term sparingly and with great care.

6.   The spirit of the valley never dies.
          It is called the subtle and profound female.
      The gate of the subtle and profound female
          Is the root of Heaven and Earth.
      It is continuous, and seems to be always existing.
      Use it and you will never wear it out.

7.   Heaven is eternal and Earth everlasting.
      They can be eternal and everlasting because they
          do not exist for themselves,
      And for this reason can exist forever.
      Therefore the sage places himself in the background,
          but finds himself in the foreground.
      He puts himself away, and yet he always remains.
      Is it not because he has no personal interests?
      This is the reason why his personal interests
          are fulfilled.

8.   The best (man) is like water.
      Water is good; it benefits all things and does not
          compete with them.
      It dwells in (lowly) places that all disdain.
      This is why it is so near to Tao.
      [The best man] in his dwelling loves the earth.
          In his heart, he loves what is profound.
          In his associations, he loves humanity.
          In his words, he loves faithfulness.
          In government, he loves order.
      In handling affairs, he loves competence.
      In his activities, he loves timeliness.
      It is because he does not compete that he is
          without reproach.

Comment. Water, the female, and the infant are Lao Tzu's famous symbols of Tao. The emphasis of the symbolism is ethical rather than metaphysical. It is interesting to note that while early Indians associated water with creation and the Greeks looked upon it as a natural phenomenon, ancient Chinese philosophers, whether Lao Tzu or Confucius,

preferred to learn moral lessons from it. Broadly speaking, these different approaches
have characterized Indian, Western, and East Asian civilizations, respectively.

9. To hold and fill to overflowing
    Is not as good as to stop in time.
    Sharpen a sword-edge to its very sharpest,
    And the (edge) will not last long.
    When gold and jade fill your hall,
    You will not be able to keep them.
    To be proud with honor and wealth
    Is to cause one's own downfall.
    Withdraw as soon as your work is done.
    Such is Heaven's Way.

    Comment. Note that one should withdraw only after his work is done. The Taoist way
    of life is not that of a hermit, although hermits have taken its name. The idea of
    withdrawal is not entirely absent even in Confucianism. Mencius said that it was the
    way of Confucius "to withdraw quickly from office when it was proper to do so."

10. Can you keep the spirit and embrace the One without departing from them?
    Can you concentrate your vital force (*ch'i*) and achieve the highest degree of
       weakness like an infant?
    Can you clean and purify your profound insight so it will be spotless?
    Can you love the people and govern the state without knowledge (cunning)?
    Can you play the role of the female in the opening and closing of the gates of
       Heaven?
    Can you understand all and penetrate all without taking any action?
    To produce things and to rear them,
    To produce, but not to take possession of them,
    To act, but not to rely on one's own ability,
    To lead them, but not to master them—
    This is called profound and secret virtue (*hsüan-te*).

    Comment. The concentration of *ch'i* (vital force, breath) is not yoga, as Waley thinks
    it is. Yoga aims at transcending the self and the external environment. Nothing of the
    sort is intended here. It is true that in the *Huai-nan Tzu*, ch. 12, the story of Yen Hui's
    "sitting down and forgetting everything" is recited to explain Lao Tzu's saying. But
    note that "the concentration" is followed by "loving the people" and "governing the
    state." Because the yoga breathing technique was later promoted by the religious
    Taoists, some scholars have unjustifiably read it into earlier texts. Wu Ch'eng

(1249–1333), for example, thought that the "continuous" operation in ch. 6 was breathing, which is certainly going too far.

11. Thirty spokes are united around the hub to make a wheel,
     But it is on its non-being that the utility of the carriage
          depends.
   Clay is molded to form a utensil,
     But it is on its non-being that the utility of the utensil
          depends.
   Doors and windows are cut out to make a room,
     But it is on its non-being that the utility of the room
          depends.
   Therefore turn being into advantage, and turn non-being into utility.

12. The five colors cause one's eyes to be blind.
   The five tones cause one's ears to be deaf.
   The five flavors cause one's palate to be spoiled.
   Racing and hunting cause one's mind to be mad.
   Goods that are hard to get injure one's activities.
   For this reason the sage is concerned with the belly and not the eyes,
   Therefore he rejects the one but accepts the other.

13. Be apprehensive when receiving favor or disgrace.
   Regard great trouble as seriously as you regard your body.
   What is meant by being apprehensive when receiving favor or disgrace?
   Favor is considered inferior.
   Be apprehensive when you receive them and also be
        apprehensive when you lose them.
   This is what is meant by being apprehensive when receiving favor or disgrace.
   What does it mean to regard great trouble as seriously as you regard the body?
   The reason why I have great trouble is that I have a body (and am attached to
        it).
   If I have no body,
   What trouble could I have?
   Therefore he who values the world as his body may be entrusted with the
        empire.
   He who loves the world as his body may be entrusted with the empire.

Comment. On the basis of this attitude toward the body, it is difficult to accept the theory that Yang Chu, who would preserve one's own life under any circumstances, was an early Taoist, as Fung has maintained.

14. We look at it and do not see it;
    Its name is The Invisible.
    We listen to it and do not hear it;
    Its name is The Inaudible.
    We touch it and do not find it;
    its name is The Subtle (formless).
    These three cannot be further inquired into,
    And hence merge into one.
    Going up high, it is not bright, and coming down low, it is not dark.
    Infinite and boundless, it cannot be given any name;
    It reverts to nothingness.
    This is called shape without shape,
    Form (*hsiang*) without object.
    It is The Vague and Elusive.
    Meet it and you will not see its head.
    Follow it and you will not see its back.
    Hold on to the Tao of old in order to master the things of the present.
    From this one may know the primeval beginning [of the universe].
    This is called the bond of Tao.

Comment. Subtlety is an important characteristic of Tao and is more important than its manifestations. The Confucianists, on the other hand, emphasized manifestation. There is nothing more manifest than the hidden (subtle), they said, and a man who knows that the subtle will be manifested "can enter into virtue." The Buddhists and Neo-Confucianists eventually achieved a synthesis and said that "there is no distinction between the manifest and the hidden."

15. Of old those who were the best rulers were
    subtly mysterious and profoundly penetrating;
    Too deep to comprehend.
    And because they cannot be comprehended,
    I can only describe them arbitrarily:
    Cautious, like crossing a frozen stream in the winter,
    Being at a loss, like one fearing danger on all sides,
    Reserved, like one visiting,
    Supple and pliant, like ice about to melt,

Genuine, like a piece of uncarved wood,
Open and broad, like a valley,
Merged and undifferentiated, like muddy water.
Who can make muddy water gradually clear through tranquillity?
Who can make the still gradually come to life through activity?
He who embraces this Tao does not want to ill himself to overflowing.
It is precisely because there is no overflowing that he is beyond wearing out
    and renewal.

16. Attain complete vacuity,
Maintain steadfast quietude.
All things come into being,
And I see thereby their return.
All things flourish,
But each one returns to its root.
This return to its root means tranquillity.
It is called returning to its destiny.
To return to destiny is called the eternal (Tao).
To know the eternal is called enlightenment.
Not to know the eternal is to act blindly to result in disaster.
He who knows the eternal is all-embracing.
Being all-embracing, he is impartial.
Being impartial, he is kingly (universal).
Being kingly, he is one with Nature.
Being one with Nature, he is in accord with Tao.
Being in accord with Tao, he is everlasting,
And is free from danger throughout his lifetime.

Comment. In the philosophy of Lao Tzu, Tao is revealed most fully through tranquillity. The position of the Neo-Confucianists is just the opposite. They said that only through activity can the mind of Heaven and Earth be seen.

17. The best (rulers) are those whose existence is (merely)
        known by the people.
The next best are those who are loved and praised.
The next are those who are feared.
And the next are those who are despised.
It is only when one does not have enough faith in others
        that others will have no faith in him.
[The great rulers] value their words highly.

They accomplish their task; they complete their work.
Nevertheless their people say that they simply follow Nature
    (*Tzu-jan*).

18. When the great Tao declined,
The doctrines of humanity (*jen*) and righteousness (*i*) arose.
When knowledge and wisdom appeared,
There emerged great hypocrisy.
When the six family relationships are not in harmony,
There will be the advocacy of filial piety and deep love to children.
When a country is in disorder,
There will be praise of loyal ministers.

19. Abandon sageliness and discard wisdom;
Then the people will benefit a hundredfold.
Abandon humanity and discard righteousness;
Then the people will return to filial piety and deep love.
Abandon skill and discard profit;
Then there will be no thieves or robbers.
However, these three things are ornament (*wen*) and not adequate.
Therefore let people hold on to these:
    Manifest plainness,
    Embrace simplicity,
    Reduce selfishness,
    Have few desires.

Comment. The sage as the idea human being and the ideal ruler is mentioned thirty times in the book. And yet here sageliness is condemned. There is no contradiction, for sageliness here means a particular characteristic, that of broad and extensive learning, and is therefore mentioned along with wisdom, humanity, and righteousness. With regard to the sage, it is curious that while ancient kings were regarded as models by most ancient schools, and even by Chuang Tzu, they were ignored by Lao Tzu. It is not that Lao Tzu did not look to the past but rather that to him the sage transcended time.

20. Abandon learning and there will be no sorrow.
How much difference is there between "Yes, sir," and "Of course not"?
How much difference is there between "good" and "evil"?
What people dread, do not fail to dread.
But, alas, how confused, and the end is not yet.

The multitude are merry, as though feasting on a day of sacrifice,
Or like ascending a tower at springtime.
I alone am inert, showing no sign (of desires),
Like an infant that has not yet smiled.
Wearied, indeed, I seem to be without a home.
The multitude all possess more than enough,
I alone seem to have lost all.
Mine is indeed the mind of an ignorant man,
Indiscriminate and dull!
Common folks are indeed brilliant;
I alone seem to be in the dark.

Comment. A Confucianist would never say, "Abandon learning." Also he would sharply distinguish between good and evil. The Neo-Confucianist, Ch'eng Hao (Ch'eng Ming-tao, 1032–1085), has been severely criticized for his saying that "both good and evil in the world are both the Principle of Nature," and Wang Yang-ming was likewise widely attacked for teaching that "in the original substance of the mind there is no distinction between good and evil."

Common folks see differences and are clear-cut;
I alone make no distinctions.
I seem drifting as the sea;
Like the wind blowing about, seemingly without destination.
The multitude all have a purpose;
I alone seem to be stubborn and rustic.
I alone differ from others,
And value drawing sustenance from Mother (Tao).

21. The all-embracing quality of the great virtue (*te*) follows alone from the Tao.
The thing that is called Tao is eluding and vague.
    Vague and eluding, there is in it the form.
    Eluding and vague, in it are things.
Deep and obscure, in it is the essence.
The essence is very real; in it are evidences.
From the time of old until now, its name (manifestations) ever remains,
By which we may see the beginning of all things.
How do I know that the beginnings of all things are so?
Through this (Tao).

Comment. Philosophically this is the most important chapter of the book. The sentence "The essence is very real" virtually formed the backbone of Chou Tun-i's (Chou Lien-hsi, 1017–1073) *Explanation of the Diagram of the Great Ultimate*, which centers on the "reality of the Non-Ultimate and the essence of yin and yang." And Chou's work laid the foundation of the entire Neo-Confucian metaphysics. Of course Neo-Confucian metaphysics is more directly derived from the *Book of Changes*, but the concepts of reality in the *Book of Changes* and in this chapter are surprisingly similar.

22. To yield is to be preserved whole.
    To be bent is to become straight.
    To be empty is to be full.
    To be worn out is to be renewed.
    To have little is to possess.
    To have plenty is to be perplexed.
    Therefore the sage embraces the One
    And becomes the model of the world.
    He does not show himself; therefore he is luminous.
    He does not justify himself; therefore he becomes prominent.
    He does not boast of himself: therefore he is given credit.
    He does not brag; therefore he can endure for long.
    It is precisely because he does not compete that the world
        cannot compete with him.
    Is the ancient saying, "To yield is to be preserved whole," empty words?
    Truly he will be preserved and (prominence, etc.) will come to him.

23. Nature says few words.
    For the same reason a whirlwind does not last a whole morning,
    Nor does a rainstorm last a whole day.
    What causes them?
    It is Heaven and Earth (Nature).
    If even Heaven and Earth cannot make them last long,
    How much less can man?
    Therefore he who follows Tao is identified with Tao.
    He who follows virtue is identified with virtue.
    He who abandons (Tao) is identified with the abandonment (of Tao).
    He who is identified with Tao—Tao is also happy to have him.
    He who is identified with virtue—virtue is also happy to have him.
    And he who is identified with the abandonment (of Tao)—the abandonment (of
        Tao) is also happy to abandon him.

It is only when one does not have enough faith in others that others will have no faith in him.

24. He who stands on tiptoe is not steady.
He who strides forward does not go.
He who shows himself is not luminous.
He who justifies himself is not prominent.
He who boasts of himself is not given credit.
He who brags does not endure for long.
From the point of view of Tao, these are like remnants of food and tumors of action,
Which all creatures detest.
Therefore those who possess Tao turn away from them.

25. There was something undifferentiated and yet complete
Which existed before heaven and earth.
Soundless and formless, it depends on nothing
and does not change.
It operates everywhere and is free from danger.
It may be considered the mother of the universe.
I do not know its name; I call it Tao.
If forced to give it a name, I shall call it Great.
Now being great means functioning everywhere.
Functioning everywhere means far-reaching.
Being far-reaching means returning to the original point.
Therefore Tao is great.
Heaven is great.
Earth is great.
And the king is also great.
There are four great things in the universe, and the king is one of them.
Man models himself after Earth.
Earth models itself after Heaven.
Heaven models itself after Tao.
And Tao models itself after Nature.

Comment. The doctrine of returning to the original is prominent in Lao Tzu. It has contributed in no small degree to the common Chinese cyclical concept, which teaches that both history and reality operate in cycles.

26. The heavy is the root of the light.

The tranquil is the ruler of the hasty.
Therefore the sage travels all day
Without leaving his baggage.
Even at the sight of magnificent scenes,
He remains leisurely and indifferent.
How is it that a lord with ten thousand chariots
Should behave lightheartedly in his empire?
If he is lighthearted, the minister will be destroyed.
If he is hasty, the ruler is lost.

27. A good traveler leaves no track or trace.
A good speech leaves no flaws.
A good reckoner uses no counters.
A well-shut door needs no bolts, and yet it cannot be opened.
A well-tied knot needs no rope and yet none can untie it.
Therefore the sage is always good in saving men and consequently no man is
    rejected.
He is always good in saving things and consequently nothing is rejected.
This is called following the light (of Nature)
Therefore the good man is the teacher of the bad,
And the bad is the material from which the good may learn.
He who does not value the teacher,
Or greatly care for the material.
Is greatly deluded although he may be learned.
Such is the essential mystery.

28. He who knows the male (active force) and keeps to the female (the passive
    force or receptive element)
Becomes the ravine of the world.
Being the ravine of the world,
He will never depart from eternal virtue,
But returns to the state of infancy.
He who knows the white (glory) and yet keeps to the black (humility),
Becomes the model for the world.
Being the model for the world,
He will never deviate from eternal virtue,
But returns to the state of the Ultimate of Non-being.
He who knows glory but keeps to humility,
Becomes the valley of the world.
Being the valley of the world,

He will be proficient in eternal virtue,
And returns to the state of simplicity (uncarved wood).
When the uncarved wood is broken up, it is turned into concrete things (as Tao
    is transformed into the myriad things).
But when the sage uses it, he becomes the leading official.
Therefore the great ruler does not cut up.

29. When one desires to take over the empire and act on it (interfere with it),
    I see that he will not succeed.
    The empire is a spiritual thing, and should not be acted on.
    He who acts on it harms it.
    He who holds on to it loses it.
    Among creatures some lead and some follow.
    Some blow hot and some blow cold.
    Some are strong and some are weak.
    Some may break and some may fall.
    Therefore the sage discards the extremes, the extravagant, and the excessive.

30. He who assists the ruler with Tao does not dominate the world with force.
    The use of force usually brings requital.
    Wherever armies are stationed, briers and thorns grow.
    Great wars are always followed by famines.
    A good (general) achieves his purpose and stops,
    But dares not seek to dominate the world.
    He achieves his purpose but does not brag about it.
    He achieves his purpose but does not boast about it.
    He achieves his purpose but is not proud of it.
    He achieves his purpose but only as an unavoidable step.
    He achieves his purpose but does not aim to dominate.
    (For) after things reach their prime, they begin to grow old,
    Which means being contrary to Tao.
    Whatever is contrary to Tao will soon perish.

31. Fine weapons are instruments of evil.
    They are hated by men.
    Therefore those who possess Tao turn away from them.
    The good ruler when at home honors the left (symbolic of good omens).
    When at war he honors the right (symbolic of evil omens).
    Weapons are instruments of evil, not the instruments of a good ruler.
    When he uses them unavoidably, he regards calm restraint as the best principle.

Even when he is victorious, he does not regard it as praiseworthy,
For to praise victory is to delight in the slaughter of men.
He who delights in the slaughter of men will not succeed in the empire.
In auspicious affairs, the left is honored.
In unauspicious affairs, the right is honored.
The lieutenant-general stands on the left.
The senior general stands on the right.
That is to say that the arrangement follows that of funeral ceremonies.
For the slaughter of the multitude, let us weep with sorrow and grief.
For a victory, let us observe the occasion with funeral ceremonies.

32. Tao is eternal and has no name.
Though its simplicity seems insignificant, none in the world can master it.
If kings and barons would hold on to it, all things would submit to them
    spontaneously.
Heaven and earth unite to drip sweet dew.
Without the command of men, it drips evenly over all.
As soon as there were regulations and institutions, there were names (differen-
    tiation of things).
 As soon as there are names, know that it is time to stop.
It is by knowing when to stop that one can be free from danger.
Analogically, Tao in the world (where everything is embraced by it), may be
    compared to rivers and streams running into the sea.

33. He who knows others is wise;
He who knows himself is enlightened.
He who conquers others has physical strength.
He who conquers himself is strong.
He who is contented is rich.
He who acts with vigor has will.
He who does not lose his place (with Tao) will endure.
He who dies but does not really perish enjoys long life.

Comment. What is it that dies but does not perish? Wang Pi said it was Tao on which
human life depended, and Wu Ch'eng said it was the human mind. Other commentators
have given different answers. Most of them, however, believe that Lao Tzu meant the
immortality of virtue. Thus the Taoists conformed to the traditional belief which had
already been expressed in the *Tso chuan* (Tso's Commentary on the *Spring and Autumn
Annals*), namely, the immortality of virtue, achievement, and words, and which has
continued to be the typical Chinese idea of immortality. It is to be noted that unlike

Chuang Tzu. Lao Tzu showed no tendency to believe in earthly immortals (*hsien*, a fairy), although his exaltation of everlasting life undoubtedly contributed to the development of the belief.

34. The Great Tao flows everywhere.
    It may go left or right.
    All things depend on it for life, and it does not turn away from them.
    It accomplishes its task, but does not claim credit for it.
    It clothes and feeds a things but does not claim to be master over them.
    Always without desires, it may be called The Small.
    All things come to it and it does not master them;
        it may be called The Great.
    Therefore (the sage) never strives himself for the great, and thereby the great
        is achieved.

35. Hold fast to the great form (Tao),
    And all the world will come.
    They come and will encounter no harm;
    But enjoy comfort, peace, and health.
    When there are music and dainties,
    Passing strangers will stay.
    But the words uttered by Tao,
    How insipid and tasteless!
    We look at Tao; it is imperceptible.
    We listen to it; it is inaudible.
    We use it; it is inexhaustible.

36. In order to contract,
        It is necessary first to expand.
    In order to weaken,
        It is necessary first to strengthen.
    In order to destroy,
        It is necessary first to promote.
    In order to grasp,
        It is necessary first to give.
    This is called subtle light.
    The weak and the tender overcome the hard and the strong.
    Fish should not be taken away from water.
    And sharp weapons of the state should not be displayed to the people.

Comment. The Confucianists have never excused Lao Tzu for teaching such a doctrine of "deceit."

37. Tao invariably takes no action, and yet there is nothing left undone.
    If kings and barons can keep it, all things will transform spontaneously.
    If, after transformation, they should desire to be active,
    I would restrain them with simplicity, which has no name.
    Simplicity, which has no name, is free of desires.
    Being free of desires, it is tranquil.
    And the world will be at peace of its own accord.

38. The man of superior virtue is not (conscious of) his virtue,
    And in this way he really possesses virtue.
    The man of inferior virtue never loses (sight of) his virtue,
    And in this way he loses his virtue.
    The man of superior virtue takes no action, but has no ulterior motive to do so.
    The man of inferior virtue takes action, and has an ulterior motive to do so.
    The man of superior humanity takes action, but has no ulterior motive to do so.
    The man of superior righteousness takes action, and has an ulterior motive to
        do so.
    The man of superior propriety takes action,
    And when people do not respond to it, he will stretch his arms and force it on
        them.
    Therefore, only when Tao is lost does the doctrine of virtue arise.
    When virtue is lost, only then does the doctrine of humanity arise.
    When humanity is lost, only then does the doctrine of righteousness arise.
    When righteousness is lost, only then does the doctrine of propriety arise.
    Now, propriety is a superficial expression of loyalty and faithfulness, and the
        beginning of disorder.
    Those who are the first to know have the flowers (appearance) of Tao but are
        the beginning of ignorance.
    For this reason the great man dwells in the thick (substantial), and does not rest
        with the thin (superficial).
    He dwells in the fruit (reality), and does not rest with the flower (appearance).
    Therefore he rejects the one, and accepts the other.

Comment. Wang Pi, who wrote the best and most philosophical commentary on the *Lao Tzu*, wrote the longest of his comments on this chapter. It is in this commentary that the important Chinese concepts of *t'i-yung* (substance and function) first appeared. Han

Fei Tzu, the first commentator on the *Lao Tzu*, wrote one of his longest and best comments on this chapter also.

39. Of old those that obtained the One:
    Heaven obtained the One and became clear.
    Earth obtained the One and became tranquil.
    The spiritual beings obtained the One and became divine.
    The valley obtained the One and became full.
    The myriad things obtained the One and lived and grew.
    Kings and barons obtained the One and became rulers of the empire.
    What made them so is the One.
    If heaven had not thus become clear,
    It would soon crack.
    If the earth had not thus become tranquil,
    It would soon be shaken.
    If the spiritual beings had not thus become divine,
    They would soon wither away.
    If the valley had not thus become full,
    It would soon become exhausted.
    If the myriad things had not thus lived and grown,
    They would soon become extinct.
    If kings and barons had not thus become honorable and high in position,
    They would soon fall.
    Therefore humble station is the basis of honor.
    The low is the foundation of the high.
    For this reason kings and barons call themselves the orphaned, the lonely ones,
        the unworthy.
    Is this not regarding humble station as the basis of honor?
    Is it not?
    Therefore enumerate all the parts of a chariot as you may, and you still have
        no chariot.
    Rather than jingle like the jade,
    Rumble like the rocks.

40. Reversion is the action of Tao.
    Weakness is the function of Tao.
    All things in the world come from being.
    And being comes from non-being.

41. When the highest type of men hear Tao,

They diligently practice it.
When the average type of men hear Tao,
They half believe in it.
When the lowest type of men hear Tao,
They laugh heartily at it.
If they did not laugh at it, it would not be Tao.
Therefore there is the established saying:
The Tao which is bright appears to be dark.
The Tao which goes forward appears to fall backward.
The Tao which is level appears uneven.
Great virtue appears like a valley (hollow).
Great purity appears like disgrace.
Far-reaching virtue appears as if insufficient.
Solid virtue appears as if unsteady.
True substance appears to be changeable.
The great square has no corners.
The great implement (or talent) is slow to finish (or mature).
Great music sounds faint.
Great form has no shape.
Tao is hidden and nameless.
Yet it is Tao alone that skillfully provides for all and brings them to perfection.

42. Tao produced the One.
The One produced the two.
The two produced the three.
And the three produced the ten thousand things.
The ten thousand things carry the yin and embrace the yang, and through the
blending of the material force (*ch'i*) they achieve harmony.
People hate to be the orphaned, the lonelys, one and the unworthy.
And yet kings and lords call themselves by these names.
Therefore it is often the case that things gain by
losing and lose by gaining.
What others have taught, I teach also:
"Violent and fierce people do not die a natural death."
I shall make this the father (basis or starting point)
of my teaching.

Comment. It is often understood that the One is the original material force or the Great
Ultimate, the two are yin and yang, the three are their blending with the original
material force, and the ten thousand things are things carrying yin and embracing yang.

However, there is no need to be specific. The important point is the natural evolution from the simple to the complex without any act of creation. This theory is common to practically all Chinese philosophical schools.

43. The softest things in the world overcome the hardest
        things in the world.
    Non-being penetrates that in which there is no space.
    Through this I know the advantage of taking no action.
    Few in the world can understand teaching without words and the advantage of
        taking no action.

44. Which does one love more, fame or one's own life?
    Which is more valuable, one's own life or wealth?
    Which is worse, gain or loss?
    Therefore he who has lavish desires will spend extravagantly.
    He who hoards most will lose heavily.
    He who is contented suffers no disgrace.
    He who knows when to stop is free from danger.
    Therefore he can long endure.

45. What is most perfect seems to be incomplete;
    But its utility is unimpaired.
    What is most full seems to be empty;
    But its usefulness is inexhaustible.
    What is most straight seems to be crooked.
    The greatest skills seems to be clumsy.
    The greatest eloquence seems to stutter.
    Hasty movement overcomes cold,
    (But) tranquillity overcomes heat.
    By being greatly tranquil,
    One is qualified to be the ruler of the world.

46. When Tao prevails in the world, galloping horses are turned back to fertilize
        (the fields with their dung).
    When Tao does not prevail in the world, war horses
        thrive in the suburbs.
    There is no calamity greater than lavish desires.
    There is no greater guilt than discontentment.
    And there is no greater disaster than greed.
    He who is contented with contentment is always contented.

47. One may know the world without going out of doors.
    One may see the Way of Heaven without looking through the windows.
    The further one goes, the less one knows.
    Therefore the sage knows without going about,
    Understands without seeing,
    And accomplishes without any action.

48. The pursuit of learning is to increase day after day.
    The pursuit of Tao is to decrease day after day.
    It is to decrease and further decrease until one reaches the point of taking no
      action.
    No action is undertaken, and yet nothing is left undone.
    An empire is often brought to order by having no activity (laissez-faire).
    If one (likes to) undertake activity, he is not qualified to govern the empire.

49. The sage has no fixed (personal) ideas.
    He regards the people's ideas is his own.
    I treat those who are good with goodness.
    And I so treat those who are not good with goodness.
    Thus goodness is attained.
    I am honest to those who are honest,
    And I am also honest to those who are not honest.
    Thus honesty is attained.
    The sage, in the government of his empire, has no subjective viewpoint.
    His mind forms a harmonious whole with that of his people.
    They all lend their eyes and ears, and he treats them all as infants.

50. Man comes into life and goes out to death.
    Three out of ten are companions of life.
    Three out of ten are companions of death.
    And three out of ten in their lives lead from activity to death.
    And for what reason?
    Because of man's intensive striving after life.
    I have heard that one who is a good preserver of his life will not meet tigers or
      wild buffalos,
    And in fighting will not try to escape from weapons of war.
    The wild buffalo cannot butt its horns against him.
    The tiger cannot fasten its claws in him.
    And weapons of war cannot thrust their blades into him.
    And for what reason?

Because in him there his no room for death.

51. Tao produces them (the ten thousand things).
    Virtue fosters them.
    Matter gives them physical form.
    The circumstances and tendencies complete them.
    Therefore the ten thousand things esteem Tao and honor virtue.
    Tao is esteemed and virtue is honored without anyone's order.
    They always come spontaneously.
    Therefore Tao produces them and virtue fosters them.
    They rear them and develop them.
    They give them security and give them peace.
    They nurture them and protect them.
    (Tao) produces them but does not take possession of them.
    It acts, but does not rely on its own ability.
    It leads them but does not master them.
    This is called profound and secret virtue.

52. There was a beginning of the universe
    Which may be called the Mother of the Universe.
    He who has found the mother (Tao)
    And thereby understands her sons (things)
    And having understood the sons,
    Still keeps to its mother,
    Will be free from danger throughout his lifetime.
    Close the mouth.
    Shut the doors (of cunning and desire).
    And to the end of life there will be (peace) without toil.
    Open the mouth.
    Meddle with affairs,
    And to the end of life there will be no salvation.
    Seeing what is small is called enlightenment.
    Keeping to weakness is called strength.
    Use the light.
    Revert to enlightenment,
    And thereby avoid danger to one's life—
    This is called practicing the eternal.

53. If I had but little knowledge
    I should, in walking on a broad way,

Fear getting off the road.
Broad ways are extremely even.
But people are fond of by-paths.
The courts are exceedingly splendid,
While the fields are exceedingly weedy,
And the granaries are exceedingly empty.
Elegant clothes are worn
Sharp weapons are carried,
Foods and drinks are enjoyed beyond limit,
And wealth and treasures are accumulated in excess.
This is robbery and extravagance.
This is indeed not Tao (the way).

54. He who is well established (in Tao) cannot be pulled away.
He who has a firm grasp (of Tao) cannot be separated from it.
Thus from generation to generation his ancestral sacrifice will never be suspended.
When one cultivates virtue in his person, it becomes genuine virtue.
When one cultivates virtue in his family, it becomes overflowing virtue.
When one cultivates virtue in his community, it becomes lasting virtue.
When one cultivates virtue in his country, it becomes abundant virtue.
When one cultivates virtue in the world, it becomes universal.
Therefore the person should be viewed as a person.
The family should be viewed as a family.
The community should be viewed as a community.
The country should be viewed as a country.
And the world should be viewed as the world.
How do I know this to be the case in the world?
Through this (from the cultivation of virtue in the person to that in the world).

55. He who possesses virtue in abundance
May be compared to an infant.
Poisonous insects will not sting him.
Fierce beasts will not seize him.
Birds of prey will not strike him.
His bones are weak, his sinews tender, but his grasp is firm.
He does not yet know the union of male and female,
But his organ is aroused.
This means that his essence is at its height.
He may cry all day without becoming hoarse,

This means that his (natural) harmony is perfect.
To know harmony means to be in accord with the eternal.
To be in accord with the eternal means to be enlightened.
To force the growth of life means ill omen.
For the mind to employ the vital force without restraint means violence.
After things reach their prime, they begin to grow old,
Which means being contrary to Tao.
Whatever is contrary to Tao will soon perish.

56. He who knows does not speak.
He who speaks does not know.
Close the mouth.
Shut the doors (of cunning and desires).
Blunt the sharpness.
Untie the tangles.
Soften the light.
Become one with the dusty world.
This is called profound identification.
Therefore it is impossible either to be intimate and close to him or to be distant
    and indifferent to him.
It is impossible either to benefit him or to harm him,
It is impossible either to honor him or to disgrace him.
For this reason he is honored by the world.

57. Govern the state with correctness.
Operate the army with surprise tactics.
Administer the empire by engaging in no activity.
How do I know that this should be so?
Through this:
    The more taboos and prohibitions there are in the world,
        The poorer the people will be.
    The more sharp weapons the people have,
        The more troubled the state will be.
    The more cunning and skill man possesses,
        The more vicious things will appear.
    The more laws and orders are made prominent,
        The more thieves and robbers there will be.
Therefore the sage says:
    I take no action and the people of themselves are transformed.
    I love tranquillity and the people of themselves become correct.

I engage in no activity and the people of themselves become prosperous.
I have no desires and the people of themselves become simple.

Comment. Laissez-faire government. Even Confucius shared this ideal.

58. When the government is nondiscriminative and dull,
The people are contented and generous.
When the government is searching and discriminative,
The people are disappointed and contentious.
Calamity is that upon which happiness depends;
Happiness is that in which calamity is latent.
Who knows when the limit will be reached?
Is there no correctness (used to govern the world?)
Then the correct again becomes the perverse
And the good will again become evil.
The people have been deluded for a long time.
Therefore the sage is as pointed as a square but does not pierce.
He is as acute as a knife but does not cut.
He is as straight as an unbent line but does not extend.
He is as bright as light but does not dazzle.

59. To role people and to serve Heaven there is nothing better than to be frugal.
Only by being frugal can one recover quickly.
To recover quickly means to accumulate virtue heavily.
By the heavy accumulation of virtue one can overcome everything.
If one can overcome everything, then he will acquire a capacity the limit of
which is beyond anyone's knowledge.
When his capacity is beyond anyone's knowledge, he is fit to rule a state.
He who possesses the Mother (Tao) of the state will last long.
This means that the roots are deep and the stalks are firm, which is the way of
long life and everlasting existence.

60. Ruling a big country is like cooking a small fish.
If Tao is employed to rule the empire,
Spiritual beings will lose their supernatural power.
Not that they lose their spiritual power,
But their spiritual power can no longer harm people.
Not only will their supernatural power not harm people,
But the sage also will not harm people.
When both do not harm each other,

Virtue will be accumulated in both for the benefit [of the people].

61. A big country may be compared to the lower part of a river.
    It is the converging point of the world;
        It is the female of the world.
    The female always overcomes the male by tranquillity,
        And by tranquillity she is underneath.
    A big state can take over a small state if it places itself below the small state;
    And the small state can take over a big state if it places itself below the big state.
    Thus some, by placing themselves below, take over (others),
    And some, by being (naturally) low, take over (other states).
    After all, what a big state wants is but to annex and herd others,
    And what a small state wants is merely to join and serve others.
    Since both big and small states get what they want,
    The big state should place itself low.

62. Tao is the storehouse of all things.
    It is the good man's treasure and the bad man's refuge.
    Fine words can buy honor,
    And fine deeds can gain respect from others.
    Even if a man is bad, when has (Tao) rejected him?
    Therefore on the occasion of crowning an emperor or installing the three ministers,
    Rather than present large pieces of jade preceded by teams of four horses,
    It is better to kneel and offer this Tao.
    Why did the ancients highly value this Tao?
    Did they not say, "Those who seek shall have it and those who sin shall be freed"?
    For this reason it is valued by the world.

63. Act without action.
    Do without ado.
    Taste without tasting.
    Whether it is big or small, many or few, repay hatred with virtue.
    Prepare for the difficult while it is still easy.
    Deal with the big while it is still small.
    Difficult undertakings have always started with what is easy,
    And great undertakings have always started with what is small.
    Therefore the sage never strives for the great,

And thereby the great is achieved.
He who makes rash promises surely lacks faith.
He who takes things too easily will surely encounter
    much difficulty.
For this reason even the sage regards things as difficult.
And therefore he encounters no difficulty.

Comment. The Taoist doctrine of walking the second mile, which was unacceptable to Confucius.

64. What remains still is easy to hold.
What is not yet manifest is easy to plan for.
What is brittle is easy to crack.
What is minute is easy to scatter.
Deal with things before they appear.
Put things in order before disorder arises.
A tree as big as a man's embrace grows from a tiny shoot.
A tower of nine storeys begins with a heap of earth.
The journey of a thousand *li* starts from where one stands.
He who takes an action fails.
He who grasps things loses them.
For this reason the sage takes no action and therefore does not fail.
He grasps nothing and therefore he does not lose anything.
People in their handling of affairs often fail when they are about to succeed.
If one remains as careful at the end as he was at the
    beginning, there will be no failure.
Therefore the sage desires to have no desire.
He does not value rare treasures.
He learns to be unlearned, and returns to what the
    multitude has missed (Tao).
Thus he supports all things in their natural state but does not take any action.

65. In ancient times those who practiced Tao well
Did not seek to enlighten the people, but to make them ignorant.
People are difficult to govern because they have too much knowledge.
Therefore he who rules the state through knowledge is a robber of the state;
He who rules a state not through knowledge is a blessing to the state.
One who knows these two things also (knows) the standard.
Always to know the standard is called profound and secret virtue.
Virtue becomes deep and far-reaching,

And with it all things return to their original natural state.
Then complete harmony will be reached.

66. The great rivers and seas are kings of all mountain streams
Because they skillfully stay below them.
That is why they can be their kings.
Therefore, in order to be the superior of the people,
    One must, in the use of words, place himself below them.
And in order to be ahead of the people
    One must, in one's own person, follow them.
Therefore the sage places himself above the people and they do not feel his weight.
He places himself in front of them and the people do not harm him.
Therefore the world rejoices in praising him without getting tired of it.
It is precisely because he does not compete that the world cannot compete with him.

67. All the world says that my Tao is great and does not seem to resemble (the ordinary).
It is precisely because it is great that it does not resemble (the ordinary).
If it did resemble, it would have been small for a long time.
I have three treasures. Guard and keep them:
    The first is deep love,
    The second is frugality,
    And the third is not to dare to be ahead of the world.
Because of deep love, one is courageous.
Because of frugality one is generous.
Because of not daring to be ahead of the world, one becomes the leader of the world.
Now, to be courageous by forsaking deep love,
To be generous by forsaking frugality,
And so be ahead of the world by forsaking following
    behind—
    This is fatal.
For deep love helps one to win in the case of attack,
    And to be firm in the case of defense.
When Heaven is to save a person,
    Heaven will protect him through deep love.

68. A skillful leader of troops is not oppressive with his military strength.

A skillful fighter does not become angry.
A skillful conqueror does not compete with people.
One who is skillful in using men puts himself below them.
This is called the virtue of not-competing.
This is called the strength to use men.
This is called matching Heaven, the highest principle of old.

69. The strategists say:
     "I dare not take the offensive but I take the defensive;
     I dare not advance an inch but I retreat a foot."
This means:
     To march without formation,
     To stretch one's arm without showing it,
     To confront enemies without seeming to meet them,
     To hold weapons without seeming to have them.
There is no greater disaster than to make light of the enemy.
Making light of the enemy will destroy my treasures.
Therefore when armies are mobilized and issues joined,
The man who is sorry over the fact will win.

70. My doctrines are very easy to understand and very easy to practice,
     But none in the world can understand or practice them.
     My doctrines have a source (Nature); my deeds have a master (Tao).
     It is because people do not understand this that they do not understand me.
     Few people know me, and therefore I am highly valued.
     Therefore the sage wears a coarse cloth on top and carries jade within his
        bosom.

71. To know that you do not know is the best.
     To pretend to know when you do not know is a disease.
     Only when one recognizes this disease is a disease can one be free from the disease.
     The sage is free from the disease.
     Because he recognizes this disease to be disease, he is free from it.

     Comment. Note the similarity with the Confucian teaching: say that you know when you
     do know and say that you do not know when you do not know.

72. When the people do not fear of what is dreadful,
     Then what is greatly dreadful will descend on them.
     Do not reduce the living space of their dwellings.

Do not oppress their lives.
It is because you do not oppress them that they are not oppressed.
Therefore the sage knows himself but does not show himself,
He loves himself but does not exalt himself.
Therefore he rejects the one but accepts the other.

73. He who is brave in daring will be killed.
He who is brave in not daring will live.
Of these two, one is advantageous and one is harmful.
Who knows why Heaven dislikes what it dislikes?
Even the sage considers it a difficult question.
The Way of Heaven does not compete, and yet it skillfully achieves victory.
It does not speak, and yet it skillfully responds to things.
It comes to you without your invitation.
It is not anxious about things and yet it plans well.
Heaven's net is indeed vast.
Though its meshes are wide, it misses nothing.

Comment. The analogy of Heaven's net has strongly strengthened the Chinese belief in retribution and formed the basis of popular Taoist religious treatises such as the *T'ai-shang kan-ying p'ien* (Tract of Influence and Responses of the Most Exalted One).

74. The people are not afraid of death.
Why, then, threaten them with death?
Suppose the people are always afraid of death and we can seize those who are vicious, and kill them,
Who would dare to do so?
There is always the master executioner (Heaven) who kills.
To undertake executions for the master executioner is like hewing wood for the master carpenter.
Whoever undertakes to hew wood for the master carpenter rarely escapes injuring his own hands.

75. The people starve because the ruler eats too much tax-grain.
Therefore they starve.
They are difficult to rule because their ruler does too many things.
Therefore they are difficult to rule.
The people take death lightly because their ruler strives for life too vigorously.
Therefore they take death lightly.
It is only those who do not seek after life that excel in making life valuable.

76. When man is born, he is tender and weak.
At death, he is stiff and hard.
All things, the grass as well as trees, are tender and supple while alive.
When dead, they are withered and dried.
Therefore the stiff and the hard are companions of death.
The tender and the weak are companions of life.
Therefore if the army is strong, it will not win.
If a tree is stiff, it will break.
The strong and the great are inferior, while the tender and the weak are superior.

77. Heaven's Way is indeed like the bending of a bow.
When (the string) is high, bring it down.
When it is low, raise it up.
When it is excessive, reduce it.
When it is insufficient, supplement it.
The Way of Heaven reduces whatever is excessive and supplements whatever is insufficient.
The way of man is different.
It reduces the insufficient to offer to the excessive.
Who is able to have excess to offer to the world?
Only the man of Tao.
Therefore the sage acts, but does not rely on his own ability.
He accomplishes his task, but does not claim credit for it.
He has no desire to display his excellence.

78. There is nothing softer and weaker than water,
And yet there is nothing better for attacking hard and strong things.
For this reason there is no substitute for it.
All the world knows that the weak overcomes the strong and the soft overcomes the hard.
But none can practice it.
Therefore the sage says:
He who suffers disgrace for his country
Is called the lord of the land.
He who takes upon himself the country's misfortunes
Becomes the king of the empire.
Straight words seem to be their opposite.

79. To patch up great hatred is surely to leave some hatred behind.

How can this be regarded as good?
Therefore the sage keeps the left-hand portion (obligation) of a contract
And does not blame the other party.
Virtuous people attend to their left-hand portions,
While those without virtue attend to other people's mistakes.
"The Way of Heaven has no favorites.
It is always with the good man."

80. Let there be a small country with few people.
Let there be ten times and a hundred times as many utensils
But let them not be used.
Let the people value their lives highly and not migrate far.
Even if there are ships and carriages, none will ride in them.
Even if there are armor and weapons, none will display them.
Let the people again knot cords and use them (in place of writing).
Let them relish their food, beautify their clothing, be content with their homes,
   and delight in their customs.
Though neighboring communities overlook one another and the crowing of
   cocks and barking of dogs can be heard,
Yet the people there may grow old and die without ever visiting one another.

81. True words are not beautiful:
Beautiful words are not true.
A good man does not argue;
He who argues is not a good man.
A wise man has no extensive knowledge;
He who has extensive knowledge is not a wise man.
The sage does not accumulate for himself.
The more he uses for others, the more he has himself.
The more he gives to others, the more he possesses of his own.
The Way of Heaven is to benefit others and not to injure.
The Way of the sage is to act but not to compete.

Reflections

Little is known of the author of the *Tao te-Ching*, yet the enigmatic verses of the *Tao te-Ching* were instrumental in shaping Chinese attitudes toward nature, human nature, and human action. The *Tao te-Ching*, attributed to Lao Tzu and probably written between the sixth and third centuries B.C., continues to inspire to modern readers. Key elements of Taoist thought include the following: 1) The "Tao" is the nameless origin of all things, but it is also the way in which all things in nature pursue their course. 2) There is a fundamental harmony and balance in nature: the sage tries to "fit in" with that fundamental "flow" which is the Tao. 3) The polarities of existence symbolized by the principles of *yin* (associated with female, water, moistness, darkness, passivity or non-action, emptiness, space, flexibility) and *yang* (associated with male, mountain, dryness, brightness, activity, fullness, rigidity) are not seen as contradictory, but as complementary; they are needed to complete each other. 4) While nature's polarities and "distinctions" are seen as complementary and necessary, the *Tao te-Ching* clearly emphasizes the importance, perhaps primacy, of the "yin," the polar element associated with female, water, and non-action. Being like water is remaining close to Tao.

After reading the verses of the *Tao te-Ching*, students should choose one on which to focus and comment. Discuss how the Taoist perspective might affect thinking about the cosmos, the environment, human actions and interactions, international affairs, education, and the creation of art.

VI

Judaism
and
Christianity

The New American Bible: Hebrew Scriptures/ Old Testament

Genesis 1–4:16

1 First Story of Creation

In the beginning, when God created the heavens and the earth, the earth was a formless wasteland, and darkness covered the abyss, while a mighty wind swept over the waters.

Then God said, "Let there be light," and there was light." God saw how good the light was. God then separated the light from the darkness. God called the light "day," and the darkness he called "night." Thus evening came, and morning followed—the first day.

Then God said, "Let there be a dome in the middle of the waters, to separate one body of water from the other." And so it happened: God made the dome, and it separated the water above the dome from the water below it. God called the dome "the sky." Evening came, and morning followed—the second day.

Then God said, "Let the water under the sky be gathered into a single basin, so that the dry land may appear." And so it happened: the water under the sky was gathered into its basin, and the dry land appeared. God called the dry land "the earth," and the basin of the water he called "the sea." God saw how good it was. Then God said, "Let the earth bring forth vegetation: every kind of plant that bears seed and every kind of fruit tree on earth that bears fruit with its seed in it." And so it happened: the earth brought forth every kind of plant that bears seed and every kind of fruit tree on earth that bears fruit with its seed in it. God saw how good it was. Evening came, and morning followed—the third day.

Then God said: "Let there be lights in the dome of the sky, to separate day from night. Let them mark the fixed times, the days and the years, and serve as luminaries in the dome of the sky, to shed light upon the earth." And so it happened: God made the two great lights, the greater one to govern the day, and the lesser one to govern the night; and he made the stars. God set them in the dome of the sky to shed light upon the earth, to govern the day and the night, and to separate the light from the darkness. God saw how good it was. Evening came, and morning followed—the fourth day.

Then God said, "Let the water teem with an abundance of living creatures, and on the earth let birds fly beneath the dome of the sky." And so it happened: God created the great sea monsters and all kinds of swimming creatures with which the water teems, and all kinds of winged birds. God saw how good it was and God blessed them, saying, "Be fertile, multiply, and fill the water of the seas: and let the birds multiply on the earth." Evening came, and morning followed—the fifth day.

Then God said, "Let the earth bring forth all kinds of living creatures: cattle, creeping things, and wild animals of all kinds." And so it happened: God made all kinds of wild animals, all kinds of cattle, and all kinds of creeping things of the earth. God saw how good it was. Then God said: "Let us make man in our image, after our likeness. Let them have dominion over the fish of the sea, the birds of the air, and the cattle, and over all the wild animals and all the creatures that crawl on the ground."

> God created man in his image;
> > in the divine image he created him;
> > male and female he created them.

God blessed them, saying: "Be fertile the multiply; fill the earth and subdue it. Have dominion over the fish of the sea, the birds of the air, and all the living things that move on the earth." God also said: "See, I give you every seed-bearing plant all over the earth and every tree that has seed-bearing fruit on it to be your food; and to all the animals of the land, all the birds of the air, and all the living creatures that crawl on the ground, I give all the green plants for food." And so it happened. God looked at everything he had made, and he found it very good. Evening came, and morning followed—the sixth day.

2

Thus the heavens and the earth and all their array were completed. Since on the seventh day God was finished with the work he had been doing, he rested on the seventh day from all the work he had undertaken. So God blessed the seventh day and made it holy, because on it he rested from all the work he had done in creation.

Such is the story of the heavens and the earth at their creation.

Second Story of Creation

At the time when the LORD God made the earth and the heavens—while as yet there was no field shrub on earth and no grass of the field had sprouted, for the LORD God had sent no rain upon the earth and there was no man to till the soil, but a stream was welling up out of the earth and was watering all the surface of the ground—the LORD God formed man out of the clay of the ground and blew into his nostrils the breath of life, and so man became a living being.

Then the LORD God planted a garden in Eden, in the east, and he placed there the man whom he had formed. Out of the ground the LORD God made various trees grow that were delightful to look at and good for food, with the tree of life in the middle of the garden and the tree of the knowledge of good and bad.

A river rises in Eden to water the garden; beyond there it divides and becomes four branches. The name of the first is the Pishon; it is the one that winds through the whole land of Havilah, where there is gold. The gold of that land is excellent; bdellium and lapis lazuli are also there. The name of the second river is the Gihon; it is the one that winds all through the land of Cush. The name of the third river is the Tigris; it is the one that flows east of Asshur. The fourth river is the Euphrates.

The LORD God then took the man and settled him in the garden of Eden, to cultivate and care for it. The LORD God gave man this order: "You are free to eat from any of the trees of the garden except the tree of the knowledge of good and bad. From that tree you shall not eat; the moment you eat from it you are surely doomed to die."

The LORD God said: "It is not good for the man to be alone. I will make a suitable partner for him." So the LORD God formed out of the ground various wild animals and various birds of the air, and he brought them to the man to see what he would call them; whatever the man called each of them would be its name. The man gave names to all the cattle, all the birds of the air, and all the wild animals; but none proved to be the suitable partner for the man.

So the LORD God cast a deep sleep on the man, and while he was asleep, he took out one of his ribs and closed up its place with flesh. The LORD God then built up into a woman the rib that he had taken from the man. When he brought her to the man, the man said:

> "This one, at last, is bone of my bones
>   and flesh of my flesh;
> This one shall be called 'woman,'
>   for out of 'her man' this one has been taken."

That is why a man leaves his father and mother and clings to his wife, and the two of them become one body.

The man and his wife were both naked, yet they felt no shame.

3   The Fall of Man

Now the serpent was the most cunning of all the animals that the LORD God had made. The serpent asked the woman, "Did God really tell you not to eat from any of the trees in the garden?" The woman answered the serpent: "We may eat of the fruit of the trees in the garden; it is only about the fruit of the tree in the middle of the garden that God said, 'You shall not eat it or even touch it, lest you die.'" But the serpent said to the woman: "You certainly will not die! No, God knows well that the moment you eat of it your eyes will be opened and you will be like gods who know what is good and what is bad." The woman saw that the tree was good for food, pleasing to the eyes, and desirable for gaining wisdom. So she took some of its fruit and ate it; and she also gave some to her husband, who was with her, and he ate it. Then the eyes of both of them were opened, and they realized that they were naked; so they sewed fig leaves together and made loincloths for themselves.

When they heard the sound of the LORD God moving about in the garden at the breezy time of the day, the man and his wife hid themselves from the LORD God among the trees of the garden. The LORD God then called to the man and asked him, "Where are you?" He answered, "I heard you in the garden; but I was afraid, because I was naked, so I hid myself." Then he asked, "Who told you that you were naked? You have eaten, then, from the tree of which I had forbidden you to eat!" The man replied, "The woman whom you put here with me—she gave me fruit from the tree, and so I ate it." The LORD

God then asked the woman, "Why did you do such a thing?" The woman answered, "The serpent tricked me into it, so I ate it."

Then the LORD God said to the serpent:

> "Because you have done this, you
>> shall be banned
>> from all the animals
>> and from all the wild creatures;
> On your belly shall you crawl,
>> and dirt shall you eat
>> all the days of your life.
> I will put enmity between you and the woman,
>> and between your offspring and hers
> He will strike at your head,
>> while you strike at his heel."

To the woman he said:

> "I will intensify the pangs of your childbearing;
>> in pain shall you bring forth children.
> Yet your urge shall be for your husband,
>> and he shall be your master."

To the man he said: "Because you listened to your wife and ate from the tree of which I had forbidden you to eat,

> "Cursed be the ground because of you!
> In toil shall you eat its yield
>> all the days of your life.
> Thorns and thistles shall it bring forth to you,
>> as you eat of the plants of the field.
> By the sweat of your face
>> shall you get bread to eat,
> Until you return to the ground,
>> from which you were taken;
> For you are dirt,
>> and to dirt you shall return."

The man called his wife Eve, because she became the mother of all the living.

For the man and his wife the LORD God made leather garment, with which he clothed them. Then the LORD God said: See! The man has become like one of us, knowing what is good and what is bad! Therefore, he must not be allowed to put out his hand to take fruit from the tree of life also, and thus eat of it and live forever." The LORD God therefore banished him from the garden of Eden, to till the ground from which he had been taken. When he expelled the man, he settled him east of the garden of Eden; and he stationed the cherubim and the fiery revolving sword, to guard the way to the tree of life.

4 Cain and Abel

The man had relations with his wife Eve, and she conceived and bore Cain, saying, "I have produced a man with the help of the LORD." Next she bore his brother Abel. Abel became a keeper of flocks, and Cain a tiller of the soil. In the course of time Cain brought an offering to the LORD from the fruit of the soil, while Abel, for his part, brought one of the best firstlings of his flock. The LORD looked with favor on Abel and his offering, but on Cain and his offering he did not. Cain greatly resented this and was crestfallen. So the LORD said to Cain: "Why are you so resentful and crestfallen? If you do well, you can hold up your head; but if not, sin is a demon lurking at the door: his urge is toward you, yet you can be his master."

Cain said to his brother Abel, "Let us go out in the field." When they were in the field, Cain attacked his brother Abel and killed him. Then the LORD asked Cain, "Where is your brother Abel?" He answered, "I do not know. Am I my brother's keeper?" The LORD then said: "What have you done! Listen: your brother's blood cries out to me from the soil! Therefore you shall be banned from the soil that opened its mouth to receive your brother's blood from your hand. If you till the soil, it shall no longer give you its produce. You shall become a restless wanderer on the earth." Cain said to the LORD: "My punishment is too great to bear. Since you have now banished me from the soil, and I must avoid your presence and become a restless wanderer on the earth, anyone may kill me at sight." "Not so!" the LORD said to him. "If anyone kills Cain, Cain shall be avenged sevenfold." So the LORD put a mark on Cain, lest anyone should kill him at sight. Cain then left the LORD's presence and settled in the land of Nod, east of Eden.

Genesis 15–17

15 The Covenant with Abram

S ome time after these events, this word of the LORD came to Abram in a vision:

> "Fear not, Abram!
> I am your shield;
> I will make your reward very great."

But Abram said, "O Lord God, what good will your gifts be, if I keep on being childless and have as my heir the steward of my house, Eliezer?" Abram continued, "See, you have given me no offspring, and so one of my servants will be my heir." Then the word of the LORD came to him: "No, that one shall not be your heir; your own issue shall be your heir." He took him outside and said: "Look up at the sky and count the stars, if you can. Just so," he added, "shall your descendants be." Abram put his faith in the LORD, who credited it to him as an act of righteousness.

He then said to him, "I am the LORD who brought you from Ur of the Chaldeans to give you this land as a possession." "O Lord God," he asked, "how am I to know that I shall possess it?" He answered him, "Bring me a three-year-old heifer, a three-year-old she-goat, a three-year-old ram, a turtledove, and a young pigeon." He brought him all these, split them in two, and placed each half opposite the other; but the birds he did not cut up. Birds of prey swooped down on the carcasses, but Abram stayed with them. As the sun was about to set, a trance fell upon Abram, and a deep, terrifying darkness enveloped him.

Then the LORD said to Abram: "Know for certain that your descendants shall be aliens in a land not their own, where they shall be enslaved and oppressed for four hundred years. But I will bring judgment on the nation they must serve, and in the end they will depart with great wealth. You, however, shall join your forefathers in peace; you shall be buried at a contented old age. In the fourth time-span the others shall come back here; the wickedness of the Amorites will not have reached its full measure until then."

When the sun had set and it was dark, there appeared a smoking brazier and a flaming torch, which passed between those pieces. It was on that occasion that the LORD made a covenant with Abram, saying: "To your descendants I give this land, from the Wadi of Egypt to the Great River [the Euphrates], the land of the Kenites, the Kenizzites, the

Kadmonites, the Hittites, the Perizzites, the Rephaim, the Amorites, the Canaanites, the Girgashites, and the Jebusites."

16 Birth of Ishmael

Abram's wife Sarai had borne him no children. She had, however, an Egyptian maid-servant named Hagar. Sarai said to Abram: The LORD has kept me from bearing children. Have intercourse, then, with my maid; perhaps I shall have sons through her." Abram heeded Sarai's request. Thus, after Abram had lived ten years in the land of Canaan, his wife Sarai took her maid, Hagar the Egyptian, and gave her to her husband Abram to be his concubine. He had intercourse with her, and she became pregnant. When she became aware of her pregnancy, she looked on her mistress with disdain. So Sarai said to Abram: "You are responsible for this outrage against me. I myself gave my maid to your embrace; but ever since she became aware of her pregnancy, she has been looking on me with disdain. May the LORD decide between you and me!" Abram told Sarai: "Your maid is in your power. Do to her whatever you please." Sarai then abused her so much that Hagar ran away from her.

The LORD's messenger found her by a spring in the wilderness, the spring on the road to Shur, and he asked, "Hagar, maid of Sarai, where have you come from and where are you going?" She answered, I am running away from my mistress, Sarai." But the LORD's messenger told her: "Go back to your mistress and submit to her abusive treatment. I will make your descendants so numerous," added the LORD's messenger, "that they will be too many to count. Besides," the LORD's messenger said to her:

> "You are now pregnant and shall bear a son
>   you shall name him Ishmael,
> For the LORD has heard you,
>   God has answered you.
> He shall be a wild ass of a man,
>   his hand against everyone,
>   and everyone's hand against him;
> In opposition to all his kin
>   shall he encamp."

To the LORD who spoke to her she gave a name, saying, "You are the God of Vision"; she meant, "Have I really seen God and remained alive after my vision?" That is why the well is called Beer-lahai-roi. It is between Kadesh and Bered.

Hagar bore Abram a son, and Abram named the son whom Hagar bore him Ishmael. Abram was eighty-six years old when Hagar bore him Ishmael.

17 Covenant of Circumcision

When Abram was ninety-nine years old, the LORD appeared to him and said: "I am God the Almighty. Walk in my presence and be blameless. Between you and me I will establish my covenant, and I will multiply you exceedingly."

When Abram prostrated himself, God continued to speak to him: "My covenant with you is this: you are to become the father of a host of nations. No longer shall you be called Abram; your name shall be Abraham, for I am making you the father of a host of nations. I will render you exceedingly fertile; I will make nations of you; kings shall stem from you. I will maintain my covenant with you and your descendants after you throughout the ages as an everlasting pact, to be your God and the God of your descendants after you. I will give to you and to your descendants after you the land in which you are now staying, the whole land of Canaan, as a permanent possession; and I will be their God."

God also said to Abraham: "On your part, you and your descendants after you must keep my covenant throughout the ages. This is my covenant with you and your descendants after you that you must keep: every male among you shall be circumcised. Circumcise the flesh of your foreskin, and that shall be the mark of the covenant between you and me. Throughout the ages, every male among you, when he is eight days old, shall be circumcised, including houseborn slaves and those acquired with money from any foreigner who is not of your blood. Yes, both the houseborn slaves and those acquired with money must be circumcised. Thus my covenant shall be in your flesh as an everlasting pact. "If a male is uncircumcised, that is, if the flesh of his foreskin has not been cut away, such a one shall be cut off from his people; he has broken my covenant."

God further said to Abraham: "As for your wife Sarai, do not call her Sarai; her name shall be Sarah. I will bless her, and I will give you a son by her. Him also will I bless; he shall give rise to nations, and rulers of peoples shall issue from him." Abraham prostrated himself and laughed as he said to himself, "Can a child be born to a man who is a hundred years old? Or can Sarah give birth at ninety?" Then Abraham said to God, Let but Ishmael live on by your favor!" "God replied: "Nevertheless, your wife Sarah is to bear you a son, and you shall call him Isaac. I will maintain my covenant with him as an everlasting pact, to be his God and the God of his descendants after him. As for Ishmael, I am heeding you: I hereby bless him. I will make him fertile and will multiply him exceedingly. He shall become the father of twelve chieftains, and I will make of him a great nation. But my covenant I will maintain with Isaac, whom Sarah shall bear to you by this time next year." When he had finished speaking with him, God departed from Abraham.

Then Abraham took his son Ishmael and all his slaves, whether born in his house or acquired with his money—every male among the members of Abraham's household—and he circumcised the flesh of their foreskins on that same day, as God had told him to do. Abraham was ninety-nine years old when the flesh of his foreskin was circumcised, and his son Ishmael was thirteen years old when the flesh of his foreskin was circumcised. Thus, on that same day Abraham and his son Ishmael were circumcised; and all the male members of his household, including the slaves born in his house or acquired with his money from foreigners, were circumcised with him.

Exodus 3

3

Meanwhile Moses was tending the flock of his father-in-law Jethro, the priest of Midian. Leading the flock across the desert, he came to Horeb, the mountain of God. There an angel of the Lord appeared to him in fire flaming out of a bush. As he looked on, he was surprised to see that the bush, though on fire, was not consumed. So Moses decided, "I must go over to look at this remarkable sight, and see why the bush is not burned."

The Call of Moses

When the LORD saw him coming over to look at it more closely, God called out to him from the bush, "Moses! Moses!" He answered, "Here I am." God said, "Come no nearer! Remove the sandals from your feet, for the place where you stand is holy ground. I am the God of your father," he continued, "the God of Abraham, the God of Isaac, the God of Jacob." Moses hid his face, for he was afraid to look at God. "But the LORD said, "I have witnessed the affliction of my people in Egypt and have heard their cry of complaint against their slave drivers, so I know well what they are suffering. Therefore I have come down to rescue them from the hands of the Egyptians and lead them out of that land into a good and spacious land, a land flowing with milk and honey, the country of the Canaanites, Hittites, Amorites, Perizzites, Hivites and Jebusites. So indeed the cry of the Israelites has reached me, and I have truly noted that the Egyptians are oppressing them. Come, now! I will send you to Pharaoh to lead my people, the Israelites, out of Egypt."

But Moses said to God, "Who am I that I should go to Pharaoh and lead the Israelites out of Egypt?" He answered, "I will be with you; and this shall be your proof that it is I who have sent you: when you bring my people out of Egypt, you will worship God on this very mountain." "But," said Moses to God, "when I go to the Israelites and say to them, 'The God of your fathers has sent me to you,' if they ask me, 'What is his name?' What am I to tell them?" God replied, I am who am." Then he added, "This is what you shall tell the Israelites: I AM sent me to you."

God spoke further to Moses, "Thus shall you say to the Israelites: The LORD, the God of your fathers, the God of Abraham, the God of Isaac, the God of Jacob, has sent me to you.

> "This is my name forever;
>   this is my title for all generations.

"Go and assemble the elders of the Israelites, and tell them: The LORD, the God of your fathers, the God of Abraham, Isaac and Jacob, has appeared to me and said: I am concerned about you and about the way you are being treated in Egypt; so I have decided to lead you up out of the misery of Egypt into the land of the Canaanites, Hittites, Amorites, Perizzites, Hivites and Jebusites, a land flowing with milk and honey.

Thus they will heed your message. Then you and the elders of Israel shall go to the king of Egypt and say to him: The LORD, the God of the Hebrews, has sent us word. Permit us, then, to go a three days' journey in the desert, that we may offer sacrifice to the LORD, our God.

"Yet I know that the king of Egypt will not allow you to go unless he is forced. I will stretch out my hand, therefore, and smite Egypt by doing all kinds of wondrous deeds there. After that he will send you away. I will even make the Egyptians so well disposed toward this people that when you leave, you will not go empty-handed. Every woman shall ask her neighbor and her house guest for silver and gold articles and for clothing to put on your sons and daughters. Thus you will despoil the Egyptians."

Exodus 19–20

19 Arrival at Sinai

In the third month after their departure from the land of Egypt, on its first day, the Israelites came to the desert of Sinai. After the journey from Rephidim to the desert of Sinai, they pitched camp.

While Israel was encamped here in front of the mountain, Moses went up the mountain to God. Then the LORD called to him and said, "Thus shall you say to the house of Jacob; tell the Israelites: You have seen for yourselves how I treated the Egyptians and how I bore you up on eagle wings and brought you here to myself. Therefore, if you hearken to my voice and keep my covenant,you shall be my special possession, dearer to me than all other people, though all the earth is mine. You shall be to me a kingdom of priests, a holy nation. That is what you must tell the Israelites." So Moses went and summoned the elders of the people. When he set before them all that the LORD had ordered him to tell them, the people all answered together, "Everything the LORD has said, we will do." Then Moses brought back to the LORD the response of the people.

The LORD also told him, "I am coming to you in a dense cloud, so that when the people hear me speaking with you, they may always have faith in you also." When Moses, then, had reported to the LORD the response of the people, the LORD added, "Go to the people and have them sanctify themselves today and tomorrow. Make them wash their garments and be ready for the third day; for on the third day the LORD will come down on Mount Sinai before the eyes of all the people. Set limits for the people all around the mountain, and tell them: Take care not to go up the mountain, or even to touch its base. If anyone touches the mountain he must be put to death. No hand shall touch him; he must be stoned to death or killed with arrows. Such a one, man or beast, must not be allowed to live. Only when the ram's horn resounds may they go up to the mountain." Then Moses came down from the mountain to the people and had them sanctify themselves and wash their garments. He warned them, "Be ready for the third day. Have no intercourse with any woman."

The Great Theophany

On the morning of the third day there were peals of thunder and lightning, and a heavy cloud over the mountain, and a very loud trumpet blast, so that all the people in the camp trembled. But Moses led the people out of the camp to meet God and they stationed themselves at the foot of the mountain. Mount Sinai was all wrapped in smoke, for the LORD came down upon it in fire. The smoke rose from it as though from a furnace, and the whole mountain trembled violently. The trumpet blast grew louder and louder, while Moses was speaking and God answering him with thunder.

When the LORD came down to the top of Mount Sinai, he summoned Moses to the top of the mountain, and Moses went up to him. Then the LORD told Moses, "Go down and warn the people not to break through toward the LORD in order to see him; otherwise many of them will be struck down. The priests, too who approach the LORD must sanctify themselves; else he will vent his anger upon them." Moses said to the LORD,

"The people cannot go up to Mount Sinai, for you yourself warned us to set limits around the mountain to make it sacred." The LORD repeated, "Go down now! Then come up again along with Aaron. But the priests and the people must not break through to come up to the LORD; else he will vent his anger upon them." So Moses went down to the people and told them this.

20 The Ten Commandments

Then God delivered all these commandments:

"I, the LORD, am your God, who brought you out of the land of Egypt, that place of slavery. You shall not have other gods besides me. You shall not carve idols for yourselves in the shape of anything in the sky above or on the earth below or in the waters beneath the earth; you shall not bow down before them or worship them. For I, the LORD, your God, am a jealous God, inflicting punishment for their fathers' wickedness on the children of those who hate me, down to the third and fourth generation; but bestowing mercy down to the thousandth generation, on the children of those who love me and keep my commandments."

"You shall not take the name of the LORD, your God, in vain. For the LORD will not leave unpunished him who takes his name in vain."

"Remember to keep holy the sabbath day. Six days you may labor and do all your work, but the seventh day is the sabbath of the LORD, your God. No work may be done then either by you, or your son or daughter, or your male or female slave, or your beast, or by the alien who lives with you. In six days the LORD made the heavens and the earth, the sea and all that is in them, but on the seventh day he rested. That is why the LORD has blessed the sabbath day and made it holy."

"Honor your father and your mother that you may have a long life in the land which the LORD, your God, is giving you."

"You shall not kill."

"You shall not commit adultery."

"You shall not steal."

"You shall not false witness against your neighbor."

"You shall not covet your neighbor's house. You shall not covet your neighbor's wife, nor his male or female slave, nor his ox or ass, nor anything else that belongs to him."

The Fear of God

When the people witnessed the thunder and lightning, the trumpet blast and the mountain smoking, they all feared and trembled. So they took up a position much farther away and said to Moses, "You speak to us and we will listen; but let not God speak to us, or we shall die." Moses answered the people, "Do not be afraid, for God has come to you only to test you and put his fear upon you, lest you should sin." Still the people remained at a distance, while Moses approached the cloud where God was.

The LORD told Moses, "Thus shall you speak to the Israelites: You have seen for yourselves that I have spoken to you from heaven. Do not make anything to rank with me; neither gods of silver nor gods of gold shall you make for yourselves."

"An altar of earth you shall make for me, and upon it you shall sacrifice your holocausts and peace offerings, your sheep and your oxen. In whatever place I choose for the remembrance of my name I will come to you and bless you. If you make an altar of stone for me, do not build it of cut stone, for by putting a tool to it you desecrate it. You shall not go up by steps to my altar, on which you must not be indecently uncovered."

Deuteronomy 6

6

"These then are the commandments, the statutes and decrees which the LORD, your God, has ordered that you be taught to observe in the land into which you are crossing for conquest so that you and your son and your grandson may fear the LORD, your God, and keep, throughout the days of your lives, all his statutes and commandments which I enjoin on you, and thus have long life. Hear then, Israel, and be careful to observe them, that you may grow and prosper the more, in keeping with the promise of the LORD, the God of your fathers, to give you a land flowing with milk and honey.

The Great Commandment

"Hear O Israel! The LORD is our God, the LORD alone! Therefore, you shall serve the LORD, your God, with all your heart, and with all your soul, and with all your strength. Take to heart these words which I enjoin on you today. Drill them into your children. Speak of them at home and abroad, whether you busy or at rest. Bind them at your wrist as sign and let them be as a pendant on your forehead. Write them on the doorposts of your houses and on your gates.

Fidelity in Prosperity

When the LORD, your God, brings you into the land which he swore to your fathers, Abraham, Isaac and Jacob, that he would give you, a land with fine, large cities that you did not build, with houses full of goods of all sorts that you did not garner, with cisterns that you did not dig, with vineyards and olive groves that you did not plant; and when, therefore, you eat your fill, take care not to forget the LORD, who brought you out of the land of Egypt, that place of slavery. The LORD, your God, shall you fear; him shall you serve, and by his name shall you swear. You shall not follow other gods, such as those of the surrounding nations, lest the wrath of the LORD, your God, flare up against you and he destroy you from the face of the land; for the LORD, your God, who is in your midst, is a jealous God.

You shall not put the LORD, your God, to the test, as you did at Massah. But keep the commandments of the LORD, your God, and the ordinances and statutes he has enjoined on you. Do what is right and good in the sight of the LORD, that you may, according to his word, prosper, and may enter in and possess the good land which the LORD promised on oath to your fathers, thrusting all your enemies out of your way.

Instruction to Children

"Later on, when your son asks you what these ordinances, statutes and decrees mean which the LORD, our God, has enjoined on you, you shall say to your son, 'We were once slaves of Pharaoh in Egypt, but the LORD brought us out of Egypt with his strong hand and wrought before our eyes signs and wonders, great and dire, against Egypt and against Pharaoh and his whole house. He brought us from there to lead us into the land he promised on oath to our fathers, and to give it to us. Therefore, the LORD commanded us to observe all these statutes in fear of the LORD, our God, that we may always have as prosperous and happy a life as we have to day; and our justice before the LORD, our God, is to consist in carefully observing all these commandments he has enjoined on us.'"

The Book of Ezekiel 1

The Vision: God on the Cherubim

In the thirtieth year on the fifth day of the fourth month, while I was among the exiles by the river Chebar, the heavens opened, and I saw divine visions. On the fifth day of the month, the fifth year, that is, of King Jehoiachin's exile, the word of the LORD came to the priest Ezekiel, the son of Buzi, in the land of the Chaldeans by the river Chebar.—There the hand of the LORD came upon me.

As I looked, a stormwind came from the North, a huge cloud with flashing fire [enveloped in brightness], from the midst of which [the midst of the fire] something gleamed like electrum. Within it were figures resembling four living creatures that looked like this: their form was human, but each had four faces and four wings, and their legs went straight down; the soles of their feet were round. They sparkled with a gleam like burnished bronze.

Their faces were like this: each of the four had the face of a man, but on the right side was the face of a lion, and on the left side the face of an ox, and finally each had the face of an eagle. Their faces [and their wings] looked out on all their four sides; they did not turn when they moved, but each went straight forward. [Each went straight forward; wherever the spirit wished to go, there they went; they did not turn when they moved.]

Human hands were under their wings, and the wings of one touched those of another. Each had two wings spread out above so that they touched one another's, while the other two wings of each covered his body. In among the living creatures something like burning coals of fire could be seen; they seemed like torches, moving to and fro among the living creatures. The fire gleamed, and from it came forth flashes of lightning.

As I looked at the living creatures, I saw wheels on the ground, one beside each of the four living creatures. The wheels had the sparkling appearance of chrysolite, and all four of them looked the same: they were constructed as though one wheel were within another. They could move in any of the four directions they faced, with veering as they moved. The four of them had rims, and I saw that their rims were full of eyes all around. When the living creatures moved, the wheels moved with them; and when the living creatures were raised from the ground, the wheels also were raised. Wherever the spirit wished to go, there the wheels went, and they were raised together with the living creatures; for the spirit of the living creatures was in the wheels.

Over the heads of the living creatures, something like a firmament could be seen, seeming like glittering crystal, stretched straight out above their heads. Beneath the firmament their wings were stretched out one toward the other. [Each of them had two covering his body.] Then I heard the sound of their wings, like the roaring of mighty waters, like the voice of the Almighty. When they moved, the sound of the tumult was like the din of an army. [And when they stood still, they lowered their wings.]

Above the firmament over their heads something like a throne could be seen, looking like sapphire. Upon it was seated, up above, one who had the appearance of a man. Upward from what resembled his waist I saw what gleamed like electrum; downward from what resembled his waist I saw what looked like fire; he was surrounded with splendor. Like the bow which appears in the clouds on a rainy day was the splendor that surrounded him. Such was the vision of the likeness of the glory of the LORD.

The Book of Ezekiel 37

Vision of the Dry Bones

The hand of the LORD came upon me, and he led me out in the spirit of the LORD and set me in the center of the plain, which was now filled with bones. He made me walk among them in every direction so that I saw how many they were on the surface of the plain. How dry they were! He asked me: Son of man, can these bones come to life? "Lord God," I answered, "you alone know that." Then he said to me: Prophesy over these bones, and say to them: Dry bones, hear the word of the LORD! Thus says the Lord GOD to these bones: See! I will bring spirit into you, that you may come to life. I will put sinews upon you, make flesh grow over you, cover you with skin, and put spirit in you so that you may come to life and know that I am the LORD. I prophesied as I had been told, and even as I was prophesying I heard a noise; it was a rattling as the bones came together, bone joining bone. I saw the sinews and the flesh come upon them, and the skin cover them, but there was no spirit in them. Then he said to me: Prophesy to the spirit, prophesy, son of man, and say to the spirit: Thus says the Lord GOD: From the four winds come, O spirit, and breathe into these slain that they may come to life. I prophesied as he told me, and the spirit came into them; they came alive and stood upright, a vast army. Then he said to me: Son of man, these bones are the whole house of Israel. They have been saying, "Our bones are dried up, our hope is lost, and we are cut off." Therefore, prophesy and say to them: Thus says the Lord GOD: O my people, I will open your graves and have you rise from them, and bring you back to the land of Israel. Then you shall know that I am the LORD, when I open your graves and have you rise from them, O my people! I will put my spirit in you that you may live, and I will settle you upon your land; thus you shall know that I am the LORD. I have promised, and I will do it, says the LORD.

Psalm 22–23

I

My God, my God, why have you forsaken me,
 far from my prayer, from the words of my cry?
O my God, I cry out by day, and you answer not;
 by night, and there is no relief for me.
Yet you are enthroned in the holy place,
  O glory of Israel!
In you our fathers trusted;
  they trusted, and you delivered them.
To you they cried, and they escaped;
  in you they trusted, and they were not put to shame.

But I am a worm, not a man;
  the scorn of men, despised by the people.
All who see me scoff at me;
  they mock me with parted lips, they wag their heads:
"He relied on the LORD; let him deliver him,
  let him rescue him, if he loves him."
You have been my guide since I was first formed,
  my security at my mother's breast.
To you I was committed at birth,
  from my mother's womb you are my God.

Be not far from me, for I am in distress
  be near, for I have no one to help me.

II

Many bullocks surround me;
  the strong bulls of Bashan encircle me.
They open their mouths against me
  like ravening and roaring lions.

I am like water poured out;
  all my bones are racked.
My heart has become like wax
  melting away within my bosom.
My throat is dried up like baked clay,

my tongue cleaves to my jaws;
   to the dust of death you have brought me down.

Indeed, many dogs surround me,
   a pack of evildoers closes in upon me;
They have pierced my hands and my feet;
   I can count all my bones.
They look on and gloat over me;
   they divide my garments among them,
   and for my vesture they cast lots.

III

But you, O LORD, be not far from me;
   O my help, hasten to aid me.
Rescue my soul from the sword,
   my loneliness from the grip of the dog.
Save me from the lion's mouth;
   from the horns of the wild bulls,
   my wretched life.

B

I

I will proclaim your name to my brethren;
   in the midst of the assembly I will praise you:
You who fear the Lord, praise him;
   all you descendants of Jacob, give glory to him;
   revere him, all you descendants of Israel!
For he has not spurned nor disdained
   the wretched man in his misery,
Nor did he turn his face away from him,
   but when he cried out to him, he heard him.
So by your gift will I utter praise in the vast assembly;
   I will fulfill my vows before those who fear him.
The lowly shall eat their fill;
   they who seek the LORD shall praise him:
"May your hearts be ever merry."

II

All the ends of the earth
    shall remember and turn to the LORD
All the families of the nations
    shall bow down before him.
For dominion is the LORD's,
    and he rules the nations.
To him alone shall bow down
    all who sleep in the earth;
Before him shall bend
    all who go down into the dust.

III

And to him my soul shall live;
    my descendants shall serve him.
Let the coming generation be told of the LORD
    that they may proclaim to a people yet to be born
    the justice he has shown.

Psalm 23
The Lord, Shepherd and Host

A psalm of David.

I

The LORD is my shepherd; I shall not want.
    In verdant pastures he gives me repose
Beside restful waters he leads me;
    he refreshes my soul.
He guides me in right paths
    for his name's sake.
Even though I walk in the dark valley
    I fear no evil; for you are at my side
With your rod and your staff
    that give me courage.

II

You spread the table before me
    in the sight of my foes;
You anoint my head with oil;
    my cup overflows.
Only goodness and kindness follow me
    all the days of my life;
And I shall dwell in the house of the LORD
    for years to come.

Proverbs 9–10

9 The Two Banquets

Wisdom has built her house,
    she has set up her seven columns;
She has dressed her meat, mixed her wine,
    yes, she has spread her table.
She has sent out her maidens; she calls
    from the heights out over the city:
"Let whoever is simple turn in here;
    to him who lacks understanding, I say,
Come, eat of my food,
    and drink of the wine I have mixed!
Forsake foolishness that you may live;
    advance in the way of understanding.
For by me your days will be multiplied
    and the years of your life increased

He who corrects an arrogant man earns insult;
    and he who reproves a wicked man incurs opprobrium.
Reprove not an arrogant man, lest he hate you;
    reprove a wise man, and he will love you.
Instruct a wise man, and he becomes still wiser;
    teach a just man, and he advaances in learning.

The beginning of wisdom is the fear of the LORD,
    and knowledge of the Holy One is understanding.
If you are wise, it is to your own advantage;

and if you are arrogant, you alone shall bear it.

The woman Folly is fickle,
    she is inane, and knows nothing.
She sits at the door of her house
    upon a seat on the city heights.
Calling to passers-by
    as they go on their straight way:
Let whoever is simple turn in here,
    or who lacks understanding; for to him I say,
Stolen water is sweet,
    and bread gotten secretly is pleasing!"
Little he knows that the shades are there,
    that in the depths of the nether world are her guests!

10

The proverbs of Solomon:
A wise son makes his father glad,
    but a foolish son is a grief to his mother.

Ill-gotten treasures profit nothing,
    but virtue saves from death.

The LORD permits not the just to hunger,
    but the craving of the wicked he thwarts.

The slack hand impoverishes,
    but the hand of the diligent enriches.

A son who fills the granaries in summer is a credit;
    a son who slumbers during harvest, a disgrace.

Blessings are for the head of the just,
    but a rod for the back of the fool.

The memory of the just will be blessed,
    but the name of the wicked will rot.

A wise man heeds commands,
    but a prating fool will be overthrown.

He who walks honestly walks securely,
    but he whose ways are crooked will fare badly.

He who winks at a fault causes trouble,
    but he who frankly reproves promotes peace.

A fountain of life is the mouth of the just,
>   but the mouth of the wicked conceals violence.

Hatred stirs up disputes,
>   but love covers all offenses.

On the lips of the intelligent is found wisdom,
>   [but the mouth of the wicked conceals violence].

Wise men store up knowledge,
>   but the mouth of a fool is imminent ruin.

The rich man's wealth is his strong city;
>   the ruination of the lowly is their poverty.

The just man's recompense leads to life,
>   the gains of the wicked, to sin.

A path to life is his who heeds admonition,
>   but he who disregards reproof goes astray.

It is the lips of the liar that conceal hostility;
>   but he who spreads accusations is a fool.

Where words are many, sin is not wanting;
>   but he who restrains his lips does well.

The Song of Songs 1–6

1 Love's Desires

L et him kiss me with kisses of his mouth!
More delightful is your love than wine!
>   Your name spoken is a spreading perfume—
>   that is why the maidens love you.
Draw me!—
>   We will follow you eagerly!
Bring me, O king, to your chambers.
With you we rejoice and exult,
>   we extol your love; it is beyond wine:
>   how rightly you are loved!

Love's Boast

I am as dark—but lovely
    O daughters of Jerusalem—
    As the tents of Kedar,
    as the curtains of Salma.
Do not stare at me because I am swarthy
    because the sun has burned me.
My brothers have been angry with me;
    they charged me with the care of the vineyards:
    my own vineyard I have not cared for.

Love's Inquiry

Tell me, you whom my heart loves,
    where you pasture your flock,
    where you give them rest at midday,
Lest I be found wandering
    after the flocks of your companions.

If you do not know,
    O most beautiful among women,
Follow the tracks of the flock
    and pasture the young ones
    near the shepherds' camps.

Love's Vision

To the steeds of Pharaoh's chariots
    would I liken you, my beloved:
Your cheeks lovely in pendants,
    your neck in jewels.
We will make pendants of gold for you,
    and silver ornaments.

Love's Union

For the king's banquet
 my nard gives forth its fragrance.
My lover is for me a sachet of myrrh
 to rest in my bosom.
My lover is for me a cluster of henna
 from the vineyards of Engedi.

Ah, you a beautiful, my beloved,
 ah, you are beautiful; your eyes are doves!
Ah you are beautiful, my lover—
 yes, you are lovely.
Our couch, too, is verdant;
 the beams of our house are cedars,
 our rafters, cypresses.

2

I am a flower of Sharon,
 a lily of the valley.

As a lily among thorns,
 so is my beloved among women

As an apple tree among the trees of the woods,
 so is my lover among men.
I delight to rest in his shadow,
 and his fruit is sweet to my mouth.
He brings me into the banquet hall
 and his emblem over me is love.

Strengthen me with raisin cakes,
 refresh me with apples,
  for I am faint with love.
His left hand is under my head
 and his right arm embraces me.
I adjure you, daughters of Jerusalem,
 by the gazelles and hinds of the field,
Do not arouse, do not stir up love
 before its own time.

A Tryst in the Spring

Hark! my lover—here he comes
    springing across the mountains,
    leaping across the hills.
My lover is like a gazelle or a young stag.
Here he stands behind our wall,
    gazing through the windows,
    peering through the lattices.
My lover speaks; he says to me,
    Arise, my beloved, my beautiful one,
    and come!
For see, the winter is past,
    the rains are over and gone.
The flowers appear on the earth,
    the time of pruning the vines has come,
    and the song of the dove is heard in our land.
The fig tree puts forth its figs,
    and the vines, in bloom, give forth fragrance.
Arise, my beloved, my beautiful one,
    and come!

O my dove in the clefts of the rock,
    in the secret recesses of the cliff,
Let me see you,
    let me hear your voice,
For your voice is sweet,
    and you are lovely."

Catch us the foxes, the little foxes
    that damage the vineyards; for
      our vineyards are in bloom!

My lover belongs to me and I to him;
    he browses among the lilies.
Until the day breathes cool and the shadows lengthen,
    roam, my lover,
Like a gazelle or a young stag
    upon the mountains of Bether.

3 Loss and Discovery

On my bed at night I sought him
    whom my heart loves—
    I sought him but I did not find him.
I will rise then and go about the city;
    in the streets and crossings I will seek
Him whom my heart loves.
    I sought him but I did not find him.
The watchmen came upon me
    as they made their rounds of the city:
    Have you seen him whom my heart loves?
I had hardly left them
    when I found him whom my heart loves.
I took hold of him and would not let him go
    till I should bring him to the
        home of my mother,
    to the room of my parent.
I adjure you, daughters of Jerusalem,
    by the gazelles and hinds of the field,
Do not arouse, do not stir up love
    before its own time.

Regal State of the Bridegroom

What is this coming up from the desert,
    like a column of smoke
Laden with myrrh, with frankincense,
    and with the perfume of every exotic dust?
Ah, it is the litter of Solomon;
    sixty valiant men surround it,
    of the valiant men of Israel:
All of them expert with the sword,
    skilled in battle,
Each with his sword at his side
    against danger in the watches of the night.

King Solomon made himself a carriage
    of wood from Lebanon.

He made its columns of silver,
    its roof of gold,
Its seat of purple cloth,
    its framework inlaid with ivory.
Daughters of Jerusalem, come forth
    and look upon King Solomon
In the crown with which his
      mother has crowned him
    on the day of his marriage,
    on the day of the joy of his heart.

4 The Charms of the Beloved

Ah, you are beautiful, my beloved,
    ah, you are beautiful!
Your eyes are doves
    behind your veil.

Your hair is like a flock of goats
    streaming down the mountains of Gilead.
Your teeth are like a flock of ewes to be shorn,
    which come up from the washing,
All of them big with twins,
    none of them thin and barren
Your lips are like a scarlet strand,
    your mouth is lovely.
Your cheek is like a half-pomegranate
    behind your veil.

Your neck is like David's tower
    girt with battlements;
A thousand bucklers hang upon it,
    all the shields of valiant men.
Your breasts are like twin fawns,
    the young of a gazelle
    that browse among the lilies.
Until the day breathes cool and the shadows lengthen,
    I will go to the mountain of myrrh,
    to the hill of incense.

You are all-beautiful, my beloved,
    and there is no blemish in you.

Come from Lebanon, my bride,
    come from Lebanon, come!
Descend from the top of Amana,
    from the top of Senir and Hermon,
From the haunts of lions,
    from the leopards' mountains.
You have ravished my heart, my sister, my bride
    you have ravished my heart with one glance of your eyes,
    with one bead of your necklace.
How beautiful is your love, my sister, my bride,
    how much more delightful is your love than wine,
    and the fragrance of your ointments than all spices!
Your lips drip honey, my bride,
    sweetmeats and milk are under your tongue;
And the fragrance of your garments
    is the fragrance of Lebanon.

The Lover and His Garden

You are an enclosed garden, my sister, my bride,
    an enclosed garden, a fountain sealed.
You are a park that puts forth pomegranates,
    with all choice fruits;
Nard and saffron, calamus and cinnamon,
    with all kinds of incense;
Myrrh and aloes,
    with all the finest spices.
You are a garden fountain, a well of water
    flowing fresh from Lebanon.
Arise, north wind! Come, south wind!
    blow upon my garden
    that its perfumes may spread abroad.

Let my lover come to his garden
and eat its choice fruits.

5

I have come to my garden, my sister, my bride;
    I gather my myrrh and my spices,
I eat my honey and my sweetmeats,
    I drink my wine and my milk.

Eat, friends; drink! Drink freely of love!

A Fruitless Search

I was sleeping, but my heart kept vigil;
    I heard my lover knocking:
"Open to me, my sister, my beloved,
    my dove, my perfect one!
For my head is wet with dew,
    my locks with the moisture of the night."
I have taken off my robe,
    am I then to put it on?
I have bathed my feet,
    am I then to soil them?

My lover put his hand through the opening;
    my heart trembled within me,
    and I grew faint when he spoke.
I rose to open to my lover
    with my hands dripping myrrh:
With my fingers dripping choice myrrh
    upon the fittings of the lock.
I opened to my lover—
    but my lover had departed, gone.
I sought him but I did not find him;
    I called to him but he did not answer me.

The watchmen came upon me
    as they made their rounds of the city;
They struck me, and wounded me,
    and took my mantle from me,
    the guardians of the walls.
I adjure you, daughters of Jerusalem,
    if you find my lover—

What shall you tell him?—
    that I am faint with love.

The Charms of the Lost Lover

How does your lover differ from any other,
    O most beautiful among women?
How does your lover differ from any other,
    that you adjure us so?

My lover is radiant and ruddy;
    he stands out among thousands.
His head is pure gold;
    his locks are palm fronds,
    black as the raven.
His eyes are like doves
    beside running waters,
His teeth would seem bathed in milk,
    and are set like jewels.
His cheeks are like beds of spice
    with ripening aromatic herbs.
His lips are red blossoms;
    they drip choice myrrh.

His arms are rods of gold
    adorned with chrysolites.
His body is a work of ivory
    covered with sapphires.
His legs are columns of marble
    resting on golden bases.
His stature is like the trees on Lebanon,
    imposing as the cedars.
His mouth is sweetness itself;
    he is all delight.
Such is my lover, and such my friend,
    O daughters of Jerusalem.

6 Discovery

Where has your lover gone,
    O most beautiful among women?
Where has your lover gone
    that we may seek him with you?

My lover has come down to his garden,
    to the beds of spice,
To browse in the garden
    and to gather lilies.
My lover belongs to me and I to him;
    he browses among the lilies.

The Charms of the Beloved

You are as beautiful as Tirzai, my beloved.
    as lovely as Jerusalem,
    as awe-inspiring as bannered troops.
Turn your eyes from me,
    for they torment me.
Your hair is like a flock of goats
    streaming down from Gilead.
Your teeth are like a flock of ewes
    which come up from the washing,
All of them big with twins,
    none of them thin and barren.
Your cheek is like a half-pomegranate
    behind your veil.

There are sixty queens, eighty concubines,
    and maidens without number—
One alone is my dove, my perfect one,
    her mother's chosen,
    the dear one of her parent.
The daughters saw her and declared her fortunate,
    the queens and concubines, and they sang her praises;

Who is this that comes forth like the dawn,
    as beautiful as the moon, as resplendent as the sun,
    as awe-inspiring as bannered troops?

Love's Meeting

I came down to the nut garden
    to look at the fresh growth of the valley,
To see if the vines were in bloom,
    if the pomegranates had blossomed.
Before I knew it, my heart had made me
    the blessed one of my kinswomen.

Isaiah 1

1 Israel's Sinfulness

The vision which Isaiah, son of Amoz, had concerning Judah and Jerusalem in the days of Uzziah, Jotham, Ahaz and Hezekiah, kings of Judah.
Hear, O heavens, and listen, O earth,
    for the Lord speaks:
Sons have I raised and reared,
    but they have disowned me!
An ox knows its owner,
    and an ass, its master's manger;
But Israel does not know,
    my people has not understood.
Ah! sinful nation, people laden with wickedness,
    evil race, corrupt children!
They have forsaken the Lord,
    spurned the Holy One of Israel,
    apostatized.
Where would you yet be struck,
    you that rebel again and again?
The whole head is sick,
    the whole heart faint.
From the sole of the foot to the head
    there is no sound spot:
Wound and welt and gaping gash,
    not drained, or bandaged,
    or eased with salve.

Your country is waste,
    your cities burnt with fire;
Your land before your eyes
    strangers devour
    [a waste, like Sodom overthrown]—
And daughter Zion is left
    like a hut in a vineyard,
Like a shed in a melon patch,
    like a city blockaded.

Unless the LORD of hosts
    had left us a scanty remnant,
We had become as Sodom,
    we should be like Gomorrah.
Hear the word of the LORD,
    princes of Sodom!
Listen to the instruction of our God,
    people of Gomorrah!
What care I for the number of your sacrifices?
    says the LORD.
I have had enough of whole-burnt rams
    and fat of fatlings;
In the blood of calves, lambs and goats
    I find no pleasure.

When you come in to visit me,
    who asks these things of you?
Trample my courts no more!
    Bring no more worthless offerings,
    your incense is loathsome to me.
New moon and sabbath, calling of assemblies,
    octaves with wickedness: these I cannot bear.
Your new moons and festivals I detest;
    they weigh me down, I tire of the load.
When you spread out your hands,
    I close my eyes to you;
Though you pray the more,
    I will not listen.
Your hands are full of blood!
    Wash yourselves clean!

Put away your misdeeds from before my eyes;
 cease doing evil; learn to do good.
Make justice your aim: redress the wronged,
 hear the orphan's plea, defend the widow.

Come now, let us set things right,
 says the LORD:
Though your sins be like scarlet,
 they may become white as snow;
Though they be crimson red,
 they may become white as wool.
If you are willing, and obey,
 you shall eat the good things of the land;
But if you refuse and resist,
 the sword shall consume you:
 for the mouth of the LORD has spoken!

How has she turned adulteress,
 the faithful city, so upright!
Justice used to lodge within her,
 but now, murderers.
Your silver is turned to dross,
 your wine is mixed with water.
Your princes are rebels
 and comrades of thieves;
Each one of them loves a bribe
 and looks for gifts.
The fatherless they defend not,
 and the widow's plea does not reach them.
Now, therefore, says the LORD,
 the LORD of hosts, the Mighty One of Israel:
Ah! I will take vengeance on my foes
 and fully repay my enemies!
I will turn my hand against you,
 and refine your dross in the furnace,
 removing all your alloy.
I will restore your judges as at first,
 and your counselors as in the beginning;
After that you shall be called
 city of justice, faithful city.

Zion shall be redeemed by judgment,
    and her repentant ones by justice.
Rebels and sinners alike shall be crushed,
    those who desert the LORD shall be consumed.
You shall be ashamed of the terebinths which you prized.
    and blush for the groves which you chose.
You shall become like a tree with falling leaves.
    like a garden that has no water.
The strong man shall turn to tow.
    and his work shall become a spark;
Both shall burn together,
    and there shall be none to quench the flames.

The New American Bible: New Testament

Matthew 5–7

5 The Beatitudes

When he saw the crowds he went up on the mountainside. After he had sat down his disciples gathered around him, and he began to teach them:

"How blest are the poor in spirit: the reign of God is theirs.
Blest too are the sorrowing; they shall be consoled.
[Blest are the lowly; they shall inherit the land.]
Blest are they who hunger and thirst for holiness; they shall have their fill.
Blest are they who show mercy; mercy shall be theirs.
Blest are the single-hearted for they shall see God.
Blest too the peacemakers; they shall be called sons of God.
Blest are those persecuted for holiness' sake; the reign of God is theirs.
Blest are you when they insult you and persecute you and utter every kind of
    slander against you because of me.
Be glad and rejoice, for your reward is great in heaven;
they persecuted the prophets before you in the very same way.

The Disciples

"You are the salt of the earth. But what if salt goes flat? How can you restore its flavor? Then it is good for nothing but to be thrown out and trampled underfoot.
"You are the light of the world. A city set on a hill cannot be hidden. Men do not light a lamp and then put it under a bushel basket. They set it on a stand where it gives light to all in the house. In the same way, your light must shine before men so that they may see goodness in your acts and give praise to your heavenly Father.

The Old Law and the New

"Do not think that I have come to abolish the law and the prophets. I have come, not to abolish them, but to fulfill them. "Of this much I assure you: until heaven and earth pass away, not the smallest letter of the law, not the smallest part of a letter, shall be done away with until it all comes true. That is why whoever breaks the least significant of these commands and teaches others to do so shall be called least in the kingdom of God. Whoever fulfills and teaches these commands shall be great in the kingdom of God. I tell you, unless your holiness surpasses that of the scribes and Pharisees you shall not enter the kingdom of God.

Against Anger

"You have heard the commandment imposed on your forefathers, 'You shall not commit murder; every murderer shall be liable to judgment.' What I say to you is: everyone who grows angry with his brother shall be liable to judgment; any man who uses abusive language toward his brother shall be answerable to the Sanhedrin, and if he holds him in contempt he risks the fires of Gehenna. If you bring your gift to the altar and there recall that your brother has anything against you, leave your gift at the altar, go first to be reconciled with your brother, and then come and offer your gift. Lose no time; settle with your opponent while on your way to court with him. Otherwise your opponent may hand you over to the judge, who will hand you over to the guard, who will throw you into prison. I warn you, you will not be released until you have paid the last penny.

Occasions of Impurity

"You have heard the commandment. 'You shall not commit adultery,' What I say to you is: anyone who looks lustfully at a woman has already committed adultery with her in his thoughts. If your right eye is your trouble, gouge it out and throw it away! Better to lose part of your body than to have it all cast into Gehenna. Again, if your right hand is your trouble: cut it off and throw it away! Better to lose part of your body than to have it all cast into Gehenna.

Divorce

"It was also said, 'Whenever a man divorces his wife, he must give her a decree of divorce.' What I say to you is: everyone who divorces his wife—lewd conduct is a separate case—forces her to commit adultery. The man who marries a divorced woman likewise commits adultery.

On Oaths

"You have heard the commandment imposed on your forefathers, 'Do not take a false: oath; rather, make good to the Lord all your pledges.' What I tell you is: do not swear at all. Do not swear by heaven (it is God's throne), nor by the earth (it is his footstool), nor by Jerusalem (it is the city of the great King); do not swear by your head (you cannot make a single hair white or black). "Say, 'Yes' when you mean 'Yes' and 'No' when you mean 'No.' Anything beyond that is from the evil one.

New Law of Retaliation

"You have heard the commandment, 'An eye for an eye. a tooth for a tooth.' But what I say to you is: offer no resistance to injury. When a person strikes you on the right cheek, turn and offer him the other. If anyone wants to go to law over your shirt, hand him your coat as well. Should anyone press you into service for one mile, go with him two miles. Give to the man who begs from you. Do not turn your back on the borrower.

Love of Enemies

"You have heard the commandment, 'You shall love your countryman but hate your enemy.' My command to you is: love your enemies, pray for your persecutors. This will prove that you are sons of your heavenly Father, for his sun rises on the bad and the good, he rains on the just and the unjust. If you love those who love you, what merit is there in that? Do not tax collectors do as much? And if you greet your brothers only, what is so praiseworthy about that? Do not pagans do as much? In a word, you must be made perfect as your heavenly Father is perfect.

6 Purity of Intention

"Be on guard against performing religious acts for people to see. Otherwise expect no recompense from your heavenly Father. When you give alms, for example, do not blow a horn before you in synagogues and streets like hypocrites looking for applause. You can be sure of this much, they are already repaid. In giving alms you are not to let your left hand know what your right hand is doing. Keep your deeds of mercy secret, and your Father who sees in secret will repay you.

Prayer

"When you are praying, do not behave like the hypocrites who love to stand and pray in synagogues or on street corners in order to be noticed. I give you my word, they are already repaid. Whenever you pray, go to your room, close your door, and pray to your Father in private. Then your Father, who sees what no man sees, will repay you. In your prayer do not rattle on like the pagans. They think they will win a hearing by the sheer multiplication of words. Do not imitate them. Your Father knows what you need before you as him. This is how you are to pray:

> 'Our Father in heaven,
> hallowed be your name,
> your kingdom come,
> your will be done
> on earth as it is in heaven.
> Give us today our daily bread,
> and forgive us the wrong we have done
> as we forgive those who wrong us.
> Subject us not to the trial
> but deliver us from the evil one.'

"If you forgive the faults of others, your heavenly Father will forgive you yours. If you do not forgive others, neither will your Father forgive you.

Fasting

"When you fast, you are not to look glum as the hypocrites do. They change the appearance of their faces so that others may see they are fasting. I assure you, they are already repaid. When you fast, see to it that you groom your hair and wash your face. In that way no one can see you are fasting but your Father who is hidden; and your Father who sees what is hidden will repay you.

True Riches

"Do not lay up for yourselves an earthly treasure. Moths and rust corrode; thieves break in and steal. Make it your practice instead to store up heavenly treasure, which neither moths nor rust corrode nor thieves break in and steal. Remember, where your treasure is, there your heart is also. The eye is the body's lamp. If your eyes are good, your body will be filled with light; if your eyes are bad, your body will be in darkness. And if your light is darkness, how deep will the darkness be! No man can serve two masters. He will either hate one and love the other or be attentive to one and despise the other. You cannot give yourself to God and money. I warn you, then: do not worry about your livelihood, what you are to eat or drink or use for clothing. Is not life more than food? Is not the body more valuable than clothes?

"Look at the birds in the sky. They do not sow or reap, they gather nothing into barns: yet your heavenly Father feeds them. Are not you more important than they? Which of you by worrying can add a moment to his life-span? As for clothes, why be concerned? Learn a lesson from the way the wild flowers grow. They do not work; they do not spin. Yet I assure you, not even Solomon in all his splendor was arrayed like one of these. If God can clothe in such splendor the grass of the field, which blooms today and is thrown on the fire tomorrow, will he not provide much more for you, O weak in faith! Stop worrying, then, over questions like, 'What are we to eat, or what are we to drink, or what are we to wear?' The unbelievers are always running after these things. Your heavenly Father knows all that you need. Seek first his kingship over you, his way of holiness, and all these things will be given you besides. Enough, then, of worrying about tomorrow. Let tomorrow take care of itself. Today has troubles enough of its own.

7 Avoiding Judgment

"If you want to avoid judgment, stop passing judgment. Your verdict on others will be the verdict passed on you. The measure with which you measure will be used to measure you. Why look at the speck in your brother's eye when you miss the plank in your own? How can you say to your brother, 'Let me take that speck out of your eye,' while all the time the plank remains in your own? You hypocrite! Remove the plank from your own eye first; then you will see clearly to take the speck from your brother's eye.

"Do not give what is holy to dogs or toss your pearls before swine. They will trample them under foot, at best, and perhaps even tear you to shreds.

The Power of Prayer

"Ask, and you will receive. Seek, and you will find. Knock, and it will be opened to you. For the one who asks, receives. The one who seeks, finds. The one who knocks, enters. Would one of you hand his son a stone when he asks for a loaf, or a poisonous snake when he asks for a fish? If you, with all your sins, know how to give your children what is good, how much more will your heavenly Father give good things to anyone who asks him!

The Golden Rule

"Treat others the way you would have them treat you: this sums up the law and the prophets.

"Enter through the narrow gate. The gate that leads to damnation is wide, the road is clear, and many choose to travel it. But how narrow is the gate that leads to life, how rough the road, and how few there are who find it!

"Be on your guard against false prophets, who come to you in sheep's clothing but underneath are wolves on the prowl. You will know them by their deeds. Do you ever pick grapes from thornbushes, or figs from prickly plants? Never! Any sound tree bears good fruit, while a decayed tree bears bad fruit. A sound tree cannot bear bad fruit any more than a decayed tree can bear good fruit. Every tree that does not bear fruit is cut down and thrown into the fire. You can tell a tree by its fruit. None of those who cry out, 'Lord, Lord,' will enter the kingdom of God but only the one who does the will of my Father in heaven. When that day comes, many will plead with me, 'Lord, Lord, have we not prophesied in your name? Have we not exorcised demons by its power? Did we not do many miracles in your name as well?' Then I will declare to them solemnly, 'I never knew you. Out of my sight, you evildoers!'

Conclusion of the Sermon

"Anyone who hears my words and puts them into practice is like the wise man who built his house on rock. When the rainy season set in, the torrents came and the winds blew and buffeted his house. It did not collapse; it had been solidly set on rock. Anyone who hears my words but does not put them into practice is like the foolish man who built his house on sandy ground. The rains fell, the torrents came, the winds blew and lashed against his house. It collapsed under all this and was completely ruined."

Jesus finished this discourse and left the crowds spellbound at his teaching. The reason was that he taught with authority and not like their scribes.

Matthew 22–25

22 The Wedding Banquet

Jesus began to address them, once more using parables. "The reign of God may be likened to a king who gave a wedding banquet for his son. He dispatched his servants to summon the invited guests to the wedding, but they refused to come. A second time he sent other servants, saying: Tell those who were invited, See, I have my dinner prepared! My bullocks and corn-fed cattle are killed; everything is ready. Come to the feast.' Some ignored the invitation and went their way, one to his farm, another to his business. The rest laid hold of his servants, insulted them, and killed them. At this the king grew furious and sent his army to destroy those murderers and burn their city. Then he said to his servants: 'The banquet is ready, but those who were invited were unfit to come. That is why you must go out into the byroads and invite to the wedding anyone you come upon.' The servants then went out into the byroads and rounded up everyone they met, bad as well as good. This filled the wedding hall with banqueters.

"When the king came in to meet the guests, however, he caught sight of a man not properly dressed for a wedding feast. 'My friend,' he said, 'how is it you came in here not properly dressed?' The man had nothing to say. The king then said to the attendants, 'Bind him hand and foot and throw him out into the night to wail and grind his teeth.' The invited are many, the elect are few."

Paying Tax to the Emperor

Then the Pharisees went off and began to plot how they might trap Jesus in speech. They sent their disciples to him, accompanied by Herodian sympathizers, who said: "Teacher, we know you are a truthful man and teach God's way sincerely. You court no one's favor and do not act out of human respect. Give us your opinion, then, in this case. Is it lawful to pay tax to the emperor or not?" Jesus recognized their bad faith and said to them, "Why are you trying to trip me up, you hypocrites? Show me the coin used for the tax." When they handed him a small Roman coin he asked them, "Whose head is this, and whose inscription?" "Caesar's," they replied. At that he said to them, "Then give to Caesar what is Caesar's, but give to God what is God's." Taken aback by this reply, they went off and left him.

The Sadducees and the Resurrection

That same day some Sadducees, who hold there is no resurrection, came to him with a question: "Teacher, Moses declared, 'If a man dies without children. his brother must take the wife and produce offspring for his brother.' Once there were seven brothers. The eldest died after marrying, and since he had no children, left his wife to his brother. The same thing happened to the second, the third, and so on, down to the seventh. Last of all the woman died too. At the resurrection, whose wife will she be, since all seven of them married her?" Jesus replied: "You are badly misled because you fail to understand the Scriptures and the power of God. When people rise from the dead, they neither marry nor are given in marriage but live like angels in heaven. As to the fact that the dead are raised, have you not read what God said to you,

> 'I am the God of Abraham, the God of Isaac,
> the God of Jacob'?

He is the God of the living, not of the dead." The crowds who listened were spellbound by his teaching.

The Great Commandment

When the Pharisees heard that he had silenced the Sadducees, they assembled in a body; and one of them, a lawyer, in an attempt to trip him up, asked him, "Teacher, which commandment of the law is the greatest?" Jesus said to him:

> "'You shall love the Lord your God
> with your whole heart,
> with your whole soul,
> and with all your mind.'

This is the greatest and first commandment. The second is like it:

> 'You shall love your neighbor as yourself.'

On these two commandments the whole law is based, and the prophets as well."

The Son of David

"In turn Jesus put a question to the assembled Pharisees, "What is your opinion about the Messiah? Whose son is he?" "David's," they answered. "He said to them, "Then how is it that David under the Spirit's influence calls him 'lord' as he does:

'The Lord said to my lord, Sit at my right hand,
until I humble your enemies beneath your feet'?

If David calls him 'lord,' how can he be his son?" No one could give him answer; therefore no one dared, from that day on, to ask him any questions.

23 Hypocrisy of the Scribes and Pharisees

Then Jesus told the crowds and his disciples: "The scribes and the Pharisees have succeeded Moses as teachers; therefore, do everything and observe everything they tell you. But do not follow their example. Their words are bold but their deeds are few. They bind up heavy loads, hard to carry, to lay on other men's shoulders, while they themselves will not lift a finger to budge them. All their works are performed to be seen. They widen their phylacteries and wear huge tassels. They are fond of places of honor at banquets and the front seats in synagogues, of marks of respect in public and of being called 'Rabbi.' As to you, avoid the title 'Rabbi.' One among you is your teacher, the rest are learners. Do not call anyone on earth your father. Only one is your father, the One in heaven. Avoid being called teachers. Only one is your teacher, the Messiah. The greatest among you will be the one who serves the rest. Whoever exalts himself shall be humbled, but whoever humbles himself shall be exalted.

"Woe to you scribes and Pharisees, you frauds! You shut the doors of the kingdom of God in men's faces, neither entering yourselves nor admitting those who are trying to enter. Woe to you scribes and Pharisees, you frauds! You travel over sea and land to make a single convert, but once he is converted you make a devil of him twice as wicked as yourselves. It is an evil day for you, blind guides! You declare, 'If a man swears by the temple it means nothing, but if he swears by the gold of the temple he is obligated.' "Blind fools! Which is more important, the gold or the temple which makes it sacred? Again you declare, 'If a man swears by the altar it means nothing, but if he swears by the gift on the altar he is obligated.' How blind you are! Which is more important, the offering or the altar which makes the offering sacred? The man who swears by the altar is swearing by it and by everything on it. The man who swears by the temple is swearing by it and by him who dwells there. The man who swears by heaven is swearing by God's throne and by him who is seated on that throne. Woe to you scribes and Pharisees, you frauds! You pay tithes on mint and herbs and seeds while neglecting the weightier matters of the law, justice and mercy and good faith. It is these you should have practiced, without neglecting the others.

"Blind guides! You strain out the gnat and swallow the camel! Woe to you scribes and Pharisees, you frauds! You cleanse the outside of cup and dish, and leave the inside filled with loot and lust! Blind Pharisee! First cleanse the inside of the cup so that its outside may be clean. Woe to you scribes and Pharisees, you frauds! You are like whitewashed tombs, beautiful to look at on the outside but inside full of filth and dead men's bones. Thus you present to view a holy exterior while hypocrisy and evil fill you within. Woe to you scribes and Pharisees, you frauds! You erect tombs for the prophets and decorate the monuments of the saints. You say, 'Had we lived in our forefathers' time we would not have joined them in shedding the prophets' blood.' Thus you show that you are the sons of the prophets' murderers. Now it is your turn: fill up the vessel measured out by your forefathers. Vipers' nest? Brood of serpents! How can you escape condemnation to Gehenna? For this reason I shall send you prophets and wise men and scribes. Some you will kill and crucify, others you will flog in your synagogues and hunt down from city to city; until retribution overtakes you for all the blood of the just ones shed on earth, from the blood of holy Abel to the blood of Zechariah son of Barachiah, whom you murdered between the temple building and the altar. All this, I assure you, will be the fate of the present generation. O Jerusalem, Jerusalem, murderess of prophets and stoner of those who were sent to you! How often have I yearned to gather your children, as a mother bird gathers her young under her wings, but you refused me. Recall the saying, 'You will find your temple deserted.' I tell you, you will not see me from this time on until you declare, 'Blessed is he who comes in the name of the Lord!'"

24 Beginning of Calamities

Jesus left the temple precincts then, and his disciples came up and pointed out to him the buildings of the temple area. His comment was: "Do you see all these buildings? I assure you, not one stone will be left on another—it will all be torn down. While he was seated on the Mount of Olives, his disciples came up to him privately and said: "Tell us, when will all this occur? What will be the sign of your coming and the end of the world?" In reply Jesus said to them: "Be on guard! Let no one mislead you. Many will come attempting to impersonate me. 'I am the Messiah!' they will claim, and they will deceive many. You will hear of wars and rumors of wars. Do not be alarmed. Such things are bound to happen, but that is not yet the end. Nation will rise against nation, one kingdom against another. There will be famine and pestilence and earthquakes in many places. These are the early stages of the birth pangs. They will hand you over to torture and kill you. Indeed, you will be hated by all nations on my account. Many will falter then, betraying and hating one another. False prophets will rise in great numbers to mislead many. Because of the increase of evil, the love of most will grow cold. The man who holds out to the end, however, is the one who will see salvation. This good news of the kingdom will be proclaimed throughout the world as a witness to all the nations. Only after that will the end come.

The Final Test

"When you see the abominable and destructive thing which the prophet Daniel foretold standing on holy ground (let the reader take note!), those in Judea must flee to the mountains. If a man is on the roof terrace, he must not come down to get anything out of his house. If a man is in the field, he must not turn back to pick up his cloak. It will be hard on pregnant or nursing mothers in those days. Keep praying that you will not have to flee in winter or on a sabbath, for those days will be more filled with anguish than any from the beginning of the world until now or in all ages to come. Indeed, if the period had not been shortened, not a human being would be saved. For the sake of the chosen, however, the days will be shortened. If anyone tells you at that time, 'Look, the Messiah is here,' or 'He is there,' do not believe it. False messiahs and false prophets will appear, performing signs and wonders so great as to mislead even the chosen if that were possible. Remember, I have told you all about it beforehand; so if they tell you, 'Look, he is in the desert,' do not go out there; or 'He is in the innermost rooms,' do not believe it. As the lightning from the east flashes to the west, so will the coming of the Son of Man be. Where the carcass lies, there the vultures gather.

Coming of the Son of Man

"Immediately after the stress of that period, 'the sun will be darkened, the moon will not shed her light, the stars will fall from the sky, and the hosts of heaven will be shaken loose.' Then the sign of the Son of Man will appear in the sky, and 'all the clans of earth will strike their breasts' as they see 'the Son of Man coming on the clouds of heaven' with power and great glory. He will dispatch his angels 'with a mighty trumpet blast, and they will assemble his chosen from the four winds, from one end of the heavens to the other.' From the fig tree learn a lesson. When its branch grows tender and sprouts leaves, you realize that summer is near. Likewise, when you see all these things happening, you will know that he is near, standing at your door. I assure you, the present generation will not pass away until all this takes place. The heavens and the earth will pass away but my words will not pass.

The Need or Watchfulness

"As for the exact day or hour, no one knows it, neither the angels in heaven nor the Son, but the Father only. The coming of the Son of Man will repeat what happened in Noah's time. In the days before the flood people were eating and drinking, marrying and being married, right up to the day Noah entered the ark. They were totally unconcerned until the flood came and destroyed them. So will it be at the coming of the Son of Man. Two men will be out in the field; one will be taken and one will be left. Two woman will be grinding meal; one will be taken and one will be left. Stay awake, therefore! You cannot know the day your Lord is coming.

"Be sure of this: if the owner of the house knew when the thief was coming he would keep a watchful eye and not allow his house to be broken into. You must be prepared in the same way. The Son of Man is coming at the time you least expect. Who is the faithful, farsighted servant whom the master has put in charge of his household to dispense food at need? Happy that servant whom his master discovers at work on his return! I assure you, he will put him in charge of all his property. But if the servant is worthless and tells himself, 'My master is a long time in coming,' and begins to beat his fellow servants, to eat and drink with drunkards, that man's master will return when he is not ready and least expects him. He will punish him severely and settle with him as is done with hypocrites. There will be wailing then and grinding of teeth.

25 Parable of the Ten Virgins

"The reign of God can be likened to ten bridesmaids who took their torches and went out to welcome the groom. Five of them were foolish, while the other five were sensible. The foolish ones, in taking their torches, brought no oil along, but the sensible ones took flasks of oil as well as their torches. The groom delayed his coming, so they all began to nod, then to fall asleep. At midnight someone shouted, 'The groom is here! Come out and greet him!' At the outcry all the virgins woke up and got their torches ready. The foolish ones said to the sensible, 'Give us some of your oil. Our torches are going out.' But the sensible ones replied, 'No, there may not be enough for you and us. You had better go to the dealers and buy yourselves some.' While they went off to buy it the groom arrived, and the ones who were ready went in to the wedding with him. Then the door was barred. Later the other bridesmaids came back. 'Master, master!' they cried. 'Open the door for us.' But he answered, 'I tell you, I do not know you.' The moral is: keep your eyes open, for you know not the day or the hour.

Parable of the Silver Pieces

"The case of a man who was going on a journey is similar. He called in his servants and handed his funds over to them according to each man's abilities. To one he disbursed five thousand silver pieces, to a second two thousand, and to a third a thousand. Then he went away. Immediately the man who received the five thousand went to invest it and made another five. In the same way, the man who received the two thousand doubled his figure. The man who received the thousand went off instead and dug a hole in the ground, where he buried his master's money. After a long absence, the master of those servants came home and settled accounts with them. The man who had received the five thousand came forward bringing the additional five. 'My lord,' he said, 'you let me have five thousand. See, I have made five thousand more.' His master said to him, 'Well done! You are an industrious and reliable servant. Since you were dependable in a small matter I will put you in charge of larger affairs. Come, share your master's joy!' The man who had received the two thousand then stepped forward. 'My lord,' he said, 'you entrusted me with two thousand and I have made two thousand more.' His master said to him, 'Cleverly done! You too are an industrious and reliable servant. Since you were dependable in a small matter I will put you in charge of larger affairs. Come, share your master's joy!'

"Finally the man who had received the thousand stepped forward. 'My lord,' he said, 'I knew you were a hard man. You reap where you did not sow and gather where you did not scatter, so out of fear I went of and buried your thousand silver pieces in the ground. Here is your money back.' His master exclaimed: 'You worthless, lazy lout! You know I reap where I did not sow and gather where I did not scatter. All the more reason to deposit my money with the bankers, so that on my return I could have had it back with interest. You, there! Take the thousand away from him and give it to the man with the ten thousand. Those who have will get more until they grow rich, while those who have not will lose even the little they have. Throw this worthless servant into the darkness outside, where he can wail and grind his teeth.

The Last Judgment

"When the Son of Man comes in his glory, escorted by all the angels of heaven, he will sit upon his royal throne, and all the nations will be assembled before him. Then he will separate them into two groups, as a shepherd separates sheep from goats. The sheep he will place on his right hand, the goats on his left. The king will say to those on his right: 'Come. You have my Father's blessing! Inherit the kingdom prepared for you from the creation of the world. For I was hungry and you gave me food, I was thirsty and you gave me drink. I was a stranger and you welcomed me, naked and you clothed me. I was ill and you comforted me, in prison and you came to visit me.' Then the just will ask him: 'Lord, when did we see you hungry and feed you or see you thirsty and give you drink? When did we welcome you away from home or clothe you in your nakedness? When did we visit you when you were ill or in prison?' The king will answer them: 'I assure you, as often as you did it for one of my least brothers, you did it for me.'

"Then he will say to those on his left: 'Out of my sight, you condemned, into that everlasting fire prepared for the devil and his angels! I was hungry and you gave me no food, I was thirsty and you gave me no drink. I was away from home and you gave me no welcome, naked and you gave me no clothing. I was ill and in prison and you did not come to comfort me.' Then they in turn will ask: 'Lord, when did we see you hungry or thirsty or away from home or naked, or ill or in prison and not attend you in your needs?' He will answer them: 'I assure you, as often as you neglected to do it to one of these least ones, you neglected to do it to me.' These will go off to eternal punishment and the just to eternal life."

Luke 6

The Disciples and the Sabbath

O nce on a sabbath Jesus was walking through the standing grain. His disciples were pulling off grain-heads, shelling them with their hands, and eating them. Some of the Pharisees asked, "Why are you doing what is prohibited on the sabbath?" Jesus said to them: "Have you not read what David did when he and his men were hungry—how he entered God's house and took and ate the holy bread and gave it to his men, even though only priests are allowed to eat it?" Then he said to them, "The Son of Man is Lord even of the sabbath."

On another sabbath he came to teach in a synagogue where there was a man whose right hand was withered. The scribes and Pharisees were on the watch to see if he would perform a cure on the sabbath so that they could find a charge against him. He knew their thoughts, however, and said to the man whose hand was withered, Get up and stand here in front. The man rose and remained standing. Jesus said to them, "I ask you, is it lawful to do good on the sabbath—or evil? To preserve life—or destroy it?"

He looked around at them all and said to the man, "Stretch out your hand." The man did so and his hand was perfectly restored.

At this they became frenzied and began asking one another what could be done to Jesus.

Choice of the Twelve

Then he went out to the mountain to pray, spending the night in communion with God. At daybreak he called his disciples and selected twelve of them to be his apostles: Simon, to whom he gave the name Peter, and Andrew his brother, James and John, Philip and Bartholomew, Matthew and Thomas, James son of Alphaeus, and Simon called the Zealot, Judas son of James, and Judas Iscariot, who turned traitor.

The Great Discourse

Coming down the mountain with them, he stopped at a level stretch where there were many of his disciples; a large crowd of people was with them from all Judea and Jerusalem and the coast of Tyre and Sidon, people who came to hear him and be healed of their diseases. Those who were troubled with unclean spirits were cured; indeed, the whole crowd was trying to touch him because power went out from him which cured all. Then, raising his eyes to his disciples, he said:

> "Blest are you poor; the reign of God is yours.
> Blest are you who hunger; you shall be filled.
> Blest are you who are weeping; you shall laugh.

"Blest shall you be when men hate you, when they ostracize you and insult you and proscribe your name as evil because of the Son of Man. On the day they do so, rejoice and exult, for your reward shall be great in heaven. Thus it was that their fathers treated the prophets.

> "But woe to you rich, for your consolation is now.
> Woe to you who are full; you shall go hungry.
> Woe to you who laugh now; you shall weep in your grief.

"Woe to you when all speak well of you. Their fathers treated the false prophets in just this way.

Love of One's Enemy

"To you who hear me, I say: Love your enemies, do good to those who hate you; bless those who curse you and pray for those who maltreat you. When someone slaps you on one cheek, turn and give him the other; when someone takes your coat, let him have your shirt as well. Give to all who beg from you. When a man takes what is yours, do not demand it back. Do to others what you would have them do to you. If you love those who love you, what credit is that to you? Even sinners love those who love them. If you do good to those who do good to you, how can you claim any credit? Sinners do as much. If you lend to those from whom you expect repayment, what merit is there in it for you? Even sinners lend to sinners, expecting to be repaid in full.

"Love your enemy and do good; lend without expecting repayment. Then will your recompense be great. You will rightly be called sons of the Most High, since he himself is good to the ungrateful and the wicked.

"Be compassionate, as your Father is compassionate. Do not judge, and you will not be judged. Do not condemn, and you will not be condemned. Pardon, and you shall be pardoned. Give, and it shall be given to you. Good measure pressed down, shaken together, running over, will they pour into the fold of your garment. For the measure you measure with will be measured back to you."

He also used images in speaking to them: "Can a blind man act as guide to a blind man? Will they not both fall into a ditch? A student is not above his teacher; but every student when he has finished his studies will be on a par with his teacher."

"Why look at the speck in your brother's eye when you miss the plank in your own? How can you say to your brother, 'Brother, let me remove the speck from your eye,' yet fail yourself to see the plank lodged in your own? Hypocrite, remove the plank from your own eye first; then you will see clearly enough to remove the speck from your brother's eye."

"A good tree does not produce decayed fruit any more than a decayed tree produces good fruit. Each tree is known by its yield. Figs are not taken from thornbushes, nor grapes picked from brambles. A good man produces goodness from the good in his heart; an evil man produces evil out of his store of evil. Each man speaks from his heart's abundance. Why do you call me 'Lord, Lord,' and not put into practice what I teach you? Any man who desires to come to me will hear my words and put them into practice. I will show you with whom he is to be compared. He may be likened to the man who, in building a house, dug deeply and laid the foundation on a rock. When the floods came the torrent rushed in on that house, but failed to shake it because of its solid foundation. On the other hand, anyone who has heard my words but not put them into practice is like the man who built his house on the ground without any foundation. When the torrent rushed upon it, it immediately fell in and was completely destroyed."

John 14–16

14 Last Discourse

"**D**o not let your hearts be troubled.
Have faith in God
and faith in me.
In my Father's house there are many dwelling places;
otherwise, how could I have told you
that I was going to prepare a place for you?

I am indeed going to prepare a place for you,
and then I shall come back to take you with me,
that where I am you also may be.
You know the way that leads where I go."

"Lord," said Thomas, "we do not know where you are going. How can we know the way?" Jesus told him:

"I am the way, and the truth, and the life;
no one comes to the Father but through me.
If you really knew me, you would know my Father also.
From this point on you know him; you have seen him."

"Lord," Philip said to him, show us the Father and that will be enough for us," "Philip," Jesus replied, "after I have been with you all this time, you still do not know me?

"Whoever has seen me has seen the Father.
How can you say, 'Show us the Father'?
Do you not believe that I am in the Father
and the Father is in me?
The words I speak are not spoken of myself;
it is the Father who lives in me accomplishing his works.
Believe me that I am in the Father
and the Father is in me,
or else, believe because of the works I do.
I solemnly assure you,
the man who has faith in me
will do the works I do,
and greater far than these.
Why? Because I go to the Father,
and whatever you ask in my name
I will do,
so as to glorify the Father in the Son.
Anything you ask me in my name
I will do.
If you love me
and obey the command I give you,
I will ask the Father
and he will give you another
    Paraclete—

to be with you always:
the Spirit of truth,
whom the world cannot accept,
since it neither sees him nor
    recognizes him;
but you can recognize him
because he remains with you
and will be within you.
I will not leave you orphaned;
I will come back to you.
A little while now and the world will see me no more;
but you see me
as one who has life, and you will have life.
On that day you will know
that I am in my Father,
and you in me, and I in you.
He who obeys the commandments he has from me
is the man who loves me;
and he who loves me will be loved by my Father.
I too will love him
and reveal myself to him."

Judas (not Judas Iscariot) said to him, "Lord, why is it that you will reveal yourself to us and not to the world?" Jesus answered:

"Anyone who loves me
will be true to my word,
and my Father will love him;
we will come to him
and make our dwelling place with him.
He who does not love me does not keep my words.
Yet the word you hear is not mine;
it comes from the Father who sent me.
This much have I told you while I was still with you;
the Paraclete, the Holy Spirit
whom the Father will send in my name,
will instruct you in everything,
and remind you of all that I told you.
'Peace' is my farewell to you,
my peace is my gift to you;

I do not give it to you as the world gives peace.
Do not be distressed or fearful.
You have heard me say,
'I go away for a while, and I come back to you.'
If you truly loved me
you would rejoice to have me go to the Father,
for the Father is greater than I.
I tell you this now, before it takes place,
so that when it takes place you may believe.
I shall not go on speaking to you longer;
the Prince of this world is at hand.
He has no hold on me,
but the world must know that I love the Father
and do as the Father has commanded me.
Come, then! Let us be on our way.

15 The Vine and the Branches

"I am the true vine
and my Father is the vinegrower.
He prunes away
every barren branch,
but the fruitful ones
he trims clean
to increase their yield.
You are clean already,
thanks to the word I have spoken to you.
Live on in me, as I do in you.
No more than a branch can bear fruit of itself
apart from the vine,
can you bear fruit
apart from me.
I am the vine, you are the branches.
He who lives in me and I in him,
will produce abundantly,
for apart from me you can do nothing.
A man who does not live in me
is like a withered, rejected branch,
picked up to be thrown in the fire and burnt.
If you live in me,

and my words stay part of you,
you may ask what you will—
it will be done for you.
My Father has been glorified
in your bearing much fruit
and becoming my disciples.

A Disciple's Love

"As the Father has loved me,
so I have loved you.
Live on in my love.
You will live in my love
if you keep my commandments,
even as I have kept my Father's commandments,
and live in his love.
All this I tell you
that my joy may be yours
and your joy may be complete.
This is my commandment:
love one another
as I have loved you.
There is no greater love than this:
to lay down one's life for one's friends.
You are my friends
if you do what I command you.
I no longer speak of you as slaves,
for a slave does not know what his master is about.
Instead, I call you friends,
since I have made known to you all that I heard from my Father.
It was not you who chose me,
it was I who chose you
to go forth and bear fruit.
Your fruit must endure,

The World's Hate

"If you find that the world hates you,
know it has hated me before you.
If you belonged to the world,
it would love you as its own;
the reason it hates you
is that you do not belong to the world.
But I chose you out of the world.
Remember what I told you:
no slave is greater than his master.
They will harry you
as they harried me.
They will respect your words
as much as they respected mine.
All this they will do to you because of my name,
for they know nothing of him who sent me.
If I had not come to them and spoken to them,
they would not be guilty of sin;
now, however, their sin cannot be excused.
To hate me is to hate my Father.
Had I not performed such works among them
as no one has ever done before,
they would not be guilty of sin;
but as it is, they have seen,
and they go on hating me and my Father.
However, this only fulfills the text in their law:
'They hated me without cause.'
When the Paraclete comes.
the Spirit of truth who comes from the Father—
and whom myself will send from the Father—
he will bear witness on my behalf.
You must bear witness as well,
for you have been with me from the beginning.

16

"I have told you all this
to keep your faith from being shaken.

Not only will they expel you from synagogues;
a time will come
when anyone who puts you to death
will claim to be serving God!
All this they will do [to you]
because they knew neither the Father nor me.
But I have told you these things
that when their hour comes
you may remember my telling you of them.

Jesus' Departure; Coming of the Paraclete

"I did not speak of this with you from the beginning
because I was with you.
Now that I go back to him who sent me,
not one of you asks me, 'Where are you going?'
Because I have had all this to say to you,
you are overcome with grief.
Yet I tell you the sober truth:
It is much better for you that I go.
If I fail to go,
the Paraclete will never come to you,
whereas if I go,
I will send him to you.
When he comes,
he will prove the world wrong
about sin,
about justice,
about condemnation.

Romans 6–7

6 Death to Sin, Life in God

What, then, are we to say? "Let us continue in sin that grace may abound"? Certainly not! How can we who died to sin go on living in it? Are you not aware that we who were baptized into Christ Jesus were baptized into his death? Through baptism into his death we were buried with him, so that, just as Christ was raised from the dead by the glory of the Father, we too might live a new life. If we have been united with him through likeness to his death, so shall we be through a like resurrection. This we know: our old self was crucified with him so that the sinful body might be destroyed and we might be slaves to sin no longer. A man who is dead has been freed from sin. If we have died with Christ, we believe that we are also to live with him. We know that Christ, once raised from the dead, will never die again; death has no more power over him. His death was death to sin, once for all; his life is life for God. In the same way, you must consider yourselves dead to sin but alive for God in Christ Jesus.

Do not, therefore, let sin rule your mortal body and make you obey its lusts; no more shall you offer the members of your body to sin as weapons for evil. Rather, offer yourselves to God as men who have come back from the dead to life, and your bodies to God as weapons for justice. Sin will no longer have power over you; you are now under grace, not under the law.

What does all this lead to? Just because we are not under the law but under grace, are we free to sin? By no means! You must realize that, when you offer yourselves to someone as obedient slaves, you are the slaves of the one you obey, whether yours is the slavery of sin, which leads to death, or of obedience, which leads to justice. Thanks be to God, though once you were slaves of sin, you sincerely obeyed that rule of teaching which was imparted to you; freed from your sin, you became slaves of justice. (I use the following example from human affairs because of your weak human nature.) Just as formerly you enslaved your bodies to impurity and licentiousness for their degradation, make them now the servants of justice for their sanctification. When you were slaves of sin, you had freedom from justice. What benefit did you then enjoy? Things you are now ashamed of, all of them tending toward death. But now that you are freed from sin and have become slaves of God, your benefit is sanctification as you tend toward eternal life. The wages of sin is death, but the gift of God is eternal life in Christ Jesus our Lord.

7 Freedom from the Law

Are you not aware, my brothers (I am speaking to men who know what law is), that the law has power over a man only so long as he lives? For example, a married woman is bound to her husband by law while he lives, but if he dies she is delivered from the law regarding husband. She will be called an adulteress if, while her husband is still alive, she gives herself to another. But if her husband dies she is freed from that law, and does not commit adultery by consorting with another man. In the same way, my brothers, you died to the law through the body of Christ, that you might belong to that Other who was raised from the dead, so that we might bear fruit for God. When we were in the flesh, the sinful passions roused by the law worked in our members and we bore fruit for death.

Now we have been released from the law—for we have died to what bound us—and we serve in the new spirit, not the antiquated letter.

Knowledge of Sin through the Law

What follows from what I have said? That the law is the same as sin? Certainly not! Yet it was only through the law that I came to know sin. I should never have known what evil desire was unless the law had said, "You shall not covet." Sin seized that opportunity: it used the commandment to rouse in me every kind of evil desire. Without law sin is dead, and at first I lived without law. Then the commandment came; with it sin came to life, and I died. The commandment that should have led to life brought me death. Sin found its opportunity and used the commandment: first to deceive me, then to kill me. Yet the law is holy and the commandment is holy and just and good.

Sin and Death

Did this good thing then become death for me? Not that either! Rather, sin, in order to be seen clearly as sin, used what was good to bring about my death. It did so that, by misusing the commandment, sin might go to the limit of sinfulness. We know that the law is spiritual, whereas I am weak flesh sold into the slavery of sin. I cannot even understand my own actions. I do not do what I want to do but what I hate. When I act against my own will, by that very fact I agree that the law is good. This indicates that it is not I who do it but sin which resides in me. I know that no good dwells in me, that is in my flesh; the desire to do right is there but not the power. What happens is that I do, not the good I will to do, but the evil I do not intend. But if I do what is against my will, it is not I who do it, but sin which dwells in me. This means that even though I want to do what is right, a law that leads to wrongdoing is always ready at hand. My inner self agrees with the law of God, but I see in my body's members another law at war with the law of my mind; this makes me the prisoner of the law of sin in my members. What a wretched man I am! Who can free me from this body under the power of death? All praise to God, through Jesus Christ our Lord! So with my mind I serve the law of God but with my flesh the law of sin.

I Corinthians 13–15:44

13 Excellence of the Gift of Love

N ow I will show you the way which surpasses all the others. If I speak with human tongues and angelic as well, but do not have love, I am a noisy gong, a clanging cymbal. If I have the gift of prophecy and, with full knowledge, comprehend all mysteries, if I have faith great enough to move mountains but have not love, I am nothing. If I give everything I have to feed the poor and hand over my body to be burned, but have not love, I gain nothing.

Love is patient; love is kind. Love is not jealous, it does not put on airs, it is not snobbish. Love is never rude, it is not self-seeking, it is not prone to anger; neither does it brood over injuries. Love does not rejoice in what is wrong but rejoices with the truth. There is no limit to love's forbearance, to its trust, its hope, its power to endure.

Love never fails. Prophecies will cease, tongues will be silent, knowledge will pass away. Our knowledge is imperfect and our prophesying is imperfect. When the perfect comes, the imperfect will pass away. When I was a child I used to talk like a child, think like a child, reason like a child. When I became a man I put childish ways aside. Now we see indistinctly, as in a mirror; then we shall see face to face. My knowledge is imperfect now; then I shall know even as I am known. There are in the end three things that last: faith, hope, and love, and the greatest of these is love.

14 Gift of Prophecy

Seek eagerly after love. Set your hearts on spiritual gifts—above all, the gift of prophecy. A man who speaks in tongue is talking not to men but to God. No one understands him, because he utters mysteries in the Spirit. The prophet, on the other hand, speaks to men for their upbuilding, their encouragement, their consolation. He who speaks in a tongue builds up himself, but he who prophesies builds up the church. I should like it if all of you spoke in tongues, but I much prefer that you prophesy. The prophet is greater than one who speaks in tongues, unless the speaker can also interpret for the upbuilding of the church.

Interpretation of Tongues

Just suppose, brothers, that I should come to you speaking in tongues. What good will I do you if my speech does not have some revelation, or knowledge, or prophecy, or instruction for you? Even in the case of lifeless things which produce a sound, such as a flute or a harp, how will anyone know what is being played if there is no distinction among the notes? If the bugle's sound is uncertain, who will get ready for battle? Similarly, if you do not utter intelligible speech because you are speaking in a tongue, how will anyone know what you are saying? You will be talking to the air. There are many different languages in the world and all are marked by sound; but if I do not know the meaning, I shall be a foreigner to the speaker and he a foreigner to me. Since you have set your hearts on spiritual gifts, try to be rich in those that build up the church.

This means that the man who speaks in a tongue should pray for the gift of interpretation. If I pray in a tongue my spirit is at prayer but my mind contributes nothing. What is my point here? I want to pray with my spirit, and also to pray with my mind. I want to sing with my spirit and with my mind as well. If your praise of God is solely with the spirit, how will the one who does not comprehend be able to say "Amen" to your thanksgiving? He will not know what you are saying. You will be uttering praise very well indeed, but the other man will not be helped. Thank God, I speak in tongues more than any of you, but in the church I would rather say five intelligible words to instruct others than ten thousand words in a tongue.

Function of These Gifts

Brothers, do not be childish in your outlook. Be like children as far as evil is concerned, but in mind be mature. It is written in the law, "In strange tongues and in alien speech I will speak to this people, and even so they will not heed me, says the Lord." The gift of tongues is a sign, not for those who believe but for those who do not believe, while prophecy is not for those who are without faith but for those who have faith. If the uninitiated or unbelievers should come in when the whole church is assembled and everyone is speaking in tongues, would they not say that you are out of your minds? But if an unbeliever or an uninitiated enters while all are uttering prophecy, he will be taken to task by all and called to account by all, and the secret of his heart will be laid bare. Falling prostrate, he will worship God, crying out, "God is truly among you."

Rules of Order

What do we propose, brothers? When you assemble, one has a psalm, another some instruction to give, still another a revelation to share; one speaks in a tongue, another interprets. All well and good, so long as everything is done with a constrictive purpose. If any are going to talk in tongues let it be at most two or three, each in turn, with another to interpret what they are saying. But if there is no one to interpret, there should be silence in the assembly, each one speaking only to himself and to God. Let no more than two or three prophets speak, and let the rest judge the worth of what they say. If another, sitting by, should happen to receive a revelation, the first ones should then keep quiet. You can all speak your prophecies, but one by one, so that all may be instructed and encouraged. The spirits of the prophets are under the prophets' control, since God is a God, not a confusion, but of peace.

According to the rule observed in all the assemblies of believers, women should keep silent in such gatherings. They may not speak. Rather, as the law states, submissiveness is indicated for them. If they want to learn anything, they should ask their husbands at home. It is a disgrace when a woman speaks in the assembly. Did the preaching of God's word originate with you? Are you the only ones to whom it has come?

If anyone thinks he is a prophet or a man of the Spirit, he should know that what I have written you is the Lord's commandment. If anyone ignores it, he in turn should be ignored. Set your hearts on prophecy, my brothers, and do not forbid those who speak in tongues, but make sure that everything is done properly and in order.

15 Christ's Resurrection

Brothers, I want to remind you of the gospel I preached to you, which you received and in which you stand firm. You are being saved by it at this very moment if you hold fast to it as I preached it to you. Otherwise you have believed in vain. I handed on to you first of all what I myself received, that Christ died for our sins in accordance with the Scriptures; that he was buried and, in accordance with the Scriptures, rose on the third day; that he was seen by Cephas, then by the Twelve. After that he was seen by five hundred brothers at once, most of whom are still alive, although some have fallen asleep. Next he was seen by James; then by all the apostles. Last of all he was seen by me, as one born out of the normal course. I am the least of the apostles; in fact, because I persecuted the church of God, I do not even deserve the name. But by God's favor I am what I am. This favor of his to me has not proved fruitless. Indeed, I have worked harder than all the others, not on my own but through the favor of God. In any case, whether it be I or they, this is what we preach and this is what you believed.

The Resurrection and Faith

Tell me, if Christ is preached as raised from the dead, how is it that some of you say there is no resurrection of the dead? If there is no resurrection of the dead, Christ himself has not been raised. And if Christ has not been raised, our preaching is void of content and your faith is empty too. Indeed, we should then be exposed as false witnesses of God, for we have bore witness before him that he raised up Christ; but he certainly did not raise him up if the dead are not raised. Why? Because if the dead are not raised, then Christ was not raised; and if Christ was not raised, your faith is worthless. You are still in your sins, and those who have fallen asleep in Christ are the deadest of the dead. If our hopes in Christ are limited to this life only, we are the most pitiable of men.

Christ, the First Fruits

But as it is, Christ is now raised from the dead, the first fruits of those who have fallen asleep. Death came through a man: hence the resurrection of the dead comes through a man also. Just as in Adam all die, so in Christ all will come to life again, but each one in proper order: Christ the first fruits and then, at his coming, all those who belong to him. After that will come the end, when, after having destroyed every sovereignty, authority, and power, he will hand over the kingdom to God the Father. Christ must reign until God has put all enemies under his feet, and the last enemy to be destroyed is death. Scripture reads that God "has placed all things under his feet." But when it says that everything has been made subject, it is clear that he who has made everything subject to Christ is excluded. When, finally, all has been subjected to the Son, he will then subject himself to the One who made all things subject to him, so that God may be all in all.

Practical Faith

If the dead are not raised, what about those who have themselves baptized on behalf of the dead? If the raising of the dead is not a reality, why be baptized on their behalf? And why are we continually putting ourselves in danger? I swear to you, brothers, by the very pride you take in me, which I cherish in Christ Jesus our Lord, that I face death every day. If I fought those beasts at Ephesus for purely human motives, what profit was there for me? If the dead are not raised, "Let us eat and drink, for tomorrow we die!" Do not be led astray any longer. "Bad company corrupts good morals." Return to reason, as you ought, and stop sinning. Some of you are quite ignorant of God; I say it to your shame.

Manner of the Resurrection

Perhaps someone will say "How are the dead to be raised up? What kind of body will they have?" A nonsensical question! The seed you sow does not germinate unless it dies. When you sow, you do not sow the full-blown plant, but a kernel of wheat or some other grain. God gives body to it as he pleases—to each seed its own fruition. Not all bodily nature is the same. Men have one kind of body, animals another. Birds are of their kind, fish are of theirs. There are heavenly bodies and there are earthly bodies. The splendor of the heavenly bodies is one thing, that of the earthly another. The sun has a splendor of its own, so has the moon, and the stars have theirs. Even among the stars, one differs from another in brightness. So it is with the resurrection of the dead. What is sown in the earth is subject to decay, what rises is incorruptible. What is sown is ignoble, what rises is glorious. Weakness is sown, strength rises up. A natural body is put down and a spiritual body comes up.

Thessalonians 4–5

4 Chastity and Charity

N ow, my brothers, we beg and exhort you in the Lord Jesus that even as you learned from us how to conduct yourselves in a way pleasing to God—which you are indeed doing—so you must learn to make still greater progress. You know the instructions we gave you in the Lord Jesus. It is God's will that you grow in holiness: that you abstain from immorality, each of you guarding his member in sanctity and honor, not in passionate desire as do the Gentiles who know not God; and that each refrain from overreaching or cheating his brother in the matter at hand; for the Lord is an avenger of all such things, as we once indicated to you by our testimony. God has not called us to immorality but to holiness, hence, whoever rejects these instructions rejects, not man, but God who sends his Holy Spirit upon you.

As regards brotherly love, there is no need for me to write you. God himself has taught you to love one another, and this you are doing with respect to all the brothers throughout Macedonia. Yet we exhort you to even greater progress, brothers. Make it a point of honor to remain at peace and attend to your own affairs. Work with your hands as we directed you to do, so that you will give good example to outsiders and want for nothing.

The Lord's Second Coming
Witnessed by the Dead

We would have you be clear about those who sleep in death, brothers; otherwise you might yield to grief, like those who have no hope. For if we believe that Jesus died and rose, God will bring forth with him from the dead those also who have fallen asleep believing in him. We say to you, as if the Lord himself had said it, that we who live, who survive until his coming, will in no way have an advantage over those who have fallen asleep. No, the Lord himself will come down from heaven at the word of command, at the sound of the archangel's voice and God's trumpet; and those who have died in Christ will rise first. Then we the living, the survivors, will be caught up with them in the clouds to meet the Lord in the air. Thenceforth we shall be with the Lord unceasingly. Console one another with this message.

5 The Need for Preparation

As regards specific times and moments, brothers, we do not need to write you; you know very well that the day of the Lord is coming like a thief in the night. Just when people are saying, "Peace and security," ruin will fall on them with the suddenness of pains overtaking a woman in labor, and there will be no escape. You are not in the dark, brothers, that the day should catch you off guard, like a thief. No, all of you are children of light and of the day. We belong neither to darkness nor to night; therefore let us not be asleep like the rest, but awake and sober! Sleepers sleep by night and drunkards drink by night. We who live by day must be alert, putting on faith and love as a breastplate and the hope of salvation as a helmet, God has not destined us for wrath but for acquiring salvation through our Lord Jesus Christ. He died for us, that all of us, whether awake or asleep, together might live with him. Therefore, comfort and upbuild one another, as indeed you are doing.

Christian Conduct

We beg you, brothers, respect those among you whose task it is to exercise authority in the Lord and admonish you; esteem them with the greatest love because of their work. Remain at peace with one another. We exhort you to admonish the unruly; cheer the fainthearted; support the weak; be patient toward all. See that no one returns evil to any other; always seek one another's good and, for that matter, the good of all.

Rejoice always, never cease praying, render constant thanks; such is God's will for you in Christ Jesus.

Do not stifle the Spirit. Do not despise prophecies. Test everything; retain what is good. Avoid any semblance of evil.

Blessing and Greeting

May the God of peace make you perfect in holiness. May he preserve you whole and entire, spirit, soul, and body, irreproachable at the coming of our Lord Jesus Christ. He who calls us is trustworthy, therefore he will do it.

Brothers pray for us too.

Greet all the brothers with a holy embrace. I adjure you by the Lord that this letter be read to them all.

May the grace of our Lord Jesus Christ be with you.

Revelation 4–6

4 Vision of Heavenly Worship

After this I had another vision: above me there was an open door to heaven, and I heard the trumpetlike voice which had spoken to me before. It said, "Come up here and I will show you what must take place in time to come." At once I was caught up in ecstasy. A throne was standing there in heaven, and on the throne was seated One whose appearance had a gemlike sparkle as of jasper and carnelian. Around the throne was a rainbow as brilliant as emerald. Surrounding this throne were twenty-four other thrones upon which were seated twenty-four elders; they were clothed in white garments and had crowns of gold on their heads. From the throne came flashes of lightning and peals of thunder; before it burned seven flaming torches, the seven spirits of God. The floor around the throne was like a sea of glass that was crystal-clear.

At the very center, around the throne itself, stood four living creatures covered with eyes front and back. The first creature resembled a lion, the second an ox; the third had the face of a man, while the fourth looked like an eagle in flight. Each of the four living creatures had six wings and eyes all over, inside and out.

Day and night, without pause, they sing:
"Holy, holy, holy, is the Lord God Almighty,
He who was, and who is, and who is to come!"

Whenever these creatures give glory and honor and praise to the One seated on the throne, who lives forever and ever, the twenty-four elders fall down before the One seated on the throne, and worship him who lives forever and ever. They throw down their crowns before the throne and sing:

"O Lord our God, you are worthy
to receive glory and honor and power!
For you have created all things;
by your will they came to be and were made!"

5 The Scroll and the Lamb

In the right hand of the One who sat on the throne I saw a scroll. It had writing on both sides and was sealed with seven seals. Then I saw a mighty angel who proclaimed in a loud voice: "Who is worthy to open the scroll and break its seals?" But no one in heaven or on earth or under the earth could be found to open the scroll or examine its contents. I wept bitterly because no one could be found worthy to open or examine the scroll. One of the elders said to me: "Do not weep. The Lion of the tribe of Judah, the Root of David, has won the right by his victory to open the scroll with the seven seals."

Then, between the throne with the four living creatures and the elders, I saw a Lamb standing, a Lamb that had been slain. He had seven horns and seven eyes; these eyes are the seven spirits of God, sent to all parts of the world. The Lamb came and received the scroll from the right hand of the One who sat on the throne. When he had taken the scroll, the four living creatures and the twenty-four elders fell down before the Lamb. Along with their harps, the elders were holding vessels of gold filled with aromatic spices, which were the prayers of God's holy people. This is the new hymn they sang:

> "Worthy are you to receive the scroll and break open its seals,
>> for you were slain.
> With your blood you purchased for God
>> men of every race and tongue,
>> of every people and nation.
> You made of them a kingdom,
>> and priests to serve our God,
>> and they shall reign on the earth."

As my vision continued, I heard the voices of many angels who surrounded the throne and the living creatures and the elders. They were countless in number, thousands and tens of thousands, and they all cried out:

> "Worthy is the Lamb that was slain
>> to receive power and riches,
>>> wisdom and strength,
>>> honor and glory and praise!"

Then I heard the voices of every creature in heaven and on earth and under the earth and in the sea; everything in the universe cried aloud:

> "To the One seated on the throne,
>> and to the Lamb.
> be praise and honor, glory and might,
>> forever and ever!"

The four living creatures answered, "Amen," and the elders fell down and worshiped.

6 The First Six Seals

Then I watched while the Lamb broke open the first of the seven seals, and I heard one of the four living creatures cry out in a voice like thunder, "Come forward!" To my surprise I saw a white horse; its rider had a bow, and he was given a crown. He rode forth victorious, to conquer yet again.

When the Lamb broke open the second seal, I heard the second living creature cry out, "Come forward!" Another horse came forth, a red one. Its rider was given power to rob the earth of peace by allowing men to slaughter one another. For this he was given a huge sword.

When the Lamb broke open the third seal, I heard the third living creature cry out, "Come forward!" This time I saw a black horse, the rider of which held a pair of scales in his hand. I heard what seemed to be a voice coming from in among the four living creatures. It said: "A day's pay for a ration of wheat and the same for three of barley! But spare the olive oil and the wine!"

When the Lamb broke open the fourth seal, I heard the voice of the fourth living creature cry out, "Come forward!" Now I saw a horse sickly green in color. Its rider was named Death, and the nether world was in his train. These four were given authority over one quarter of the earth, to kill with sword and famine and plague and the wild beasts of the earth.

When the Lamb broke open the fifth seal, I saw under the altar the spirits of those who had been martyred because of the witness they bore to the word of God. They cried out at the top of their voices: "How long will it be, O Master, holy and true, before you judge our cause and avenge our blood among the inhabitants of the earth?" Each of the martyrs was given a long white robe, and they were told to be patient a little while longer until the quota was filled of their fellow servants and brothers to be slain, as they had been.

When I saw the Lamb break open the sixth seal, there was a violent earthquake; the sun turned black as a goat's-hair tentcloth and the moon grew red as blood. The stars in the sky fell crashing to earth like figs shaken loose by a nighty wind. Then the sky disappeared as if it were a scroll being rolled up; every mountain and island was uprooted from its base. The kings of the earth, the nobles and those in command, the wealthy and powerful, the slave and the free—all hid themselves in caves and mountain crags. They cried out to the mountains and rocks, Fall on us! Hide us from the face of the One who sits on the throne and from the wrath of the Lamb! The great day of their vengeance has come. Who can withstand it?"

Reflections

The selections from the Hebrew Scriptures, the "Tenakh," or for Christians, the Old Testament, contain a number of paradigmatic stories and genres of literature. Students should reflect on the language and imagery of the passages, how Jews and Christians have come to understand these verses in terms of their "meaning," and how the world views expressed are similar to, or different from, religious world views studied thus far. One could spend hours simply on the Genesis 1 and 2 stories, looking at the process of extracting the meaning and intentionality of the texts. The paradigmatic events of the Exodus story and the language of the Psalms should be looked at in the interpretative context of Jewish and Christian histories. The role of the prophet, prophetic language, and apocalyptic imagery should be investigated in light of the texts. The Song of Songs provides an opportunity for discussion on both the divine/human relationship as envisaged in the Biblical tradition and the implied assumptions about intimacy, sexuality, and gender.

Selections from the New Testament provide materials for looking at the teachings of Jesus: his ethics, his eschatological teachings, his understanding of his relationship to his disciples and to his "Father." The readings lend themselves to discussion of the development of canon and "orthodoxy," the variety of perspectives reflected in Gospels (compare the "Beatitudes" in Matthew and Luke for an understanding of hermeneutics), and the language that informed theological doctrine, reflection, and ritual. Paul's understanding of the Christ event was crucial in the development of Christian thought and practice, and his discussions on sin, death, and baptism form an important exposition of the existential dilemma and its overcoming. Again, eschatological imagery needs to be looked at in terms of what it meant to the early Christian community and how that imagery has been utilized at different periods of history by Christian and non-Christian communities (including modern-day "cults"). Models for mystical expression in Judaism include Ezekiel and The Song of Songs; in Christianity, they include The Song of Songs and the Gospel of John. Indeed, one way to organize scriptural themes important to Judaism, Christianity, and Islam is to scrutinize the imagery related to God; the prophets; human tendencies and ethical demands; end time; and the mystical/visionary/unitive experience.

Sabbath, Day of Re-Creation

Daily observance is the pulse beat supplying Jews with the lifeblood of the divine. The Sabbath re-creates them, giving them the strength for meaningful daily living. It is linked to God's creative act itself (Genesis 2:1–4). Goal rested from His work and hallowed the Sabbath. It is the only holy day ordained in the Ten Commandments, both in Exodus (20:8–11) and in Deuteronomy (5:12–15). But God needs no rest; the meaning of the term lies deeper. God ceased from making the world all by Himself; henceforth people must be His co-workers. As Creator, God is the world's owner and may ordain rest for those who toil in His domain. In obeying this command, Jews acknowledge God's ownership of the world and constitute themselves not its master but its stewards.

They are to become aware that people are called to carry on God's work during the six days of labor. This task has two distinct features: First, nature and all its produce must be utilized for beneficent purposes: we may neither squander its riches nor selfishly claim them all for ourselves. Hence the commandment emphasizes that God is nature's creator. Secondly, society and every one of its members is equally God's; all humankind must be given that dignity which comes from being God's children. Servants, too, must be allowed to rest, as is doubly emphasized in the version of the Commandments found in Deuteronomy, "that your servants may rest as well as you." The meaning of the Sabbath thus synthesizes the religious element and the social element, the spiritualizing of daily work and the promotion of humanity's basic rights. Judaism considers one without the other to be meaningless.

To Jews, the Sabbath has become not merely a day of rest, but a day of spiritual re-creation for the tasks which form the functions of the week's labor. As such, it has given

From JUDAISM: DEVELOPMENT AND LIFE, 3RD EDITION by Leo Trepp. Copyright ©1982 by Wadsworth Publishing Company, a Division of Wadsworth, Inc. Edited and reprinted by permission.

the Jews strength, hope, and confidence. Truly, human beings, so charged with a divine duty, are dear to God. The Sabbath became a Covenant between God and Israel (Exodus 13:12-17); its desecration spells denial of God Himself and His creatorship (Numbers 15:32-36). It guarantees Israel's eternity, for the servant's life has meaning as long as the Master's work needs to be done, and this work is eternal. It has given Jews the strength to endure and preserve their mental balance. In the terms of the German poet (of Jewish background) Heinrich Heine: a dog during the week, the Jew is restored to his true character as a prince of God one day a week. If he must, he can return to the degradation the world may impose upon him, for he knows his true identity. According to the rabbis, the Sabbath thus provides Jews with "a taste of the world to come." Sagely they remark: "As Israel has kept the Sabbath, the Sabbath has kept Israel alive."

Prohibition of Work

The meaning of *rest* had to be defined, lest a person rationalize that his work, or that imposed upon his servants, could not really be called work. A simple yardstick was used in this definition. All of God's world is His sanctuary; as His co-workers, Israel once built a sanctuary in the desert, a small symbol of His presence, though He pervades the entire universe. All types of work once connected with the building of the tabernacle in the desert are therefore prohibited. In this manner the principle of, rest in God's behest is realized by those who are called to build the greater sanctuary of a God-centered society.

This led to the prohibition of thirty-nine basic kinds of work, arranged in several general categories: (1) the growing and preparation of food (eleven prohibitions); (2) clothing in all its processes (thirteen prohibitions) (3) leather work and writing (nine prohibitions); (4) the building of shelter (two prohibitions); (5) the use of fire (two prohibitions); (6) work completion, the final hammer stroke (one prohibition); and (7) transportation (one prohibition). Around these primary prohibitions, the rabbis added secondary ones to prevent violation of the basic ones. Thus the Sabbath became a day of complete spirituality. The toil of daily living fell, away and thoughts and preoccupation with daily events were completely banished. A truly divine peace settled upon those who fully observed it.

Observance of the Sabbath

The Jewish Day of Rest always starts with the preceding evening. Scripture states: "It was evening and it was morning" (Genesis 1), putting the night before the day. This is a natural arrangement also for the farmer and artisan, whose days end when the sun sets;

their thoughts then turn to the morrow. All Jewish holy days begin with the preceding evening.

Friday evening thus becomes a night of solemn observance. The food is prepared during the day, the body beautified, a festive table is laid out.

Traditionally the mother, guardian of the home, kindles the Sabbath lights, blessing God and invoking His blessing upon her household. There must be at least two candles on the table—a double portion, compared to the single dim light that was once the only illumination during the week.

Also traditionally, the father would attend worship accompanied by only the male members of the family. The mother stayed home with the female members and the infants. This gave her an hour of relaxation and meditation after strenuous Sabbath preparations, and refreshed her for the Sabbath meal that was to follow. Today, women frequently accompany their husbands to worship and the family prays together. It is also hoped that the men in the family assist the women in the Sabbath preparations.

After the opening Psalms, the welcome hymn to the Sabbath Bride is sung, and, following the habit of the mystics, the congregation turns to the door, welcoming the Bride. Sabbath Psalms (Psalms 92, 93) follow. The evening prayer is offered, followed by the Kiddush.

When the father returns home, the family welcome the Sabbath angels, which, according to tradition, accompany him home to bless his festive table. The father praises his wife, diligent mother, as a "woman of valor," knowing that the joyful family Sabbath is her work (Proverbs 31:10–31). Both parents bless their children with the biblical blessing (Numbers 6:25–26) and bestow upon them their Sabbath kiss.

On the table stands the cup of wine, and beside it lie two loaves of bread (hallah) covered by an embroidered cloth. The loaves are a reminder of the double portion of Manna, covered by a layer of dew allotted Israel in the desert every Friday.

The father raises the cup, blessing God for the Sabbath. This is the **Kiddush**, the sanctification of the Sabbath. Every family member shares in the wine. He cuts the hallah, praising God for bread, and each member partakes of it. The festive meal follows, concluded by songs and grace.

The following morning, the family attends worship, which includes the reading of Torah, a special section for each week. Seven people are "called up" to follow the reader, who recites from the sacred scroll. Each offers a blessing of thanksgiving for the gift of Torah. An eighth person reads the Haftarah, the prophetic selection of the day. The service may also include a sermon, an interpretation of Torah.

The family then returns home for Kiddush and a joyful meal. The rest of the day belongs to the people, as the morning belonged to God. Torah study may be included. An afternoon nap after the midday meal has become an accepted folk habit. A leisurely stroll in nature can also be part of the observance.

The afternoon prayer calls the worshippers back to the synagogue. Torah is read again—the first section of next week's portion. In this manner, a bridge is built across the hardships of the week; a new Sabbath beckons.

The *Third Meal*, between the afternoon and evening prayers, was for the mystics a time of immersion into the eternal. It has been adapted in Israel and among some Jewish groups elsewhere as an hour of song, praise, and fellowship.

Evening worship commences when three stars have appeared in the sky: night has fallen. (Generally, the Jewish calendar gives the exact time.) **Habdalah** follows: the "separation" from the holy day. The cup is filled to overflowing, and a portion of the wine caught in a plate beneath it, symbolizing the hope that happiness may overflow during the week. A twisted candle is lit; it is held high by the youngest. The father begins to recite the Habdalah. He then takes a box filled with spices—often in the form of a tower, for God is tower of salvation—sniffs the sweet-smelling contents, and passes the box around. May each member of the family take a last whiff of the Sabbath aroma into the week.

The father speaks the blessing over the flame of the candle. This is the beginning of the first day of the week, when God created the light (Genesis 1). God is praised for the light. After giving thanks, he makes use of this light by watching the play of light and shadow on his hands. On conclusion of the Habdalah, the candle is dipped into the overflow of the wine to be extinguished.

The greeting of the Sabbath is "*Shabbat Shalom*," or, in Yiddish, "*Gut Schabbes*." After Habdalah, the wish expressed in greeting is "*Shabua tov*," or, in Yiddish, "*A gute Woch*" —both meaning "a good week."

A short repast is offered, to "accompany the Queen (Sabbath)" on her retreat. Pleas for divine protection during the week are rendered to God. May Elijah, guardian of Israel, accompany the members of the family on their chores and soon herald the arrival of the Messiah.

In medieval times, Jewish families had a special "Sabbath lamp," lit only on the Sabbath, which could be lowered and raised. This led to a common saying: "As the lamp is lowered [on Friday], sorrow rises and vanishes; as the lamp is raised [after Habdalah], sorrow descends again."

The best expression of the essence of the Sabbath is perhaps found in the following paragraph from the Mussaf prayer:

> They who observe the Sabbath and call it a delight rejoice in Your kingdom. The people that hallow the seventh day are all seated and given delight out of Your goodness. For upon the seventh day You poured out Your grace and hallowed it; You called it the most precious of days, in remembrance of the works of creation.

Variations

Having described the traditional observance at its most complete, we should note that there are many variations in Sabbath celebration and observance. For instance, many American congregations have instituted a late Friday night service for those who cannot observe the Sabbath in the home, followed by **Oneg Shabbat**, a fellowship hour. Reform Jews do not consider themselves bound by work prohibitions.

Of Wine and Bread

Wine and bread are widely used in Jewish observances. They are indeed most precious gifts resulting from the partnership of God and human beings. The divine gifts of nature are transformed into perfect food through human ingenuity. In raising the cup of wine, the head of the house proclaims an even deeper meaning. **Kos**, the Hebrew word for cup, is derived from *kosas*, to measure out. It stands, therefore, for the gifts God has measured out, be they plentiful or scanty, pleasant or full of sorrow. As Jews raise the cup, they give thanks for all.

Reflections

This short discussion brings to life the specific intentions and duties related to the Jewish Sabbath. It is particularly important in communicating the importance of ritual within the family context. Christians will see something of how the Christian eucharistic liturgy has its roots in Jewish custom. Does the discussion in "Sabbath, Day of Re-creation" support Eliade's contentions regarding the function of myth and ritual?

VIII

Islam

The Koran Interpreted: Selections especially important in Muslim faith and piety

I

The Opening

In the Name of God, the Merciful, the Compassionate

Praise belongs to God, the Lord of all Being,
the All-merciful, the All-compassionate,
   the Master of the Day of Doom.

Thee only we serve; to Thee alone we pray for succour.
   Guide us in the straight path,
the path of those whom Thou hast blessed,
not of those against whom Thou art wrathful,
   nor of those who are astray.

CXII

Sincere Religion .

In the Name of God, the Merciful, the Compassionate

Say: 'He is God, One,
God, the Everlasting Refuge,
who has not begotten, and has not been begotten,
and equal to Him is not any one.'

CVII

Charity

In the Name of God, the Merciful, the Compassionate

Hast thou seen him who cries lies to the Doom?
That is he who repulses the orphan
and urges not the feeding of the needy.

So woe to those that pray
and are heedless of their prayers,
to those who make display
and refuse charity.

CI

The Clatterer

In the Name of God, the Merciful, the Compassionate

The Clatterer! What is the Clatterer?
And what shall teach thee what is the Clatterer?
The day that men shall be like scattered moths,
and the mountains shall be like plucked wool-tufts.

Then he whose deeds weigh heavy in the Balance
shall inherit a pleasing life,
but he whose deeds weigh light in the Balance
shall plunge in the womb of the Pit.
And what shall teach thee what is the Pit?
A blazing Fire!

C

The Chargers

In the Name of God, the Merciful, the Compassionate

By the snorting chargers,
by the strikers of fire,
by the dawn-raiders
blazing a trail of dust,
cleaving there with a host!
Surely Man is ungrateful to his Lord,
and surely he is a witness against that!
Surely he is passionate in his love for good things.
Knows he not that when that which is in the tombs is overthrown,
and that which is in the breasts is brought out—
surely on that day their Lord shall be aware of them!

XCVI

The Blood-Clot

In the Name of God, the Merciful, the Compassionate

Recite: In the Name of thy Lord who created,
created Man of a blood-clot.
Recite: And thy Lord is the Most Generous,
who taught by the Pen,
taught Man that he knew not.

No indeed; surely Man waxes insolent,
for he thinks himself self-sufficient.
Surely unto thy Lord is the Returning.

What thinkest thou? He who forbids
a servant when he prays—
What thinkest thou? If he were upon guidance
or bade to godfearing—
What thinkest thou? If he cries, lies, and turns away—
Did he not know that God sees?

No indeed; surely, if he gives not over,
We shall seize him by the forelock,
a lying, sinful forelock.
So let him call on his concourse!
We shall call on the guards of Hell.

No indeed; do thou not obey him,
and bow thyself, and draw nigh.

XCVII

Power

In the Name of God, the Merciful, the Compassionate

Behold, We sent it down on the Night of Power;
And what shall teach thee what is the Night of Power?
The Night of Power is better than a thousand months;
in it the angels and the Spirit descend,
by the leave of their Lord, upon every command.
Peace it is, till the rising of dawn.

XCIV

The Expanding

In the Name of God, the Merciful, the Compassionate

Did We not expand thy breast for thee
and lift from thee thy burden,
the burden that weighed down thy back?
Did We not exalt thy fame?

So truly with hardship comes ease,
truly with hardship comes ease.
So when thou art empty, labour,
and let thy Lord be thy Quest.

LXXXI

The Darkening

In the Name of God, the Merciful, the Compassionate

When the sun shall be darkened,
when the stars shall be thrown down,
when the mountains shall be set moving,
when the pregnant camels shall be neglected,
when the savage beasts shall be mustered,
when the seas shall be set boiling,
when the souls shall be coupled,
when the buried infant shall be asked for what sin she was slain,
when the scrolls shall be unrolled,
when the heaven shall be stripped off,
when Hell shall be set blazing,
when Paradise shall be brought nigh,
then shall a soul know what it has produced.

No! I swear by the slinkers,
the runners, the sinkers,
by the night swarming,
by the dawn sighing,
truly this is the word of a noble Messenger
having power, with the Lord of the Throne secure,
obeyed, moreover trusty.

Your companion is not possessed;
he truly saw him on the clear horizon;
he is not niggardly of the Unseen.

And it is not the word of an accursed Satan;
where then are you going?

It is naught but a Reminder
unto all beings,
for whosoever of you who would go straight;
but will you shall not, unless God wills,
the Lord of all Being.

LXVIII

The Pen

In the Name of God, the Merciful, the Compassionate

Nun

By the Pen, and what they inscribe,
thou art not, by the blessing of thy Lord,
a man possessed.
Surely thou shalt have a wage unfailing;
surely thou art upon a mighty morality.
So thou shalt see, and they will see,
which of you is the demented.

Surely thy Lord knows very well
those who have gone astray from
His way, and He knows very well
those who are guided.

LIII

The Star

In the Name of God, the Merciful, the Compassionate

By the Star when it plunges,
your comrade is not astray, neither errs,
nor speaks he out of caprice.
This is naught but a revelation revealed,
taught him by one terrible in power,
very strong; he stood poised,
being on the higher horizon,

then drew near and suspended hung,
two bows'-length away, or nearer,
then revealed to his servant that he revealed.
His heart lies not of what he saw;
what, will you dispute with him what he sees?

Indeed, he saw him another time
by the Lote-Tree of the Boundary
nigh which is the Garden of the Refuge,
when there covered the Lote-Tree that which covered;
his eye swerved not, nor swept astray.
Indeed, he saw one of the greatest signs of his Lord.

Have you considered El-Lat and El-'Uzza
and Manat the third, the other?
What have you males, and He females?
That were indeed an unjust division.
They are naught but names yourselves
have named, and your fathers; God has
sent down no authority touching them.
They follow only surmise, and what the
souls desire; and yet guidance has
come to them from their Lord.
Or shall man have whatever he fancies?
And to God belongs the First and the Last.

XXIV

Light

• • • God is the Light of the heavens and the earth;
the likeness of His Light is as a niche
wherein is a lamp
(the lamp in a glass,
the glass as it were a glittering star)
kindled from a Blessed Tree,
an olive that is neither of the East nor of the West

whose oil wellnigh would shine, even if no fire touched it;
Light upon Light;
(God guides to His Light whom He will.)
(And God strikes similitudes for men,
and God has knowledge of everything.)
in temples God has allowed to be raised up,
and His Name to be commemorated therein;
therein glorifying Him, in the mornings and the evenings,
are men whom neither commerce nor trafficking
diverts from the remembrance of God
and to perform the prayer, and to pay the alms,
fearing a day when hearts and eyes shall be turned about,
that God may recompense them for their fairest works
and give them increase of His bounty;
and God provides whomsoever He will, without reckoning...

The Koran Interpreted: Selections Related to Islamic Law and Duties

II

The Cow

...It is not piety, that you turn your faces
to the East and to the West.
    True piety is this:
to believe in God, and the Last Day,
the angels, the Book, and the Prophets,
to give of one's substance, however cherished,
    to kinsmen, and orphans,
the needy, the traveller, beggars,
    and to ransom the slave,
to perform the prayer, to pay the alms.
And they who fulfil their covenant
when they have engaged in a covenant,
    and endure with fortitude
misfortune, hardship and peril,
these are they who are true in their faith,
    these are the truly godfearing....
...O believers, prescribed for you is
the Fast, even as it was prescribed for

those that were before you—haply you
    will be godfearing—
for days numbered; and if any of you
be sick, or if he be on a journey,
then a number of other days; and for those
who are able to fast, a redemption
by feeding a poor man. Yet better
it is for him who volunteers good,
and that you should fast is better for you,
    if you but know;
the month of Ramadan, wherein the Koran
was sent down to be a guidance
to the people, and as clear signs
of the Guidance and the Salvation
So let those of you, who are present
at the month, fast it; and if any of you
be sick, or if he be on a journey,
then a number of other days; God desires
ease for you, and desires not hardship
for you; and that you fulfil the number, and
magnify God that He has guided you, and haply
    you will be thankful.

And when My servants question thee
concerning Me—I am near to answer
the call of the caller, when he calls
to Me; so let them respond to Me,
and let them believe in Me; haply so
    they will go aright.

Permitted to you, upon the night of
the Fast, is to go in to your wives;
they are a vestment for you, and you are
a vestment for them. God knows that you have been
betraying yourselves, and has turned to you
and pardoned you. So now lie with them,
and seek what God has prescribed for you.
And eat and drink, until the white thread
shows clearly to you from the black thread
at the dawn; then complete the Fast

unto the night, and do not lie with them
while you cleave to the mosques. Those are
God's bounds; keep well within them. So God
makes clear His signs to men; haply they
    will be godfearing.

Consume not your goods between you
in vanity; neither proffer it
to the judges, that you may sinfully
consume a portion of other men's goods,
    and that wittingly.

They will question thee concerning
the new moons. Say: 'They are appointed
times for the people, and the Pilgrimage.'

It is not piety to come to the houses
from the backs of them; but piety is
to be godfearing; so come to the houses
by their doors, and fear God; haply so
    you will prosper.

And fight in the way of God with those
who fight with you, but aggress not; God loves
    not the aggressors.
And slay them wherever you come upon them,
and expel them from where they expelled you;
persecution is more grievous than slaying.
But fight them not by the Holy Mosque
until they should fight you there;
then, if they fight you, slay them—
such is the recompense of unbelievers—
but if they give over, surely God is
All-forgiving, All-compassionate.

Fight them, till there is no persecution
and the religion is God's; then if they
give over, there shall be no enmity
    save for evildoers.
The holy month for the holy month;

holy things demand retaliation.
Whoso commits aggression against you,
do you commit aggression against him
like as he has committed against you;
and fear you God, and know that God is
     with the godfearing.

And expend in the way of God;
and cast not yourselves by your own hands
into destruction, but be good-doers; God
     loves the good-doers.

Fulfil the Pilgrimage and the Visitation
unto God; but if you are prevented,
then such offering as may be feasible.
And shave not your heads, till the offering
reaches its place of sacrifice. If any
of you is sick, or injured in his head,
then redemption by fast, or freewill offering,
or ritual sacrifice. When you are secure,
then whosoever enjoys the Visitation
until the Pilgrimage, let his offering
be such as may be feasible; or if he
finds none, then a fast of three days
in the Pilgrimage, and of seven when
you return, that is ten completely;
that is for him whose family are not
present at the Holy Mosque. And fear
God, and know that God is terrible
     in retribution.

The Pilgrimage is in months well-known;
whoso undertakes the duty of Pilgrimage
in them shall not go in to his womenfolk
not indulge in ungodliness and disputing
in the Pilgrimage. Whatever good you do,
God knows it. And take provision;
but the best provision is godfearing,
so fear you Me, men possessed of minds!
It is no fault in you, that you should seek

bounty from your Lord; but when you press on
from Arafat, then remember God
at the Holy Waymark, and remember Him
as He has guided you, though formerly you
    were gone astray.
Then press on from where the people
press on, and pray for God's forgiveness;
God is All-forgiving, All-compassionate.
And when you have performed your holy rites
remember God, as you remember your fathers
or yet more devoutly. Now some men
there are who say, 'Our Lord, give to us
in this world'; such men shall have no part
    in the world to come.
And others there are who say, 'Our Lord,
give to us in this world good, and good
in the world to come, and guard us against the
    chastisement of the Fire';
those—they shall have a portion from
what they have earned; and God is swift
    at the reckoning.
And remember God during certain days
numbered. If any man hastens on
in two days, that is no sin in him;
and if any delays, it is not a sin
in him, if he be godfearing. And
fear you God, and know that unto Him
    you shall be mustered...

...They will question thee concerning
the holy month, and fighting in it.
Say: 'Fighting in it is a heinous thing,
but to bar from God's way, and disbelief in Him,
and the Holy Mosque, and to expel its people
from it—that is more heinous in God's sight;
and persecution is more heinous than slaying.'
They will not cease to fight with you,

The Koran Interpreted: Selections Related to the Prophets

XIX

Mary

In the Name of God, the Merciful, the Compassionate

Kaf Ha Ya Ain Sad

The mention of thy Lord's mercy
unto His servant Zachariah;
when he called upon his Lord
    secretly
saying, 'O my Lord, behold
the bones within me are feeble
and my head is all aflame with
    hoariness.
And in calling on Thee, my Lord,
I have never been hitherto
    unprosperous.
And now I fear my kinsfolk
after I am gone; and my wife
is barren. So give me, from Thee,

a kinsman
who shall be my inheritor
and the inheritor of the House
of Jacob; and make him, my Lord,
    well-pleasing.'
'O Zachariah, We give thee
good tidings of a boy, whose name
    is John.
No namesake have We given him
    aforetime.'
He said, 'O my lord, how
shall I have a son, seeing
my wife is barren, and I
have attained to the declining
    of old age.'
Said He, 'So it shall be; thy
Lord says, "Easy is that for
Me, seeing that I created
thee aforetime, when thou wast
    nothing."'
He said, 'Lord, appoint to me
some sign. 'Said He, 'Thy sign
is that thou shalt not speak to
men, though being without fault,
    three nights.'
So he came forth unto his
people from the Sanctuary,
then he made signal to them,
'Give you glory at dawn and
    evening.'
'O John, take the Book forcefully';
and We gave him judgment, yet a
    little child,
and a tenderness from Us,
and purity; and he was
godfearing, and cherishing
his parents, not arrogant,
    rebellious.
'Peace be upon him, the day
he was born, and the day he

dies, and the day he is raised
    up alive!'

And mention in the Book Mary
when she withdrew from her people
    to an eastern place,
and she took a veil apart from them;
then We sent unto her Our Spirit
that presented himself to her
    a man without fault.
She said, 'I take refuge in
the All-merciful from thee!
    If thou fearest God....'
He said, 'I am but a messenger
come from thy Lord, to give thee
    a boy most pure.'
She said, 'How shall I have a son
whom no mortal has touched, neither
    have I been unchaste?'
He said, 'Even so thy Lord has said:
"Easy is that for Me; and that We
may appoint him a sign unto men
and a mercy from Us; it is
    a thing decreed."'
So she conceived him, and withdrew with him
    to a distant place.
And the birthpangs surprised her by
the trunk of the palm-tree. She said,
'Would I had died ere this, and become
    a thing forgotten!'
But the one that was below her
called to her, 'Nay, do not sorrow;
see, thy Lord has set below thee
    a rivulet.
Shake also to thee the palm-trunk,
and there shall come tumbling upon thee
    dates fresh and ripe.
Eat therefore, and drink, and be
comforted; and if thou shouldst see
    any mortal,

say, "I have vowed to the All-merciful
a fast, and today I will not speak
    to any man."'
Then she brought the child to her folk
carrying him; and they said,
    'Mary, thou hast surely committed
      a monstrous thing!
Sister of Aaron, thy father was not
a wicked man, nor was thy mother
    a woman unchaste.'
Mary pointed to the child then;
but they said, 'How shall we speak
to one who is still in the cradle,
    a little child?'
He said, 'Lo, I am God's servant;
God has given me the Book, and
    made me a Prophet.
Blessed He has made me, wherever
I may be; and He has enjoined me
to pray, and to give the alms, so
    long as I live,
and likewise to cherish my mother;
He has not made me arrogant,
    unprosperous.
Peace be upon me, the day I was born,
and the day I die, and the day I am
    raised up alive!'
That is Jesus, son of Mary,
in word of truth, concerning which
    they are doubting.
It is not for God to take a son
unto Him. Glory be to Him! When He
decrees a thing, He but says to it
    'Be,' and it is.
Surely God is my Lord, and your
Lord; so serve you Him. This is
    a straight path.

But the parties have fallen into variance among themselves;
then woe to those who disbelieve for the scene of a dreadful day.

How well they will hear and see on the day they come to Us!
But the evildoer even today are in error manifest.
Warn thou them of the day of anguish, when the matter
shall be determined, and they yet heedless and unbelieving.
Surely We shall inherit the earth and all that are upon it,
     and unto Us they shall be returned.

And mention in the Book Abraham;
surely he was a true man, a Prophet.
When he said to his father, 'Father,
why worshippest thou that which neither
hears nor sees, nor avails thee anything?
Father, there has come to me knowledge
such as came not to thee; so follow me,
and I will guide thee on a level path.
Father, serve not Satan; surely Satan
is a rebel against the All-merciful.
Father, I fear that some chastisement
from the All-merciful will smite thee,
so that thou becomest a friend to Satan.'
Said he, 'What, art thou shrinking
from my gods, Abraham? Surely, if thou
givest not over, I shall stone thee;
so forsake me now for some while.'
He said, 'Peace be upon thee!
I will ask my Lord to forgive thee;
surely He is ever gracious to me.
Now I will go apart from you
and that you call upon, apart from
God; I will call upon my Lord,
and haply I shall not be, in calling
upon my Lord, unprosperous.'
So, when he went apart from them
and that they were serving, apart
from God. We gave him Isaac and
Jacob, and each We made a Prophet;
and We gave them of Our mercy,
and We appointed unto them
a tongue of truthfulness, sublime.

And mention in the Book Moses;
he was devoted, and he was
    a Messenger, a Prophet.
We called to him from the right side
of the Mount, and We brought him
    near in communion.
And We gave him his brother Aaron, of
    Our mercy, a Prophet.

And mention in the Book Ishmael;
he was true to his promise, and he was
    a Messenger, a Prophet.
He bade his people to pray
and to give the alms, and he was
    pleasing to his Lord.

And mention in the Book Idris; he was
    a true man, a Prophet.
We raised him up to a high place.

These are they whom God has blessed
    among the Prophets
of the seed of Adam, and of those
We bore with Noah, and of the seed of
    Abraham and Israel,
and of those We guided and chose.
When the signs of the All-merciful were
    recited to them,
they fell down prostrate, weeping.

Then there succeeded after them a succession
who wasted the prayer, and followed lusts; so
    they shall encounter error
save him who repents, and believes, and
does a righteous deed; those—they shall
enter Paradise, and they shall not
    be wronged anything;
Gardens of Eden that the All-merciful
promised His servants in the Unseen; His
    promise is ever performed.

There they shall hear no idle talk, but only
'Peace.' There they shall have their provision
    at dawn and evening.
That is Paradise which We shall give
as an inheritance to those of Our servants
    who are godfearing.

We come not down, save at the commandment of thy Lord.
    To Him belongs
all that is before us, and all that is behind us, and all
    between that.

Say: 'Shall I seek after a Lord other
than God, who is the Lord of all things?'

Every soul earns only to its own account;
no soul laden bears the load of another.
Then to your Lord shall you return, and
He will tell you of that whereon you
    were at variance.
It is He who has appointed you viceroys
in the earth, and has raised some of you
in rank above others, that He may try you
in what He has given you. Surely thy Lord
is swift in retribution; and surely
He is All-forgiving, All compassionate.

VII

The Battlements

In the Name of God, the Merciful, the Compassionate

Alif Lam Mim Sad

A Book sent down to thee—
so let there be no impediment in thy breast

because of it—
to warn thereby, and as a reminder to believers:
Follow what has been sent down to you from your
Lord, and follow no friends other than He; little
do you remember.
How many a city We have destroyed! Our might came
upon it at night, or while they took their ease
in the noontide,
and they but cried, when Our might came upon them,
'We were evildoers.'
So We shall question those unto whom a Message was sent,
and We shall question the Envoys,
and We shall relate to them with knowledge; assuredly
We were not absent.
The weighing that day is true; he whose scales are heavy—
they are the prosperers,
and he whose scales are light—they have lost their souls
for wronging Our signs.

We have established you in the earth
and there appointed for you livelihood;
little thanks you show.
We created you, then We shaped you,
then We said to the angels: 'Bow yourselves
to Adam'; so they bowed themselves,
save Iblis—he was not of those
that bowed themselves.
Said He, 'What prevented thee to
bow thyself, when I commanded thee?'
Said he, 'I am better than he; Thou
createdst me of fire, and him Thou
createdst of clay.'
Said He, 'Get thee down out of it;
it is not for thee to wax proud here,
so go thou forth; surely thou art
among the humbled.'
Said he, 'Respite me till the day
they shall be raised.'
Said He, 'Thou art among the ones that
are respited.'

Said he, 'Now, for Thy perverting me,
I shall surely sit in ambush for them
    on Thy straight path;
then I shall come on them from before them
and from behind them, from their right hands
and their left hands; Thou wilt not find
    most of them thankful.'
Said He, 'Go thou forth from it, despised
and banished. Those of them that follow
thee—I shall assuredly fill Gehenna
    with all of you.'

'O Adam, inherit, thou and thy wife,
the Garden, and eat of where you will,
but come not nigh this tree, lest you be
    of the evildoers.'
Then Satan whispered to them, to reveal
to them that which was hidden from them
of their shameful parts. He said, 'Your Lord
has only prohibited you from this tree
lest you become angels, or lest you
    become immortals.'
And he swore to them, 'Truly, I am for you
    a sincere adviser.'
So he led them on by delusion; and when
they tasted the tree, their shameful parts
revealed to them, so they took to stitching
upon themselves leaves of the Garden.
And their Lord called to them, 'Did not I
prohibit you from this tree, and say
to you, "Verily Satan is for you
    a manifest foe"?'
They said, 'Lord, we have wronged ourselves,
and if Thou dost not forgive us, and
have mercy upon us, we shall surely be
    among the lost.'
Said He, 'Get you down, and each of you
an enemy to each. In the earth a sojourn
shall be yours, and enjoyment
    for a time.'

Said He, 'Therein you shall live, and
therein you shall die, and from there you
     shall be brought forth'...

...To God belong the Names Most Beautiful;
     so call Him by them.
and leave those who blaspheme His Names—
they shall assuredly be recompensed
     for the things they did.

III

The House of Imran

...And when the angels said,
'Mary, God has chosen
thee, and purified
thee; He has chosen
thee above all women.
Mary, be obedient to
thy Lord, prostrating
and bowing before Him.'
(That is of the tidings
of the Unseen, that We
reveal to thee; for thou
wast not with them, when
they were casting quills
which of them should have
charge of Mary; thou
wast not with them, when
they were disputing.)
When the angels said,
'Mary, God gives thee good
tidings of a Word from Him
whose name is Messiah,
Jesus, son of Mary;

high honoured shall he be
in this world and the next,
near stationed to God.
He shall speak to men
in the cradle, and of age,
and righteous he shall be.'
'Lord,' said Mary,
'how shall I have a son
seeing no mortal has
touched me?' 'Even so,'
God said, 'God
creates what He will.
When He decrees a thing
He does but say to it
"Be," and it is.
And He will teach him
the Book, the Wisdom,
the Torah, the Gospel,
to be a Messenger
to the Children of Israel
saying, "I have come to
you with a sign from
your Lord. I will create
for you out of clay as
the likeness of a bird;
then I will breathe into
it, and it will be a
bird, by the leave of God.
I will also heal
the blind and the leper,
and bring to life the
dead, by the leave of God.
I will inform you too
of what things you eat,
and what you treasure up
in your houses. Surely
in that is a sign for you,
if you are believers.
Likewise confirming the
truth of the Torah that

is before me, and to make
lawful to you certain
things that before were
forbidden unto you.
I have come to you with
a sign from your Lord;
so fear you God, and
obey you me. Surely
God is my Lord and
your Lord; so serve Him.
This is a straight path".'

And when Jesus perceived
their unbelief, he said,
'Who will be my helpers
unto God?' The Apostles
said, 'We will be helpers
of God; we believe in God;
witness thou our submission.
Lord, we believe in that
Thou hast sent down, and we
follow the Messenger.
Inscribe us therefore with
those who bear witness.'

And they devised, and God
devised, and God is
the best of devisers.

When God said, 'Jesus,
I will take thee to Me
and will raise thee to Me,
and I will purify thee
of those who believe not.
I will set thy followers
above the unbelievers
till the Resurrection Day.
Then unto Me shall you
return, and I will decide
between you, as to what

you were at variance on.
As for the unbelievers,
I will chastise them with
a terrible chastisement
in this world and the next;
they shall have no helpers.'

But as for the believers, who do
deeds of righteousness, He will pay them
in full their wages: and God loves not
        the evildoers.

This We recite to thee
of signs and wise remembrance.
Truly, the likeness of
Jesus, in God's sight,
is as Adam's likeness;
He created him of dust,
then said He unto him,
'Be,' and he was.
The truth is of God;
be not of the doubters.
And whoso disputes with thee
concerning him, after the
knowledge that has come to thee,
say: 'Come now, let us call
our sons and your sons,
our wives and your wives,
our selves and your selves,
then let us humbly pray
and so lay God's curse
upon the ones who lie.'
This is the true story.
There is no god but God,
and assuredly God is
the All-mighty, the All-wise.
And if they turn their backs,
assuredly God knows
the workers of corruption.

Say: 'People of the Book! Come now to a word
common between us and you, that we serve
none but God, and that we associate not
aught with Him, and do not some of us take
others as Lords, apart from God.' And if
they turn their backs, say: 'Bear witness that
we are Muslims.'...

IV

Women

...**S**o, for their breaking the compact, and disbelieving
in the signs of God, and slaying the Prophets
without right, and for their saying, 'Our hearts
are uncircumcised'—nay, but God sealed them
for their unbelief, so they believe not,
     except a few—
and for their unbelief, and their uttering
against Mary a mighty calumny,
and for their saying, 'We slew the Messiah,
Jesus son of Mary, the Messenger of God'—
yet they did not slay him, neither crucified him,
only a likeness of that was shown to them.
Those who are at variance concerning him surely
are in doubt regarding him; they have no knowledge
of him, except the following of surmise;
and they slew him not of a certainty—
no indeed; God raised him up to Him; God is
     All-mighty, All-wise...

...We have revealed to thee as We revealed
to Noah, and the Prophets after him,
and We revealed to Abraham, Ishmael,
Isaac, Jacob, and the Tribes,
Jesus and Job, Jonah and Aaron

and Solomon, and We gave to David
    Psalms,
and Messengers We have already told thee of
before, and Messengers We have not told thee of;
and unto Moses God spoke directly—
Messengers bearing good tidings, and warning,
so that mankind might have no argument
against God, after the Messengers; God is
    All-mighty, All-wise.
But God bears witness to that He has sent down
to thee; He has sent it down with His knowledge;
and the angels also bear witness; and God suffices
    for a witness.

Surely those who disbelieve, and bar
from the way of God, have gone astray
    into far error.
Surely the unbelievers, who have done evil,
God would not forgive them, neither guide them
    on any road
but the road to Gehenna, therein dwelling
forever and ever; and that for God is
    an easy matter.

O men, the Messenger has now come to you
with the truth from your Lord; so believe;
better is it for you. And if you disbelieve,
to God belongs all that in the heavens
and in the earth; and God is
    All-knowing, All-wise.

People of the Book, go not beyond the bounds
in your religion, and say not as to God
but the truth. The Messiah, Jesus son of Mary,
was only the Messenger of God, and His Word
that He committed to Mary, and a Spirit from
Him. So believe in God and His Messengers,
and say not, 'Three.' Refrain; better is it
for you. God is only One God. Glory be
to Him—that He should have a son!

To Him belongs all that is in the heavens
and in the earth; God suffices
    for a guardian.
The Messiah will not disdain to be a servant
of God, neither the angels who are near
    stationed to Him.
Whosoever disdains to serve Him, and waxes
proud, He will assuredly muster them to
    Him, all of them.
As for the believers, who do deeds of righteousness,
He will pay them in full their wages,
and He will give them more, of His bounty;
and as for them who disdain, and wax proud,
them He will chastise with a painful chastisement,
and they shall not find for them, apart from God,
    a friend or helper.

O men, a proof has now come to you from your Lord;
We have sent down to you a manifest light.
As for those who believe in God, and hold fast
to Him, He will surely admit them to mercy
from Him, and bounty, and will guide them to Him
    on a straight path...

Reflections

The Koran ("Quran" is another transliteration of the Arabic) is the sacred scripture of Islam and is considered to be the "word," or expression of God ("Allah" in Arabic) revealed to Muhammad through the angel Gabriel. The Koran consists of 114 chapters, or Suras, which Muhammad received and recited in the Arabic language over a twenty-year period beginning about 610 C.E. Muslims see the beauty of the Koranic Arabic as evidence of its inspired nature. For the most part, the verses which Muhammad received in the earlier part of his career are shorter and convey the powerful emotional and psychological "moment" of prophetic revelation. They contain the self-revelation of God to Muhammad (thus, many passages begin with "We," referring to God), and Muslims believe that the essential content of the Koranic revelation is the same as that which was given to Abraham, Moses, Jesus, and all the previous prophets of God. That content is the affirmation of the One, Transcendent God, "the Merciful, the Compassionate," and the duty of human beings to surrender to the Divine Will. The early verses also contain vivid warnings about social injustice and the inevitability of a Final Judgment of one's deeds at the End Time (e.g., "The Clatterer," Sura CI). "The Blood Clot" (Sura XCVI) was the first verse revealed to Muhammad. That sacred event of the "descent of the Koran into the Prophet's heart" is described in such verses as "Power" (Sura XCVII) and "Star" (Sura LIII). The "Fatiha" (Sura I) is the opening chapter and most recited verse of the Koran; it is often called the Islamic "Lord's Prayer." The Suras recited by Muhammad in his later years tend to be longer and more legalistic in nature, as they were directed at the emerging Islamic community/state in Medina (e.g., Sura II, "Cow" on the basic duties, or Pillars of Islam). It should be noted that the Koran was compiled with the longer, Medinan verses at the beginning, and the shorter, Meccan verses at the end. In this volume I have placed the shorter verses first, to convey to the student something of the chronology of Muhammad's revelatory experiences. The entire Sura named after Mary, Jesus' mother, and sections from Sura IV (Women), have been included because of their instructive quality as to fundamental Muslim beliefs and stories regarding the prophets before Muhammad, including Adam and Jesus.

Throughout Islamic history, the Koran has been the primary source of knowledge and discussion on questions related to God, human nature, law, and forms of religious piety. The Koran also provided the basis for the rich tradition of Sufi, or mystical commentary on the text. Thus the Koran should be read with an eye toward the apparent, or literal, meaning of the text, but also with an eye toward the possible hidden, or "spiritual" meaning of the text. The "Light Verse" (from Sura XXIV) for example, has lent itself to much mystical speculation on the meaning of divine illumination and wisdom.

The Traditional Biographies of the Prophet Muhammad: "The Journey to the Divine Proximity"

Now when I was brought on my Night Journey to the (place of the) Throne and drew near to it, a green *rafraf* [narrow piece of silk brocade] was let down to me, a thing too beautiful for me to describe to you, whereat Gabriel advanced and seated me on it. Then he had to withdraw from me, placing his hands over his eyes, fearing lest his sight be destroyed by the scintillating light of the Throne, and he began to weep aloud, uttering *tasbīh*, *tahmīd* and *tathniya* to Allah. By Allah's leave, as a sign of His mercy toward me and the perfection of His favor to me, that *rafraf* floated me into the (presence of the) Lord of the Throne, a thing too stupendous for the tongue to tell of or imagination to picture. My sight was so dazzled by it that I feared blindness. Therefore, I shut my eyes, which was by Allah's good favor. When I thus veiled my sight, Allah shifted my sight (from my eyes) to my heart, so with my heart I began to look at what I had been looking at with my eyes. It was a light so bright in its scintillation that I despair of ever describing to you what I saw of His majesty. Then I besought my Lord to complete His favor to me by granting me the boon of having a steadfast vision of Him with my heart. This my Lord did, giving me that favor, so I gazed at Him with my heart till it was steady and I had a steady vision of Him.

There He was, when the veil had been lifted from Him, seated on His Throne, in His dignity, His might, His glory, His exaltedness, but beyond that it is not permitted me to describe Him to you. Glory be to Him! How majestic is He! How bountiful are His works! How exalted is His position! How brilliant is His light! Then He lowered somewhat for me His dignity and drew me near to Him, which is as He has said in His book, informing you of how He would deal with me and honor me: "One possessed of strength. He stood erect when He was at the highest point of the horizon. Then He drew near and descended, so that He was two bows' lengths off, or even nearer" (LIII, 6-9). This means that when He inclined to me He drew me as near to Him as the distance between the two ends of a bow, nay, rather, nearer than the distance between the crotch of the bow and its curved ends. "Then He revealed to his servant what he revealed" (v. 10), i.e., what matters He had decided to enjoin upon me. "His heart did not falsify what it saw" (v. 11), i.e., my vision of Him with my heart. Indeed he was seeing one of the greatest signs of his Lord" (v. 18).

Now when He—glory be to Him—lowered His dignity for me He placed one of His hands between my shoulders and I felt the coldness of His fingertips for a while on my heart, whereat I experienced such a sweetness, so pleasant a perfume, so delightful a coolness, such a sense of honor in (being granted this) vision of Him, that all my terrors melted away and my fears departed from me, so my heart became tranquil. Then was I filled with joy, my eyes were refreshed, and such delight and happiness took hold of me that I began to bend and sway to right and left like one overtaken by slumber. Indeed, it seemed to me as though everyone in heaven and earth had died, for I heard no voices of angels, nor during the vision of my Lord did I see any dark bodies. My Lord left me there such time as He willed, then brought me back to my senses, and it was as though I had been asleep and had awakened. My mind returned to me and I was tranquil, realizing where I was and how I was enjoying surpassing favor and being shown manifest preference.

Then my Lord, glorified and praised be He, spoke to me, saying: "O Muhammad, do you know about what the Highest Council s disputing?" I answered: "O Lord, Thou knowest best about that, as about all things, for Thou art the One who knows the unseen" (cf. V, 109/108). They are disputing," He said, "about the degrees (*darajāt*) and the excellences. Do you know, O Muhammad, what the degrees and the excellences are?" Thou, O Lord," I answered, knowest better and art more wise." Then He said: "The degrees are concerned with performing one's ablutions at times when that is disagreeable, walking on foot to religious assemblies, watching expectantly for the next hour of prayer when one time of prayer is over. As for the excellences, they consist of feeding the hungry, spreading peace, and performing the *tahajjud* prayer at night when other folk are sleeping." Never have I heard anything sweeter or more pleasant than the melodious sound of His voice.

Such was the sweetness of His melodious voice that it gave me confidence, and so I spoke to Him of my need. I said: "O Lord, Thou didst take Abraham as a friend, Thou didst speak with Moses face to face, Thou didst raise Enoch to a high place, Thou didst give Solomon a kingdom such as none after him might attain, and didst give to David the Psalter. What then is there for me, O Lord?" He replied: "O Muhammad, I take you as a friend just as I took Abraham as a friend. I am speaking to you just as I spoke face to face with Moses. I am giving you the *Fātiha* (sura I) and the closing verses of *al-Baqara* (II, 284–286), both of which are from the treasuries of My Throne and which I have given to no prophet before you. I am sending you as a prophet to the white folk of the earth and the black folk and the red folk, to jinn and to men thereon, though never before you have I sent a prophet to the whole of them. I am appointing the earth, its dry land and its sea, for you and for your community as a place for purification and for worship. I am giving your community the right to booty which I have given as provision to no community before them. I shall aid you with such terrors as will make your enemies flee before you while you are still a month's journey away. I shall send down to you the Master of all Books and the guardian of them, a Quran which We Ourselves have parceled out (XVII, 106/107). I shall exalt your name for you (XCIV, 4), even to the extent of conjoining it with My name, so that none of the regulations of My religion will ever be mentioned without you being mentioned along with Me."

Then after this He communicated to me matters which I am not permitted to tell you, and when He had made His covenant with me and had left me there such time as He willed, He took His seat again upon His Throne. Glory be to Him in His majesty, His dignity, His might. Then I looked, and behold, something passed between us and a veil of light was drawn in front of Him, blazing ardently to a distance that none knows save Allah, and so intense that were it to be rent at any point it would burn up all Allah's creation. Then the green *rafraf* on which I was descended with me, gently rising and falling with me in 'Illiyun ['Illiyun is said to be the highest of all celestial regions] till it brought me back to Gabriel, who took me from it. Then the *rafraf* mounted up till it disappeared from my sight.

After such an overwhelming experience, during which he was declared to be inwardly the synthesis of all previous messengers and was granted assurances of Divine Succour and Glory, the Prophet was naturally reluctant to leave the Divine Presence and to return to the world of relativity and passion. He was, however, promised before his return to earth that he and his followers would experience the ecstasy of ascension in divine worship. That is why the daily prayers are called the *mi'rāj* of the faithful.

Subsequent to the return of the Prophet from the Ascension, the Meccans became all the more baffled and enraged. Their hostility now knew no bounds and the stage was set for the Prophet and his followers to migrate to Yathrib, which afterward acquired the name of Medina, (*Madīnat al-nabī* or *Madīnat al-rasūl*, the City of the Prophet or the City of the Messenger).

Reflections

Most Westerners are not aware of the devotion that many Muslims feel toward the figure of Muhammad. The exemplary conduct of the Prophet, as related in the *hadiths* (sayings of the Prophet) and traditional biographical accounts of the Prophet, has been second only to the Koran in its influence on Muslim piety and custom. "Journey to the Divine Proximity" is a portion of one of the biographies of the Prophet. It contains the famous *mi'rāj* (ascension) story of Muhammad, in which the Prophet ascends through the heavens of the Ptolemaic universe to the Throne of God. Muhammad rides a winged creature, Buraq, and is guided by Gabriel until the final stage of the journey (i.e., the human being can know that which the angels cannot). The story reminds us of Ezekiel's experience, and the *mi'rāj* became the model for the Sufis (the Islamic mystics) in their pilgrimage to the "inner throne of the heart," the locus of union with God in the human soul.

A Twentieth Century Sufi: "Everyone is Speaking of Peace"

Brothers and sisters born in this world, please listen to this wonder! The heavens and earth have always existed in peace. The sun, the moon, the stars, and the wind all perform their duty in harmony. Only man, who lives on this earth, has lost that peace. He only talks about it. He gives speeches about establishing peace, but then he disrupts the unity and sets out to rule the world. Is this not a wonder? Such is the speech of man.

In this present century, man has discarded God, truth, peacefulness, conscience, honesty, justice, and compassion. Man has changed so much! Instead of searching to discover the three thousand gracious qualities of God, he has lost all those qualities and opened the way to destruction. He seeks to ruin the lives of others and to destroy the entire world. But the world will not be destroyed; the earth and the heavens will never be destroyed. Only man will be destroyed. Man, with all the various means of destruction he has discovered, will in the end destroy only himself. He is like a certain type of moth that is attracted to the glow of a flame, thinking it is food. These moths circle around and around the flame, until finally they fly right into it and die. In the same way, man plummets into evil actions, thinking they will benefit him. He sees evil as good, but the end result is destruction.

Never has destruction been so much in evidence as in the present century. Man has changed the concept of God, who is truth, and debased the meaning of man, who is wisdom and beauty. He no longer understands what a true human being really is. If man could rediscover who he truly is and then change his present self, he would know peace.

From ISLAM AND WORLD PEACE by Bawa Muhaiyaddeen. Pp. 7–9. Copyright ©1987 by Fellowship Press. Reprinted by permission.

Man says he wants to bring peace to others, but in order to do that he must first find it within his own life. How can anyone who has not found peace within himself hope to bring peace to others? How can a man who has no compassion, no unity, and no love within himself bring peace to the world?

One who has not found justice, conscience, honesty, and truth within him self will not find these qualities in others. One who has not found the value of patience within himself will not find it in others. One who has not understood his own state will not understand the state of others. One who has not strengthened his own faith in God cannot strengthen the faith of others or be strengthened by the faith of others. One who has not acquired good qualities cannot find them in others, nor can he teach them to others. If he tries, his work will be fruitless. How can a man who carries a water bag full of holes hope to quench the thirst of others? As long as he has not repaired his own vessel, he can never fill that of another man.

To understand this and to establish peace, man must first change the thoughts and qualities within himself. He must change his qualities of selfishness and avarice, his desire for praise, and his love for earth, sensual pleasures, and gold. He must stop thinking, "My family! My wife! My children! I must rule the world! I must advance my position in life!" When a man has all these selfish ideas, how can he possibly create peace for others?

However, if he severs these qualities from himself and begins to feel the hunger, the pain, and the difficulties felt by others, and if he treats all lives as his own life, then he will find peace. If he can strive for this understanding and obtain inner patience, contentment, and trust in God, if he can imbibe God's qualities and acquire God's state, then he will know peace. And once he finds that clarity within himself, he will discover peace in every life. If everyone would do this, life in this world would be heaven on earth. But if those who live in this world and rule this world cannot find serenity within themselves, they will only end up destroying the world when they try to establish peace. We must think about this.

One who has not found peace within himself will forever be giving speeches about peace. This world is a pulpit upon which man preaches, and there is no end to this talk! For millions of years man has been speaking this way, but he has not come forward to first find peace within himself. There is no use in making speeches. Man must acquire the qualities of God and live in that state. Only then can he speak of peace, only then can he speak the speech of God and dispense the justice of God's kingdom.

The people who have come to rule the world should think about this. Every man should think about it. Peace can only be found in the heart. Good qualities, wisdom, and clarity must provide that explanation within each heart. Man will only know peace when he brings God's justice and His qualities into himself. Therefore, before we speak of peace, let us try to acquire God's words within ourselves. Let us find tranquility within ourselves. If we can do that, our speech will be fruitful. Then the whole world will be at peace.

Man must find peace, tranquility, happiness, unity, love, and every good quality within his own life, within his own innermost heart. Only a person who does that can understand the difficulties, the pain, and the misery of others. A man of wisdom will know this, understand this, and rectify his own mistakes. Then he can help others.

We must all think about this. May God help us. Amen.

Reflections

The Sufi sage, the teacher of wisdom who guides the disciple to the station of the "perfect human" (*insan al-kamil*), has been an important aspect of popular piety in Islam since the second Islamic century. This tradition was continued in the life and discourses of Bawa Muhaiyaddeen, a Sri Lankan Sufi teacher who taught in his native land for thirty years before coming to the United States in 1971. Bawa Muhaiyaddeen founded a community in the United Stares and taught there until his death in 1986. "Everyone is Speaking of Peace" presents the classic Sufi understanding of "islam," that is, the state of inner peace and unity with God that is realized in the human heart that is "surrendered," the state that must exist if there is to be peace among individuals, religions, or nations.

Bibliography

Eliade, Mircea. "Archetypes and Repetition." *The Myth of the Eternal Return*. Princeton, New Jersey: Princeton University Press, 1974 [chapter 1].

Neihardt, John. *Black Elk Speaks*. Lincoln, Nebraska: University of Nebraska Press, 1961 [pp. 1–6].

"Katha" in *The Upanisads: Breath of the Eternal*. Translated by Swami Prahbahvananda and Frederick Manchester. Hollywood, California: Vedanta Press, 1957 [pp. 14–25].

Rama, Swami, Ballentine, Rudolf M.; and Ajaya-Allan, Swami. "The Seven Centers of Consciousness." *Yoga and Psychotherapy*. Glenview, Illinois: Himalayan Institute, 1976 [ch. 7, pp. 216–228].

Burtt, E. A., ed. *The Teachings of the Compassionate Buddha*. New York: Mentor, 1982 [pp. 48–50, 128–129].

Wing-Tsit Chan, ed. and trans. "The Humanism of Confucius" and "The Natural Way of Lao Tzu." *A Sourcebook in Chinese Philosophy*. Princeton, New Jersey: Princeton University Press, 1969.

The New American Bible. Encino, California: Benziger, a division of Glencoe Publishing Co., Inc. (Collier Macmillan Canada, Ltd.), 1970.

Trepp, Leo. "Sabbath, Day of Re-Creation." *Judaism: Development and Life*, 3rd ed. Belmont, California: Wadsworth Publishing Co., 1974 [chapter 19].

The Koran Interpreted. Translated by Arberry, A.J. New York: Macmillan Publishing Company, 1955.

Qasimi, Ja'far. "The Journey to Divine Proximity." *Islamic Spirituality: Foundations*, ed. Seyyed Hossein Nasr, 65–96. New York: Crossroad Press, 1987 [pp. 78–80].

Bawa Muhaiyaddeen. *Islam and World Peace*. Philadelphia: Fellowship Press, 1987 [pp. 7–9].